Business Calculations

Business Calculations

David Spurling BSc

Geoffrey Whitehead BSc (Econ), General Editor

Pitman

PITMAN PUBLISHING LIMITED
128 Long Acre, London WC2E 9AN

PITMAN PUBLISHING INC
1020 Plain Street, Marshfield, Massachusetts 02050

Associated Companies
Pitman Publishing Pty Ltd, Melbourne
Pitman Publishing New Zealand Ltd, Wellington
Copp Clark Pitman, Toronto

First published in Great Britain 1985

British Library Cataloguing in Publication Data
Spurling, David
  Business calculations.
  1. Business mathematics
  I. Title II. Whitehead, Geoffrey
  510'.24658   HF5691

  ISBN 0-273-02040-4

Printed in Great Britain at The Bath Press, Avon

Contents

Foreword

Calculations form an important element in our lives both at home and at work, and an indication of some level of numeracy is often a basic requirement for employment or further education.

It is well known that many employers have expressed regret at the decline of ability in arithmetic in recent years, and all vocational courses now recognise this by having a core requirement of basic numeracy skills.

This book will provide students with the necessary numerical competence for entry into employment and in particular into business fields. The approach will enable all students to develop confidence in commercial arithmetic and help them to gain qualifications in this subject. All elementary syllabuses (Royal Society of Arts, London Chamber of Commerce, General Certificate examinations etc.) have been covered. A full explanation of each aspect of these syllabuses is given and adequate practice in calculations is provided.

Most elementary examinations include a separate mental arithmetic paper, and students are urged not to neglect this aspect. The book provides an Appendix of Mental Arithmetic Tests, graduated in difficulty, one for each chapter of the book.

I should like to express my appreciation of the author's forbearance in meeting criticisms of the original text and generally bearing with us in our attempts to make this book a really helpful aid to teachers, lecturers and (above all) students.

Geoffrey Whitehead
GENERAL EDITOR

1

An Introduction to Business Calculations

1.1 Why do we need business calculations?

To some extent everyone is concerned with business calculations. Obviously there are many calculations to do in such business activities as estimating, costing and quoting for contracts of every sort. The first thing everyone needs to know when considering any project is the likely cost. This requires us to know the quantities of materials required, the types and costs of labour that must be employed, and the various overhead expenses that will be involved. All these costs must be taken into account before we can decide on the price to be charged to a particular customer.

Most people would need to be able to do some calculations in their job. It is often necessary to have an idea of weights and measures as well as money. For example, if you worked in a transport department, you would need to be able to calculate the total weights of consignments so that you do not infringe vehicle- or axle-weight limits. If you worked in a general administration department you would need to be able to calculate the required quantities of stationery and other materials. If you work in a factory you may need to keep a record of the amounts of raw materials and components used. This will ensure that there has been no pilfering, as well as ensuring that production is not held up through lack of materials. You may also need to calculate the costs of storing these parts. When materials are issued for a particular job or contract, you may need to calculate the costs to be allocated to it. This is called 'job costing', or 'contract costing'. If you work in an accountant's office, you will find that accountants and book-keepers need to do many calculations in their daily lives.

Apart from business calculations as employees, we are also personally interested in calculations in our everyday domestic lives.

The author of this book was pleasantly surprised when working in a wages department to find how quickly many people could calculate quite complex overtime rates. Wages activities are often performed by computers today, but it is still worth while to check the calculations on our wages slips, as even with computerised systems mistakes can still occur.

In your home life it is helpful to be able to check you have received the right amount of change when shopping. Calculations may help you to obtain the best value for money. Many goods come in a variety of different sizes. Without the ability to perform mental calculations, it is difficult to see which is the most cost-effective method of buying.

You may need to buy on credit, in which case it is very important for you to be able to calculate the total costs. This is particularly important if you purchase a house. There are a wide variety of repayment methods, such as mortgages and endowment mortgages. The ability to calculate would help you in selecting the best method.

If you purchase a vehicle, whether it is a motor cycle or a car, calculations about buying on credit and being able to work out running costs are almost essential. If you do not own a vehicle you will almost certainly use public transport. In recent years there have been a wide variety of public transport fares available. Here again calculations will enable you to be sure that you get the best value for money.

If you are one of the increasing number of people who do your own house repairs, maintenance and decorating, calculations will be necessary. For example, if you wish to purchase carpet or other floor-covering for a new house or flat, an approximate idea of how much of either you need is helpful when budgeting. If you are decorating it is obviously essential to know that you have sufficient rolls of wallpaper and sufficient litres of paint.

In your home life you will almost certainly have to do some calculations for income tax purposes. If you ever attempt to set up business yourself you will have to do some calculations involving value added tax.

If you are budgeting for the month or the week, calculations will be essential. If you travel abroad, whether for work or for pleasure, you will almost certainly have to carry out calculations with regard to foreign exchange. You may also have to do similar calculations for your firm if it exports or imports goods or services.

We see therefore that the study of business calculations is a useful and worthwhile activity.

1.2 The role of computers and calculators

Whilst calculators and computers are now used in most modern offices and factories, it is still helpful to have ideas about the basic arithmetical processes. Without this knowledge it is easy to make elementary mistakes. There is a well known phrase in the computer industry: 'garbage in, garbage out'. This means that if bad data is given to the computer operator, the computer is sure to give bad results. Similarly, incompetent keying on a calculator or computer keyboard will produce ridiculous answers. It is essential to have a sound grasp of basic calculations, so that you know roughly what the answer will be. A ridiculous answer would then be obvious to you, and you would re-key the data to check the answer displayed.

Never lose an opportunity to gain keyboard experience on a calculator or a computer. It is an essential requirement, and greatly helped by learning to type properly. Both boys and girls

should learn typing today, and you are strongly advised to acquire this skill if the opportunity occurs.

Calculators and computers can do all our calculations at electronic speeds. An addition sum takes less than a millionth of a second, so that we can understand the tremendous savings that can be made by using these devices. For many elementary examinations you are not allowed to use them, however, as you have a similar device in your own body: your brain. If we train our brains to do simple calculations properly we shall not only find them always available, and never in need of a new battery, but also able to pick up the wrong answers that a computer occasionally gives.

1.3 How to use this book

This book teaches you how to do all the basic calculations you will meet in everyday life, at home and at work. You will notice that there are tests at the end of each chapter, which will help you to become really skilled at each type of calculation. It is advisable to work systematically through the book; a good student should aim to do every exercise.

1.4 Advice if you are taking examinations

If you are using the book to study on your own for examinations, you should obtain a copy of the relevant syllabus from the examination body. You should then check this against the different chapters within this book and concentrate on those chapters which form part of your syllabus. It is often helpful to see past copies of examination papers from the examination boards if these are available.

If you find when you look at the tests in each chapter that the first one or two questions are easy, then it is sensible to move on to the next chapter. If, by contrast, you find the first questions difficult, then do the entire set; practice makes perfect. Do not, however, get discouraged if you become completely stuck. You may find it better to move on to another chapter, go through a section of work that you do understand, and then return to the difficult chapter when you feel more confident. What seems hard one week may seem easy a month later.

2
Integers and the Basic Rules of Arithmetic

2.1 What is an integer?

An integer is a whole number. Therefore, numbers such as 1, 2, 3, 5, 27 and 133 are all examples of integers. In this chapter, we deal solely with integers. In later chapters we shall deal with fractions, that is, numbers smaller than 1. There are four basic arithmetic processes affecting integers: addition, subtraction, multiplication and division. You will find calculations where you have to use these processes in almost any job. Let us revise these four processes, which we all learn very early in our school lives.

2.2 Addition

You will probably be familiar with adding up numbers arranged in columns. When the numbers add up to less than 10 in each column, there are no problems, but difficulties arise when the numbers add up to more than 10. This is because the column arrangement has separate columns for units, tens, hundreds, thousands etc.

Our whole system of counting is based on 10, and is sometimes said to be a 'base 10' series. (If you do further studies, you may well go on to the computer system. Computers use the binary system of arithmetic, which has a base of 2.) Another name for a 'base 10' system is a 'decimal system' (from the Latin *decem*, meaning 'ten'). It is a system where 10 units make 1 ten (10), 10 tens make 1 hundred (100), 10 hundreds make 1 thousand (1000) etc.

If we take the simple example of adding 211, 312 and 413, we will place these numbers one under each other:

H	T	U
2	1	1
3	1	2
4	1	3
9	3	6

We start with the unit column adding 1, 2 and 3. This makes 6. We proceed to the tens column 1, 1 and 1, which makes 3, and then to the hundreds column 2, 3 and 4, which makes 9. In this case none of the columns added up to more than nine, so there was no need to carry over. We therefore arrived at the answer 936. Let us take a slightly more difficult example, where the columns do exceed 10 when added.

Th	H	T	U
	5	4	5
	4	6	7
	9	8	9
2	0	0	1
		2	2

In this case we would add up 5, 7 and 9, which makes 21. We cannot write 21 in the units column, because the 2 part of 21 is 2 tens. These must be carried into the tens column, and only the 1 can be put in the units column. We usually carry the 2 in our heads, but we can also write the 2 below the answer line as shown. We now proceed to add the tens column. We add 4, 6, 8 and 2, which makes 20. We therefore have 20 tens. We put 0 into the tens column, and the 20 tens make 2 hundreds. We carry this 2 into the hundreds column. We now add up 5, 4 and 9 hundreds and the additional 2, which makes 20. There are no hundreds for the hundreds column but the 20 hundreds make 2 thousands. The total is therefore 2001.

When setting out sums on a piece of paper, you will need to make sure that the columns come exactly under each other. Now try the addition sums in Section 2.3 below. Note that where we have more than three columns (hundreds, tens and units), it is helpful to leave a small space every third column. Thus the number 1 254 366 requires two spaces, as in (j) below.

2.3 Exercises: simple addition sums

Set each of these sums down, being sure to keep the columns clear, and find the totals of each.

(a)
```
    345
    592
  + 786
```
(b)
```
    578
    180
  + 400
```
(c)
```
    466
    212
  + 417
```
(d)
```
    100
    518
  + 895
```
(e)
```
   2 654
   3 910
  +4 721
```
(f)
```
   1 079
   9 543
  +2 245
```
(g)
```
   1 074
   5 294
   3 824
  +1 797
```
(h)
```
   4 395
   1 762
   1 834
  +1 726
```
(i)
```
   575 421
   986 476
  +201 113
```
(j)
```
   1 254 366
   7 591 278
  +4 987 654
```

Please note: In this exercise, as with all other exercises in this book, do not mark the book unless it is your own property.

2.4 Using sub-totals

Sometimes we have to add a very long list of numbers, in which case it is very easy to make mistakes. If you are fairly good at arithmetic, one possibility is to add up all the numbers down a column, put down the answer on the separate piece of paper and then reverse the process from the bottom upwards. If you merely repeat going downwards twice, you are likely to make the same mistake again, whereas by reversing the flow repeat errors are less likely. Another possibility is to use sub-totals. In this case, use a limited number of lines for each sub-total, and then add up the sub-totals. For example:

```
    212
    834
    436
    729
    945    3 156
    ──────
    685
    334
    197
    544
    691    2 451
    ──────
    813
    569
    954
    782
  + 213    3 331
  ───────────────
           8 938
           ═════
```

2.5 Adding horizontally

Although it is definitely quicker to do addition sums up and down the columns, we do occasionally have to add horizontally. Thus it is possible to add across the page:

$$127 + 136 + 154 = ?$$

To do this we look at the units figures first: $7 + 6 + 4 = 17$. Write down the 7 units and carry the 10 into the tens section. 2 tens + 3 tens + 5 tens + 1 ten to carry = 11 tens. As before, the 10 tens become 1 hundred. We write the 1 ten in the answer and carry 1 hundred. $1 + 1 + 1 + 1$ to carry = 4 hundreds. Therefore, the answer is:

$$127 + 136 + 154 = 417$$

In many firms, there may be a need to add both vertical and horizontal columns at the same time. For example, a sales manager may be interested in total sales for each region, whilst the transport manager might be interested in total sales delivered by each depot (see Table 2.1). Adding horizontally will give the monthly sales totals. Adding vertically will give the regional sales totals for the six-month period. The total of the final column gives the grand total of sales. Now try the addition sums in Section 2.6 below.

Sales by representatives

Month	Northern region	Eastern region	Southern region	Western region	Totals
Jan.	14 177	7 167	23 529	13 782	
Feb.	17 998	5 211	18 412	16 555	
Mar.	16 543	7 137	19 882	14 689	
Apr.	13 447	6 113	25 307	21 897	
May	12 567	3 345	57 333	49 785	
June	20 998	7 654	49 496	31 192	
Totals					

Table 2.1

2.6 Exercises: more addition sums

1 Use sub-totals to add up these sums.

(a)	(b)	(c)
562	556	1 876
231	781	4 322
321	251	9 721
496	982	5 494
783	279	7 887
269	491	2 137
131	378	8 554
456	121	7 211
772	556	9 854
223	778	3 666
597	145	4 113
159	439	9 876
468	798	4 217
243	412	8 791
+ 910	+ 768	+ 3 496

(d)	(e)	(f)
4 567	9 111	12 816
7 823	5 478	23 725
4 712	2 378	33 814
3 911	4 562	42 956
2 134	7 113	72 851
1 765	4 223	76 312
5 478	7 889	42 958
9 113	2 113	71 625
4 789	4 678	83 429
3 914	7 789	71 747
9 101	1 191	83 256
7 656	7 232	11 275
2 311	4 562	13 954
8 543	7 899	16 725
+ 7 626	+ 9 921	+ 36 384

2 Copy these sums into your exercise book and add them horizontally.

(a) $5 + 4 + 9 + 7 =$
(b) $21 + 14 + 36 + 11 =$
(c) $416 + 114 + 259 =$
(d) $572 + 776 + 1 987 =$
(e) $776 + 2 339 + 4 112 =$
(f) $817 + 546 + 4 127 =$

3 Copy these sums into your exercise book and add them horizontally.

(a) $7 + 2 + 6 + 9 + 5 =$
(b) $14 + 13 + 27 + 62 =$
(c) $174 + 238 + 147 =$
(d) $1 965 + 2 478 + 3 862 =$
(e) $27 565 + 32 726 + 49 814 =$

4 By adding vertically and horizontally find (a) the total monthly sales, (b) the total area sales, and (c) the grand total of sales for the half year.

Sales of motor vehicles

	Europe	Africa	Far East	USA	Totals
Jan.	27 321	17 294	11 712	1 814	
Feb.	46 294	19 384	23 738	2 375	
Mar.	38 176	18 264	18 256	11 856	
Apr.	42 348	7 231	9 384	8 235	
May	52 714	18 384	27 314	9 199	
June	53 828	21 397	24 236	14 376	
Totals					

2.7 Subtraction

Frequently, we will use subtraction in business. For example, if we work in a firm's transport depot, with a certain amount of diesel fuel or petrol in stock, we must subtract the amount put into lorries and cars to find how much we have left. Similarly in factories, we start off with supplies of raw materials or components, and if we record how much we have used, we can calculate how much we should have left. This detects any pilfering, and also alerts us to the need to re-order as supplies are used up.

In subtraction as with addition we start from the right-hand side, i.e. the units column, and work our way across the columns. In some cases, there are no real problems as we only have to subtract small numbers from larger numbers. Suppose, for example, we have to subtract 121 from 243:

$$\begin{array}{r} 243 \\ - 121 \\ \hline 122 \\ \hline\hline \end{array}$$

We would say: 3 units minus 1 unit equals 2 units, and put this in the units column. We would then say: 4 tens minus 2 tens equals 2 tens, and put this in the tens column. We would then go to the hundreds column: 2 hundreds minus 1 hundred equals 1 hundred, and place this in the hundreds column. The answer is therefore 122. If we want to check on our answer we can add 122 to 121 to find that the result is 243, the figure we started with.

It is always more difficult when we have to subtract a number that involves borrowing figures from the next column. Consider the example below:

$$\begin{array}{r} 1\,234 \\ - \quad 567 \\ \hline \\ \hline\hline \end{array}$$

When we try to take 7 from 4 it cannot be done and we have to borrow a 10 from the tens row. This means that the 3 tens in 1234 is reduced to only 2 tens, i.e. 1224. The 10 we have borrowed is put with the 4 to give 14. We can now say: 14 subtract 7 equals 7. This 7 is placed in the answer, in the units column. We must now subtract the tens, by saying: 2 (not 3) subtract 6. Again we cannot do this, so we must borrow 100 and turn it into 10 tens. We can now say: 12 subtract 6 equals 6. Of course, really it is 12 tens subtract 6 tens.

Put the 6 tens in the answer. Continuing in this way we find that the answer is 667.

$$\begin{array}{r} 1\,234 \\ - \quad 567 \\ \hline 667 \\ \hline\hline \end{array}$$

(Checking, we can add up 667 and 567 and we find that they do add to 1234.)

2.8 Subtracting horizontally

Just as we can add across the page it is occasionally necessary to subtract across the page. Thus we could say:

$$8 - 5 = 3$$

It is more difficult to subtract 15 from 27 ($27 - 15 = 12$), but if we start with the units figure it is quite simple. However, to subtract 89 from 175 ($175 - 89$) requires us to borrow figures from the next column. Five subtract 9, you cannot, so borrow a ten, etc. Easy subtraction sums of this sort are often set as mental arithmetic in examinations, but with large subtraction sums it is preferable to set the sum down in a proper manner and subtract vertically.

Now try the exercises in Section 2.9 below.

2.9 Exercises: Simple subtraction

1 Set down these subtraction sums in your exercise book and find the answers.

(a)	568	(b)	659	(c)	105
	− 285		− 327		− 96

(d)	534	(e)	916	(f)	9 104
	− 312		− 345		− 1 715

(g)	7 513	(h)	6 592	(i)	5 792
	− 907		− 3 782		− 3 464

(j)	49 783		
	− 4 651		

2 Set down these subtraction sums and find the

answers. Do not attempt to work them horizontally.

(a) $5\,946 - 3\,212 =$ (b) $7\,823 - 5\,454 =$
(c) $16\,722 - 9\,584 =$ (d) $17\,394 - 3\,934 =$
(e) $15\,999 - 12\,349 =$ (f) $562\,342 - 40\,234 =$
(g) $33\,467 - 23\,492 =$ (h) $343\,962 - 23\,349 =$
(i) $792\,555 - 14\,678 =$ (j) $523\,199 - 472\,897 =$

3 Copy out these subtraction sums exactly as shown and work them horizontally.

(a) $8 - 5 =$ (b) $44 - 27 =$
(c) $15 - 7 =$ (d) $56 - 13 =$
(e) $25 - 2 =$ (f) $17 - 8 =$
(g) $22 - 6 =$ (h) $24 - 9 =$
(i) $57 - 14 =$ (j) $43 - 7 =$

3

Basic Rules: Multiplication and Division

3.1 Multiplication

Multiplication is a quick way of doing additions. To a person who has not learned any multiplication tables the answer to the question 'What do eight sixes come to altogether?' can only be found by adding up eight lots of 6:

$$6 + 6 + 6 + 6 + 6 + 6 + 6 + 6 = 48$$

Using multiplication tables we can give the answer directly, because in the eight-times table one of the lines is $8 \times 6 = 48$ (eight sixes are forty-eight). Each line of the multiplication table is called a *bond*. You probably learned your multiplication tables at school, but it is more important to know the individual bonds. Bonds such as $7 \times 7 = 49$ or $9 \times 9 = 81$ should fly into your head instantaneously.

Usually we only learn tables up to the twelve-times table, which finishes $12 \times 12 = 144$. If we multiply a number up to 12 by another integer of up to 12 most people will remember the answer from their early school days. If we have numbers larger than 12 we do not know the answers and have to set down a multiplication sum. If we multiply a large number by 12 or less, the method used is called **short multiplication**. We set such a sum down, as shown:

$$\begin{array}{r} 123 \\ \times \quad 8 \\ \hline 984 \\ \hline 12 \end{array}$$

(a) Start with the units figure: $8 \times 3 = 24$. Put the 4 units in the answer and carry the 2 tens into the tens column.
(b) Now multiply the tens: $8 \times 2 = 16$. Add in the other 2 tens and we have 18 tens. Put the 8 in the answer and carry the 10 tens into the hundreds row as 1 hundred.
(c) Now multiply the hundreds: $8 \times 1 = 8$. Add the 1 hundred to the 8 hundreds and we have 9 hundreds to put into the answer. So, $8 \times 123 = 984$.

It is important to use the right word in mathematics, as in other walks of life. In the sum shown above, $123 \times 8 = 984$, the figure we are multiplying by (8) is called the **multiplier**, and the number being multiplied (123) is called the **multiplicand**. The answer to a multiplication sum (984) is called the **product**. So, in the example given, 123 is the multiplicand, 8 is the multiplier, and the product is 984.

3.2 Exercises: short multiplication

Do the following multiplication sums.

1 (a) $956 \times 7 =$ (b) $962 \times 10 =$
  (c) $922 \times 2 =$ (d) $863 \times 4 =$
  (e) $3562 \times 8 =$ (f) $5892 \times 9 =$
  (g) $9554 \times 3 =$ (h) $1213 \times 12 =$
  (i) $1067 \times 5 =$ (j) $9342 \times 6 =$

2 (a) $3586 \times 9 =$ (b) $4925 \times 11 =$
  (c) $4275 \times 7 =$ (d) $7284 \times 8 =$
  (e) $8342 \times 6 =$ (f) $8257 \times 5 =$
  (g) $15\,294 \times 10 =$ (h) $26\,923 \times 12 =$
  (i) $16\,138 \times 4 =$ (j) $38\,786 \times 9 =$

3.3 Multiplication by 10, 100 and 1000 etc.

You may have noticed in some of the short multiplication sums in Section 3.2 above, that when multiplying by 10 the answer is exactly the same as the original number except that a 0 (nought) has appeared on the extreme right-hand end of the number. Thus $962 \times 10 = 9620$, and $15\,294 \times 10 = 152\,940$.

If we multiply by 100 we get two noughts appearing, and when we multiply by 1000 three noughts appear. Thus $886 \times 100 = 88\,600$ and $886 \times 1000 = 886\,000$.

(Notice that with very large numbers we leave a small gap between the hundreds and the thousands column. This is now laid down by international agreement. The United Kingdom used to separate numbers off with commas (as in 152,940), but this is no longer correct. Do not do it.)

3.4 Long multiplication

When we multiply larger numbers together we have to have a line of calculations for each figure in the multiplier. It is helpful to put the number with the largest number of digits at the top so that it becomes the multiplicand and the smaller number is the multiplier. This reduces the number of lines of working required. Consider the example:

$$
\begin{array}{r}
12\,345 \\
\times \quad 16 \\
\hline
\end{array}
$$

The calculation would be as follows:

$$
\begin{array}{r}
12\,345 \\
\times \quad 16 \\
\hline
74\,070 \\
123\,450 \\
\hline
197\,520 \\
\hline
\end{array}
$$
(6 times 12 345)
(10 times 12 345)
(16 times 12 345)

(a) We multiply by the 6 as in a short multiplication sum. It is best to remember the carrying figures in your head, so as not to create a muddle on the page. So we multiply $6 \times 5 = 30$, put 0 in the answer and carry 3. Our next step is $6 \times 4 = 24$, and 3 makes 27, put 7 in the answer and carry 2 etc.
(b) We now have to multiply by the ten in 16. When we do this we simply have to put a 0 in the units column, and after that the figures are the same, because $1 \times 5 = 5$, $1 \times 4 = 4$ etc.

(c) We now add up the two rows to give us the total of 6 times and 10 times, which is the product (answer) we require.
(d) Suppose we had been multiplying by 26. The second line of working would not have been just 10 times, but 20 times. We would have put a 0 in the units column and then multiplied by 2 to get 20 times 12 345. Follow this idea in the further example:

$$
\begin{array}{r}
53\,284 \\
\times \quad 136 \\
\hline
319\,704 \\
1\,598\,520 \\
5\,328\,400 \\
\hline
7\,246\,624 \\
\hline
\end{array}
$$
$(6 \times 53\,284)$
$(30 \times 53\,284)$
$(100 \times 53\,284)$
$(136 \times 53\,284)$

Answer $= \underline{\underline{7\,246\,624}}$

Some people may have been taught to start with the highest number in the multiplier. In other words, in the calculation which we have now done above, to have started by multiplying by the 1 hundred, then the tens and then the units. It makes no difference to the answer, so please continue to use the method to which you have become accustomed.

3.5 Exercises: long multiplication

Do the following long multiplication sums:

1 (a) $266 \times 17 =$ (b) $234 \times 19 =$
(c) $893 \times 14 =$ (d) $546 \times 57 =$
(e) $5867 \times 22 =$ (f) $6519 \times 18 =$
(g) $4983 \times 36 =$ (h) $9105 \times 63 =$
(i) $8946 \times 27 =$ (j) $2598 \times 36 =$

2 (a) $23\,754 \times 19 =$ (b) $38\,127 \times 17 =$
(c) $49\,852 \times 23 =$ (d) $36\,841 \times 75 =$
(e) $12\,728 \times 39 =$ (f) $24\,382 \times 36 =$
(g) $42\,368 \times 48 =$ (h) $36\,817 \times 95 =$
(i) $77\,501 \times 176 =$ (j) $273\,528 \times 194 =$

3.6 Exercises: multiplication problems

1 At a museum, 367 visitors bought one postcard each, 480 bought two postcards each and 207 bought three postcards each, 945 visitors

bought packs of five postcards and 2076 visitors each bought packs of ten postcards. How many postcards were sold altogether?

2 At the World Cup football venue, 138 934 people paid for a single ticket, 173 425 paid for two persons, 13 365 paid for three persons and 12 006 group tickets for ten persons each were sold. How many seats were sold?

3 In a survey of egg yield, 84 hens laid an average of 225 eggs per year, 634 gave an average of 150 eggs per year, and 282 laid an average 120 eggs per year. What was the total yield of eggs?

4 A library computer discovers that the following issues were made in one month: 15 072 books were issued once, 1765 were issued twice, 833 were issued three times and 194 were issued four times. No book was issued more than four times in a month. What was the total number of issues made in the month?

3.7 Division

Division is a mathematical process for sharing. The sign for division is ÷, so a statement $100 \div 4$ means: 'How shall I share out 100 items among four people?' We could give each person 1 item each and there would be 96 left. We could then give them another 1 each. There would then be 92 items left. Each time we take away 4 items, the remainder left to share out is smaller. When we have taken away 4 items twenty-five times we find there are none left, because 25 fours make 100. So division could be done by repeated subtractions, but it is a tedious way to divide. The better way is to use our multiplication tables backwards. Thus we can say:

$$6 \times 10 = 60$$

or

10 into 60 goes 6 times

Note that we could also say:

6 into 60 goes 10 times

These two sums are usually written:

$$\text{10)}\overline{60} \qquad \text{6)}\overline{60}$$
$$\underline{6} \qquad \quad \underline{10}$$

Once again, as with multiplication, we can do some calculations more easily than others. If we know our tables (in other words, for dividing by numbers up to 12) we can use **short division**. For longer numbers we must use **long division**.

3.8 Short division

Consider the following division sum: $184 \div 4$ (how many fours in 184?). This is set down as shown below left, and the calculation is done as shown below right:

$$\text{4)}\overline{184} \qquad \qquad \text{4)}\overline{184}^{\;\;\;2}$$
$$\qquad \qquad \qquad \underline{46}$$

(a) We start by dividing 4 into the 1 hundred. This will not of course work out, because 1 is smaller than 4. The 1 hundred is now put with the 8 tens, making 18 tens.

(b) Four into 18 goes 4 times ($4 \times 4 = 16$) and there are 2 over. Put the answer 4 below the 8 in the answer row, and carry the 2 tens left over to the units row. This makes 24 units.

(c) Four into 24 units goes 6 times ($6 \times 4 = 24$), so 6 goes in the answer. The answer to the question is that 4 goes into 184 forty-six times.

Sometimes we get a remainder:

$$187 \div 4 = \text{4)}\overline{187}^{\;\;\;2}$$
$$\qquad \qquad \underline{46} \text{ remainder } 3$$

When we have a remainder we can either declare it in writing, as shown above, or write it as a fraction $\frac{3}{4}$. Thus the answer to the question: 'How many fours in 187?' is either '$46\frac{3}{4}$ fours in 187?' or '46 fours, and a remainder of 3'. A full explanation of fractions is given later.

In a division sum ($184 \div 4 = 46$), the number we are dividing by (4) is called the **divisor**, the number we are sharing out (184) is the **dividend** and the answer (46) is called the **quotient**.

3.9 Exercises: short division

Work out the answers to the following division sums. If there are remainders, show them as fractions.

1 (a) $695 \div 5 =$ (b) $732 \div 4 =$
  (c) $848 \div 8 =$ (d) $954 \div 3 =$
  (e) $1272 \div 12 =$ (f) $5980 \div 10 =$
  (g) $7299 \div 9 =$ (h) $8384 \div 8 =$
  (i) $7271 \div 11 =$ (j) $4382 \div 7 =$

2 (a) $594 \div 9 =$ (b) $738 \div 12 =$
  (c) $2562 \div 11 =$ (d) $3817 \div 9 =$
  (e) $4726 \div 7 =$ (f) $5832 \div 5 =$
  (g) $7281 \div 6 =$ (h) $5842 \div 9 =$
  (i) $7476 \div 5 =$ (j) $3817 \div 8 =$

3.10 Long division

When we have to divide by numbers larger than 12 (and consequently do not know our tables) we have to use a method called long division. Consider the long division calculation shown below:

$$162\tfrac{10}{27}$$
$$27\overline{)4384}$$
$$\underline{27}$$
$$168$$
$$162$$
$$\overline{64}$$
$$\underline{54}$$
$$10$$

rough workings

27	27
$\times\ 5$	$\times\ 6$
135	162
27	27
$\times\ 2$	$\times\ 3$
54	81

(a) The answer is written over the top of the dividend, to leave the space below clear.
(b) We start by saying 27 into 4 thousands will not go. The 4 thousands now goes with the 3 hundreds to give 43 hundreds. Twenty-seven into 43 goes once (two 27s are 54, as shown in the rough workings at the side). We put the 1 in the answer (over the hundreds column), and then put 27 under the 43 and subtract to find the remainder. There are 16 hundreds left. We now put this 16 hundreds with the 8 tens by bringing the 8 tens down alongside it.
(c) Now we ask 'how may 27s in 168?' Of course, it is really 168 tens. A bit more rough working helps us discover that $6 \times 27 = 162$. So there are six 27s in 168. Put 6 in the answer (over the tens column), and take 162 from 168 to find the remainder. This is 6. There are 6 tens left over.

(d) Bring down the 4 units next to the 6 tens and we have 64 units. Twenty-seven into 64 goes: $2 \times 27 = 54$ and 10 left over. Put 2 in the answer (in the units column), making an answer of 162, and show the remainder as a fraction $\tfrac{10}{27}$.

We must all know how to do long division, and in fact many readers will already be proficient at this. If you are one of these, the following sums may be done on a calculator, to give you keyboard practice.

(*Note*: A calculator will not give an answer with a fraction, other than a decimal fraction. This will make it difficult to check your answers. The best way to do this is to make a note of the fraction you get on the calculator. For example, in 2(a) below the answer is $369\tfrac{4}{85}$. The calculator gives 369.04705. If you make a note of the decimal fraction here (.04705) and then work out $4 \div 85$ on the calculator, you will see that it comes to the same figure. Your answer is therefore correct.)

3.11 Exercises: long division

Do the following long division sums, showing any remainders as fractions.

1 (a) $2608 \div 16 =$ (b) $21\,480 \div 24 =$
  (c) $1881 \div 19 =$ (d) $6084 \div 26 =$
  (e) $13\,818 \div 14 =$ (f) $6840 \div 15 =$
  (g) $11\,487 \div 21 =$ (h) $28\,971 \div 29 =$
  (i) $7004 \div 17 =$ (j) $4429 \div 22 =$

2 (a) $31\,369 \div 85 =$ (b) $42\,949 \div 51 =$
  (c) $64\,472 \div 63 =$ (d) $401\,373 \div 72 =$
  (e) $181\,059 \div 48 =$ (f) $74\,284 \div 49 =$
  (g) $35\,381 \div 92 =$ (h) $85\,720 \div 33 =$
  (i) $75\,076 \div 76 =$ (j) $28\,249 \div 27 =$

3.12 Exercises: problems involving long division

1 A wholesaler of bulk sugar on the London sugar market decides during a shortage to apportion supplies equally among his 69 customers. The total supplies reaching him are 4782 tonnes. Any remainder is to be given to

charity. How much will each customer receive, and what surplus will be available for charity?

2 If 37 350 students are allocated equally to 45 colleges, how many will each college receive?

3 A charity collects coins in bags that contain 125 coins each. The total collection is 29 375 coins. How many bags are filled?

4 Visitors to a seaside resort travel in buses holding 78 passengers each. A pensioners' organisation proposes to take 1056 passengers. What is the least number of buses that can be used?

5 An emergency relief organisation charters two aircraft, each holding 385 passengers, to move 10 000 people from a danger area. How many journeys must be made by each plane?

4
Fractions

4.1 What are fractions?

The phrase 'vulgar' or 'common' fraction is used when describing quantities that are less than one. In the United Kingdom, we now have a decimal currency which makes no use of fractions of a penny. Whilst the metric system has become far more common within the United Kingdom, we frequently have items measured in units of half a kilogram. The commonest fractions are:

$$\tfrac{1}{2}, \tfrac{1}{3}, \tfrac{1}{4}, \tfrac{1}{5}, \tfrac{1}{6}, \tfrac{1}{7}, \tfrac{1}{8}, \tfrac{1}{9}, \tfrac{1}{10} \text{ etc.}$$

The names given to these fractions are one-half, one-third, one-quarter, one-fifth, one-sixth, one-seventh, one-eighth, one-ninth and one-tenth respectively. You will notice that the fraction is in two parts, separated by a horizontal line. A simple way to look at fractions is to say that the horizontal line means 'cut in'. The fraction $\tfrac{1}{2}$ could then be read as '1 cut in 2 parts', and $\tfrac{1}{3}$ could be regarded as '1 cut in 3 parts'.

The bottom part of a fraction is called the **denominator**. This means 'the name of' and it tells us what sort of fraction we are dealing with: halves, thirds, quarters, fifths etc. The top part of the fraction is called the **numerator**. This means the 'number' of fractions we have. Consider:

$$\tfrac{1}{5}, \tfrac{2}{5}, \tfrac{3}{5}, \tfrac{4}{5}$$

The denominator tells us these are all fifths, but the numerator tells us in each case how many fifths we have: one fifth, two fifths, three fifths etc.

Suppose we have $\tfrac{5}{5}, \tfrac{6}{5}$ or $\tfrac{7}{5}$. In each of these cases we have a fraction where the numerator is as large, or larger than, the denominator. This means we must have a whole number. Five fifths makes 1 whole unit. So:

$$\tfrac{5}{5} = 1 \quad \tfrac{6}{5} = 1\tfrac{1}{5} \quad \tfrac{7}{5} = 1\tfrac{2}{5}$$

Since a fraction should always be less than one, $\tfrac{5}{5}$, $\tfrac{6}{5}$ and $\tfrac{7}{5}$ are **improper fractions** and it is best to turn them into **mixed numbers**, as shown above. A mixed number has some integers (whole numbers) and some fractions. To do this we divide the numerator by the denominator. Thus with $\tfrac{6}{5}$ we say '5 into 6 goes once, and $\tfrac{1}{5}$ over'. So:

$$\tfrac{6}{5} = 1\tfrac{1}{5}$$

Similarly $\tfrac{17}{10} = 1\tfrac{7}{10}$ and $\tfrac{25}{12} = 2\tfrac{1}{12}$.

We can also change mixed numbers into improper fractions. Thus:

$$1\tfrac{1}{2} = \tfrac{3}{2} \quad 2\tfrac{1}{4} = \tfrac{9}{4} \quad 3\tfrac{1}{5} = \tfrac{16}{5}$$

To change a mixed number to a fraction, you multiply the whole numbers by the denominator and add in the numerator. So with $1\tfrac{1}{2}$ in the line above, we say 1 (the whole number) × 2 (the denominator) = 2. Now add the numerator, 1, to 2 and we have 3 halves, i.e. $\tfrac{3}{2}$. Similarly $2\tfrac{1}{4}$ becomes $2 \times 4 = 8$; $8 + 1 = 9$; 9 quarters = $\tfrac{9}{4}$.

4.2 Exercises: changing improper fractions to mixed numbers

1 Change the following improper fractions to mixed numbers.

(a) $\tfrac{3}{2}$ (b) $\tfrac{4}{2}$ (c) $\tfrac{5}{2}$ (d) $\tfrac{4}{3}$
(e) $\tfrac{7}{3}$ (f) $\tfrac{5}{4}$ (g) $\tfrac{7}{4}$ (h) $\tfrac{11}{4}$
(i) $\tfrac{8}{5}$ (j) $\tfrac{13}{5}$ (k) $\tfrac{11}{6}$ (l) $\tfrac{17}{6}$
(m) $\tfrac{9}{8}$ (n) $\tfrac{13}{12}$ (o) $\tfrac{29}{12}$ (p) $\tfrac{45}{11}$

2 Change the following mixed numbers to improper fractions.

(a) $1\tfrac{3}{4}$ (b) $1\tfrac{3}{5}$ (c) $2\tfrac{1}{2}$ (d) $2\tfrac{3}{4}$
(e) $2\tfrac{7}{8}$ (f) $2\tfrac{11}{12}$ (g) $3\tfrac{1}{3}$ (h) $3\tfrac{3}{4}$
(i) $3\tfrac{5}{6}$ (j) $4\tfrac{7}{10}$ (k) $5\tfrac{7}{8}$ (l) $7\tfrac{3}{5}$
(m) $8\tfrac{1}{4}$ (n) $9\tfrac{1}{3}$ (o) $7\tfrac{11}{12}$ (p) $8\tfrac{5}{8}$

4.3 Cancelling fractions

Usually, we try to give fractions in their simplest possible form. For example, we would not give an answer as $\frac{3}{6}$, but would simplify it to make one half ($\frac{1}{2}$). You can follow this idea if you look at Figure 4.1.

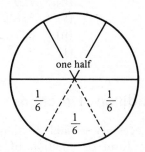

Figure 4.1 Three sixths = one half

(a) The circle is divided into two semicircles, or half circles.
(b) It has also been divided into 6 parts.
(c) As you can see there are three sixths in each half, so $\frac{3}{6} = \frac{1}{2}$.

What have we done in this example? We have divided the numerator of the fraction by 3 and the denominator of the fraction by 3. Three is said to be a **common factor**. A common factor is a small number which divides into both the numerator and the denominator. In this example, 3 divides into both 3 and 6.

If we had taken as our example $\frac{9}{12}$, then 3 would divide into both 9 and 12 and, therefore, we would arrive at the answer $\frac{3}{4}$. This process is called **cancelling**. Cancelling like this is also termed 'reducing the fraction to its lowest terms'. Sometimes we can cancel several times before we get to the lowest terms. For example:

$$\frac{66}{198}$$
$$= \frac{33}{99} \text{ (cancelling by 2)}$$
$$= \frac{11}{33} \text{ (cancelling by 3)}$$
$$= \frac{1}{3} \text{ (cancelling by 11)}$$

We usually write this as follows:

$$\frac{\cancel{66}\overset{33\,11\,1}{}}{\cancel{198}\underset{99\,33\,3}{}} = \frac{1}{3}$$

4.4 Exercises: reducing fractions to their lowest terms

1 Reduce these fractions to their lowest terms.

(a) $\frac{3}{6}$ (b) $\frac{4}{6}$ (c) $\frac{2}{8}$
(d) $\frac{4}{8}$ (e) $\frac{6}{8}$ (f) $\frac{5}{10}$
(g) $\frac{3}{12}$ (h) $\frac{4}{12}$ (i) $\frac{6}{12}$
(j) $\frac{8}{12}$ (k) $\frac{10}{12}$ (l) $\frac{7}{14}$

2 Cancel these fractions down to their lowest terms.

(a) $\frac{12}{24}$ (b) $\frac{15}{20}$ (c) $\frac{16}{36}$
(d) $\frac{14}{28}$ (e) $\frac{18}{36}$ (f) $\frac{20}{36}$
(g) $\frac{48}{64}$ (h) $\frac{48}{72}$ (i) $\frac{24}{96}$
(j) $\frac{25}{50}$ (k) $\frac{25}{75}$ (l) $\frac{45}{80}$

4.5 Prime numbers, factors and multiples

Once again we must know the right names for one or two things we shall meet in fractions, before we can discuss them properly.

A **prime number** is a number which can only be divided exactly by itself and 1. Thus 1, 2, 3, 5, 7, 11, 13, 17 and 19 are prime numbers. 19, for example, will divide by 19 (it goes once) or by 1 (it goes 19 times). However, 4, 6, 8, 9, 10, 12, 14, 15, 16 and 18 are not prime numbers. For example, 15 is not a prime number as it can be divided not only by 1 and 15 but also by 5 and 3. No even number apart from 2 is a prime number, as any even number can be divided by 2.

A **factor** is a number which will divide into another number an exact number of times. For example, 2 is a factor of 8, as we can divide it into 8 exactly 4 times. Some numbers will have a number of factors. For example, the number 60 will divide by 2, 3, 4, 5, 6, 10, 12, 15, 20 and 30 and hence has all these numbers as factors.

A **common factor** is a number which will go into two (or more) other numbers. As we have seen in fractions we often use the term 'common factor'. This is where two (or more) numbers have a factor that divides exactly into both (or all) of them. For example, all even numbers have a common factor of 2. Four is a common factor of both 8 and 12. It is these common factors which are used when we cancel a fraction down to its lowest terms.

The **highest common factor** is the highest number that divides exactly into two or more numbers. The highest common factor of 12 and 18 is 6. Six is the highest number that divides exactly into both of them. The highest common factor of 21, 30 and 36 is 3.

The term **multiple** means a number which contains another number an exact number of times. For example, we can say that 24 is a multiple of 6 as it contains it four times.

A **common multiple** contains two or more numbers an exact number of times. Therefore, we could say that eighteen is a common multiple of 2, 3, 6 and 9. Similarly, 30 is a common multiple of 2, 3, 5, 6, 10 and 15. These common multiples are very useful in the addition and subtraction of fractions.

4.6 Exercises: prime numbers, factors and multiples

1 Write down all the prime numbers between 1 and 10.
2 Write down all the prime numbers between 20 and 30.
3 Pick out the prime numbers in each of the following sets.

(a) 3, 9, 12	(b) 16, 57, 19
(c) 5, 13, 26	(d) 7, 33, 16
(e) 4, 6, 11	(f) 29, 4, 12
(g) 54, 7, 26	(h) 5, 17, 1
(i) 18, 8, 1	(j) 11, 16, 3

4 Write down the factors of each of the following numbers, not counting 1 and the number itself.

(a) 28	(b) 63
(c) 15	(d) 21
(e) 48	(f) 54
(g) 36	(h) 96
(i) 18	(j) 60

5 Find any common factors (not counting 1) for the numbers in each of the following sets.

(a) 3, 21	(b) 17, 51
(c) 15, 45	(d) 8, 28
(e) 24, 72	(f) 48, 84
(g) 4, 24	(h) 14, 49
(i) 12, 44	(j) 6, 30

6 Find a common multiple of the numbers in each of the following.

(a) 2, 7	(b) 4, 11
(c) 3, 5	(d) 5, 7, 9
(e) 4, 8	(f) 6, 5, 8
(g) 2, 9	(h) 2, 6, 7
(i) 3, 4	(j) 5, 9, 12

4.7 The addition of fractions

It is often necessary to add fractions together. The simplest form of addition of fractions is where we have the same denominator in both fractions.

For example, if we were to add $\frac{1}{10} + \frac{3}{10} + \frac{3}{10} + \frac{1}{10}$ we would arrive at the answer $\frac{8}{10}$. Having done this we can simplify the answer, as 2 will go into both the numerator and denominator and we can cancel the answer down to $\frac{4}{5}$.

If, however, we were asked to add $\frac{1}{5}$, $\frac{1}{10}$ and $\frac{1}{15}$, then it is apparent that we cannot do it immediately.

The solution to the difficulty is to find a common multiple of 5, 10, and 15, so that we can turn them all into the same type of fractions. This is called the **common denominator**. It is a common multiple of 5, 10 and 15.

So how do we find the common denominator? Take our example:

$$\frac{1}{5} + \frac{1}{10} + \frac{1}{15}.$$

To find the common denominator the rules are:
(a) Look at the largest of the denominators: in this case, 15.
(b) Will 5 go into 15? The answer is yes. Good! We need not worry about 5 any more, as the common multiple we are looking for is a multiple of 15, and if 5 goes into 15 then 5 will go into any multiple of 15.
(c) Will 10 go into 15? No! Then let us double 15: $2 \times 15 = 30$.
(d) Will 10 go into 30? Yes. Will 15 go into 30? Yes. Will 5 go into 30? Yes. Then 30 is the common denominator we require.

(e) *Special note*: Of course, there are many multiples of 5, 10 and 15 (for example, 60, 90, 120, 150 etc.). The best one to use is 30, because it is the **lowest common multiple** and gives us the **lowest common denominator**.

Consider the first example; below:

$$\tfrac{1}{2} + \tfrac{1}{4}$$
$$= \tfrac{2+1}{4} \quad \text{(4 is the common denominator)}$$
$$\qquad (\tfrac{1}{2} = \tfrac{2}{4})$$
$$= \tfrac{3}{4}$$

We can add the above fractions together as soon as we have turned them to the same type of fraction: quarters.

Consider the second example, below:

$$\tfrac{1}{3} + \tfrac{1}{6}$$
$$= \tfrac{2+1}{6} \quad \text{(6 is the common denominator)}$$
$$= \tfrac{\cancel{3}^{1}}{\cancel{6}_{2}} \quad (\tfrac{1}{3} \text{ becomes } \tfrac{2}{6} \text{ (see notes below))}$$
$$= \tfrac{1}{2} \quad \text{(3 and 6 will cancel by 3)}$$

To turn $\tfrac{1}{3}$ into $\tfrac{2}{6}$ we say:

(a) Divide the denominators into one another. (How many threes in six? Answer: 2.)
(b) Multiply the numerator by the answer to (a) $1 \times 2 = 2$.
(c) So $\tfrac{1}{3}$ becomes $\tfrac{2}{6}$. (Check—will it cancel down again to $\tfrac{1}{3}$? Yes it will.)
(d) Once the $\tfrac{1}{3}$ is changed to sixths we can add up the two fractions.

Consider the third example, below:

$$\tfrac{3}{4} + \tfrac{2}{3} + \tfrac{1}{12}$$
$$= \tfrac{9+8+1}{12} \quad \text{(the common denominator is 12)}$$
$$= \tfrac{18}{12} \quad (\tfrac{3}{4} \text{ changes to } \tfrac{9}{12} \text{ and } \tfrac{2}{3} \text{ to } \tfrac{8}{12})$$
$$\qquad \text{(when added the fraction is an improper fraction)}$$
$$= 1\tfrac{\cancel{6}^{1}}{\cancel{12}_{2}} \quad \text{(change the improper fraction to a mixed number)}$$
$$= 1\tfrac{1}{2} \quad \text{(cancel down the fractional part of the mixed number)}$$

Consider the fourth example, below:

$$1\tfrac{1}{2} + 2\tfrac{3}{4} + 3\tfrac{7}{8} \quad \text{(we have some whole numbers; add these first)}$$
$$= 6\tfrac{4+6+7}{8} \quad \text{(the common denominator is 8)}$$

$$= 6\tfrac{17}{8} \quad \text{(the fraction is improper—turn it to a mixed number} = 2\tfrac{1}{8})$$
$$= 8\tfrac{1}{8} \quad (6 + 2\tfrac{1}{8} \text{ gives us } 8\tfrac{1}{8})$$

4.8 Exercises: addition of fractions

1 Set down the following fractions and add them together.

(a) $\tfrac{2}{3} + \tfrac{4}{5} =$ (b) $\tfrac{3}{5} + \tfrac{3}{4} =$
(c) $\tfrac{3}{4} + \tfrac{7}{10} =$ (d) $\tfrac{2}{3} + \tfrac{3}{20} =$
(e) $\tfrac{5}{16} + \tfrac{1}{2} + \tfrac{5}{8} =$ (f) $\tfrac{1}{2} + \tfrac{4}{5} + \tfrac{17}{20} =$
(g) $\tfrac{7}{8} + \tfrac{2}{3} + \tfrac{7}{12} =$ (h) $\tfrac{4}{5} + \tfrac{1}{2} + \tfrac{11}{20} =$
(i) $\tfrac{4}{5} + \tfrac{3}{4} + \tfrac{1}{2} =$ (j) $\tfrac{2}{3} + \tfrac{1}{2} + \tfrac{5}{8} =$
(k) $\tfrac{7}{10} + \tfrac{4}{7} + \tfrac{3}{4} =$ (l) $\tfrac{9}{10} + \tfrac{2}{3} + \tfrac{4}{15} =$

2 Add the following mixed numbers.

(a) $2\tfrac{2}{3} + 1\tfrac{1}{2} + 4\tfrac{7}{12} =$ (b) $4\tfrac{1}{2} + 9\tfrac{3}{10} + 4\tfrac{2}{3} =$
(c) $1\tfrac{1}{3} + 3\tfrac{11}{12} + 6\tfrac{3}{4} =$ (d) $9\tfrac{1}{2} + 2\tfrac{17}{30} + 2\tfrac{5}{6} =$
(e) $4\tfrac{7}{10} + 1\tfrac{5}{6} + 3\tfrac{1}{5} =$ (f) $2\tfrac{5}{8} + 3\tfrac{1}{4} + 4\tfrac{7}{10} =$
(g) $4\tfrac{7}{10} + 1\tfrac{1}{2} + 2\tfrac{3}{4} =$ (h) $3\tfrac{1}{5} + 1\tfrac{1}{7} + 7\tfrac{1}{2} =$
(i) $1\tfrac{2}{3} + 3\tfrac{3}{8} + 6\tfrac{3}{4} =$ (j) $9\tfrac{1}{2} + 2\tfrac{7}{12} + 4\tfrac{1}{3} =$
(k) $3\tfrac{7}{8} + 4\tfrac{7}{10} + 1\tfrac{1}{4} =$ (l) $2\tfrac{7}{12} + 1\tfrac{5}{6} + 7\tfrac{1}{2} =$

4.9 Subtraction of fractions

Subtraction of fractions is very similar to addition. We again have to find a common denominator.

Suppose, for example, we wish to subtract $\tfrac{3}{8}$ from $\tfrac{7}{8}$, how would we do this? Since they both have the same denominator, we merely take the 3 from the 7. We would therefore arrive at the answer $\tfrac{4}{8}$, which we can cancel down to $\tfrac{1}{2}$.

If, however, we do not have the same denominator, then as before, we have to find a common denominator. Consider the first example, below:

$$\tfrac{6}{7} - \tfrac{2}{3} \quad \text{(the common denominator is 21)}$$
$$= \tfrac{18-14}{21} \quad (\tfrac{6}{7} \text{ changes to } \tfrac{18}{21} \text{ and } \tfrac{2}{3} \text{ to } \tfrac{14}{21})$$
$$= \tfrac{4}{21} \quad \text{(when subtracted we have an answer of } \tfrac{4}{21})$$

Consider the second example, below:

$$4\tfrac{1}{2} - 1\tfrac{1}{3} \quad \text{(subtract the whole numbers first)}$$
$$= 3\tfrac{3-2}{6}$$
$$= 3\tfrac{1}{6}$$

Consider the third example, below:

$4\frac{1}{3} - 2\frac{5}{6}$ (subtract the whole numbers first)

$= 2\frac{2-5}{6}$ (when changed to sixths, the second number is bigger than the first)

$= 1\frac{6+2-5}{6}$ (use one of the whole numbers to give $\frac{6}{6}$. Now take the 5 from the 6 (1) and add 2 to give $\frac{3}{6}$)

$= 1\frac{3}{6}$ (cancel down)

$= 1\frac{1}{2}$

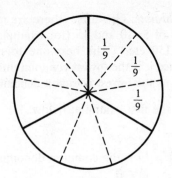

Figure 4.2 One third of one third = one ninth

4.10 Exercises: subtraction of fractions

1 Carry out the following subtractions.

(a) $\frac{3}{4} - \frac{1}{2} =$ (b) $\frac{4}{5} - \frac{11}{30} =$

(c) $\frac{2}{3} - \frac{1}{8} =$ (d) $\frac{3}{4} - \frac{3}{10} =$

(e) $\frac{6}{7} - \frac{1}{5} =$ (f) $\frac{6}{7} - \frac{1}{2} =$

(g) $\frac{5}{12} - \frac{3}{10} =$ (h) $\frac{11}{12} - \frac{1}{4} =$

(i) $\frac{7}{10} - \frac{1}{6} =$ (j) $\frac{4}{9} - \frac{3}{18} =$

2 Set down and complete the following subtractions.

(a) $5\frac{1}{2} - 4\frac{1}{3} =$ (b) $7\frac{9}{10} - 6\frac{2}{3} =$

(c) $9\frac{1}{4} - 2\frac{1}{3} =$ (d) $16\frac{7}{12} - 12\frac{4}{5} =$

(e) $11\frac{1}{3} - 8\frac{9}{10} =$ (f) $17\frac{7}{8} - 5\frac{3}{4} =$

(g) $8\frac{1}{4} - 4\frac{1}{2} =$ (h) $24\frac{17}{24} - 18\frac{9}{10} =$

(i) $17\frac{11}{12} - 2\frac{1}{8} =$ (j) $3\frac{3}{7} - 1\frac{1}{2} =$

(k) $12\frac{17}{24} - 10\frac{1}{6} =$ (l) $5\frac{1}{4} - 2\frac{9}{10} =$

(m) $8\frac{5}{9} - 2\frac{1}{3} =$ (n) $7\frac{3}{5} - 2\frac{4}{7} =$

4.11 Multiplication of fractions

In Chapter 3, on multiplication of integers, we showed that if we multiply one number by another number the answer is greater than the original number. When we multiply fractions, which are of course less than 1, the final answer will be less than the original answer. Suppose, for example, we multiply $\frac{1}{3} \times \frac{1}{3}$. The answer will be $\frac{1}{9}$. You may find this easier to understand if you change the term multiply to 'of'. If I multiply 100 by 2, there are two *of them*, which is of course 200. If I change $\frac{1}{3} \times \frac{1}{3}$ to $\frac{1}{3}$ of $\frac{1}{3}$, you can easily see that one third of $\frac{1}{3}$ is one ninth.

We see from Figure 4.2 that:

$$\frac{1}{3} \times \frac{1}{3} = \frac{1}{9}$$

Notice that we can get this result very easily if we simply multiply the numerators and multiply the denominators. Thus:

$$\frac{1}{2} \times \frac{1}{2} = \frac{1}{4}$$
$$\frac{1}{3} \times \frac{1}{4} = \frac{1}{12}$$
$$\frac{2}{3} \times \frac{1}{5} = \frac{2}{15}$$

However, consider the following example:

$$\frac{2}{3} \times \frac{3}{4} = \frac{6}{12}$$

Clearly $\frac{6}{12}$ will cancel down (cancelling by 6) to $\frac{1}{2}$. It is really better if we cancel before we multiply the numerators and multiply the denominators.

$$\frac{\overset{1}{\cancel{2}}}{\underset{1}{\cancel{3}}} \times \frac{\overset{1}{\cancel{3}}}{\underset{2}{\cancel{4}}} \qquad \text{(cancelling by 3, and by 2)}$$

$$= \frac{1}{2}$$

The rules for a simple multiplication of fractions are:

(a) Set down the calculation.

(b) Cancel if you can.

(c) Multiply the numerators and multiply the denominators.

If we try to multiply mixed numbers a serious difficulty arises. Consider the calculation $1\frac{1}{2} \times 1\frac{1}{2}$. Really this is made up of two little thoughts:

$$1\frac{1}{2} \times 1 \quad \text{and} \quad 1\frac{1}{2} \times \frac{1}{2}$$

The first part is easy: $1\frac{1}{2} \times 1 = 1\frac{1}{2}$.

The second part is more difficult. We have

$$1 \times \frac{1}{2} \quad \text{and} \quad \frac{1}{2} \times \frac{1}{2}$$
$$1 \times \frac{1}{2} = \frac{1}{2} \qquad\qquad \frac{1}{2} \times \frac{1}{2} = \frac{1}{4}$$

Therefore $1\frac{1}{2} \times 1\frac{1}{2}$ comes to $1\frac{1}{2} + \frac{1}{2} + \frac{1}{4} = 2\frac{1}{4}$

Although this looks a little complicated we can

make it easier if we change the mixed numbers to improper fractions first. We then have:

$1\frac{1}{2} \times 1\frac{1}{2}$ (set the sum down)

$= \frac{3}{2} \times \frac{3}{2}$ (change the mixed numbers to improper fractions)

$= \frac{9}{4}$ (multiply the numerators, multiply the denominators)

$= 2\frac{1}{4}$ (change the improper fraction back to a mixed number)

So this is what we do each time we do a multiplication of fractions sum involving mixed numbers. For example:

$1\frac{1}{2} \times 2\frac{2}{3} \times 3\frac{1}{4}$ (change them to improper fractions)

$= \frac{3}{2} \times \frac{8}{3} \times \frac{13}{4}$ (cancel if you can)

$= \frac{13}{1}$ (multiply the numerators and multiply the denominators)

$= 13$ (as the denominator was 1, we have 13 integers)

4.12 Exercises: multiplication of fractions

Set down these fraction sums and multiply them.

1 (a) $\frac{1}{2} \times \frac{4}{5} =$ (b) $\frac{2}{3} \times \frac{9}{10} =$
  (c) $\frac{6}{7} \times \frac{7}{15} =$ (d) $\frac{11}{12} \times \frac{6}{7} =$
  (e) $\frac{3}{4} \times \frac{5}{6} =$ (f) $\frac{20}{33} \times \frac{4}{5} =$
  (g) $\frac{2}{3} \times \frac{1}{8} =$ (h) $\frac{5}{19} \times \frac{4}{15} =$
  (i) $\frac{17}{20} \times \frac{4}{7} =$ (j) $\frac{6}{7} \times \frac{5}{12} =$

2 (a) $\frac{3}{4} \times \frac{2}{3} \times \frac{5}{8} =$ (b) $\frac{7}{10} \times \frac{3}{4} \times \frac{14}{15} =$
  (c) $\frac{9}{10} \times \frac{4}{7} \times \frac{4}{9} =$ (d) $\frac{10}{21} \times \frac{8}{11} \times \frac{11}{12} =$
  (e) $\frac{5}{8} \times \frac{4}{7} \times \frac{1}{2} =$ (f) $\frac{2}{3} \times \frac{5}{9} \times \frac{7}{10} =$
  (g) $\frac{15}{16} \times \frac{7}{12} \times \frac{8}{15} =$ (h) $\frac{1}{10} \times \frac{5}{12} \times \frac{2}{3} =$
  (i) $\frac{3}{5} \times \frac{5}{7} \times \frac{1}{2} =$ (j) $\frac{6}{11} \times \frac{3}{4} \times \frac{11}{15} =$
  (k) $\frac{4}{7} \times \frac{9}{10} \times \frac{21}{40} =$ (l) $\frac{9}{10} \times \frac{5}{3} \times \frac{4}{9} =$

3 (a) $1\frac{3}{4} \times 4\frac{1}{7} =$ (b) $3\frac{1}{5} \times 1\frac{1}{11} =$
  (c) $9\frac{7}{8} \times 6\frac{4}{5} =$ (d) $2\frac{1}{2} \times 4\frac{3}{9} =$
  (e) $6\frac{5}{6} \times 1\frac{1}{7} =$ (f) $3\frac{1}{4} \times 8\frac{1}{3} =$
  (g) $5\frac{5}{6} \times 6\frac{7}{8} =$ (h) $2\frac{4}{9} \times 9\frac{3}{4} =$
  (i) $6\frac{1}{2} \times 5\frac{5}{12} =$ (j) $7\frac{1}{5} \times 4\frac{1}{2} =$

4 (a) $7\frac{1}{3} \times 4\frac{1}{8} \times 2\frac{1}{4} =$ (b) $3\frac{3}{4} \times 4\frac{3}{5} \times 7\frac{1}{5} =$
  (c) $8\frac{1}{6} \times 2\frac{1}{4} \times 4\frac{1}{2} =$ (d) $5\frac{1}{5} \times 2\frac{2}{13} \times 4\frac{3}{7} =$
  (e) $4\frac{1}{5} \times 9\frac{1}{3} \times 8\frac{4}{7} =$ (f) $6\frac{3}{7} \times 7\frac{1}{3} \times 1\frac{2}{11} =$
  (g) $2\frac{3}{4} \times 4\frac{1}{11} \times 1\frac{4}{15} =$ (h) $2\frac{1}{5} \times 1\frac{1}{3} \times 4\frac{3}{8} =$
  (i) $1\frac{1}{3} \times 2\frac{2}{9} \times 1\frac{4}{5} =$ (j) $1\frac{1}{9} \times 2\frac{7}{10} \times 6\frac{1}{8} =$

(k) $4\frac{2}{3} \times 6\frac{1}{2} \times 3\frac{3}{4} =$ (l) $3\frac{1}{8} \times 4\frac{1}{5} \times 1\frac{3}{7} =$
(m) $3\frac{5}{8} \times 1\frac{1}{5} \times 1\frac{5}{29} =$ (n) $3\frac{2}{3} \times 1\frac{7}{11} \times 1\frac{2}{9} =$

4.13 Division of fractions

When we divide whole numbers into one another the answer is always smaller than the number we started with. For example:

$10 \div 5 = 2$ (How many fives in 10? Answer: 2)
$36 \div 6 = 6$ (How many sixes in 36? Answer: 6)

When we divide by fractions the answer is always larger, because there are a number of fractions in each whole one. For example:

$10 \div \frac{1}{2} = 20$ (there are 20 halves in 10 whole ones)
$36 \div \frac{1}{6} = 216$ (There are 216 sixths in 36 whole ones)

The simplest way to do division of fractions is to learn a little mathematical trick: *change the divisor upside down and multiply.* The divisor is the fraction that we are dividing by. When dividing we turn the divisor upside down and then multiply. For example, if we divide $\frac{1}{3}$ by $\frac{1}{6}$ we will invert the divisor $\frac{1}{6}$ and write it as $\frac{6}{1}$.

$\frac{1}{3} \div \frac{1}{6}$ (change the divisor upside down and multiply)

$= \frac{1}{3} \times \frac{6}{1}$ (cancel if you can)

$= \frac{2}{1}$ (multiply the numerators and multiply the denominators)

$= 2$ (when we have any number over 1 we can just disregard the 1)

Now consider the first example, below:

$\frac{3}{4} \div \frac{1}{2}$ (invert the divisor and multiply)

$= \frac{3}{4} \times \frac{2}{1}$ (cancel if you can)

$= \frac{3}{2}$ (multiply the numerators, multiply the denominators)

$= 1\frac{1}{2}$ (as the answer is an improper fraction change it to a mixed number)

There are $1\frac{1}{2}$ halves in three quarters; a sensible answer.

Now consider the second example below:

$\frac{3}{8} \div \frac{5}{16}$

$= \frac{3}{8} \times \frac{16}{5}$

$= \frac{6}{5}$

$= 1\frac{1}{5}$

Check: There are $1\frac{1}{5}$ lots of $\frac{5}{16}$ in $\frac{3}{8}$. Is this a sensible answer? Yes, because one lot of $\frac{5}{16} = \frac{5}{16}$ and another fifth of this is $\frac{1}{16}$. When we add $\frac{5}{16}$ and $\frac{1}{16}$ together we get $\frac{6}{16} = \frac{3}{8}$.

Now consider the third example, below:

$4\frac{1}{2} \div 1\frac{3}{4}$ (change the mixed numbers to improper fractions)

$= \frac{9}{2} \div \frac{7}{4}$ (change the divisor upside down and multiply)

$= \frac{9}{2_1} \times \frac{4^2}{7}$ (cancel if you can, then multiply the numerators and multiply the denominators)

$= \frac{18}{7}$ (change back to a mixed number)

$= 2\frac{4}{7}$

Check: Is this a sensible answer? There are $2\frac{4}{7}$ lots of $1\frac{3}{4}$ in $4\frac{1}{2}$. Yes it is, as $2 \times 1\frac{3}{4} = 3\frac{1}{2}$; $\frac{4}{7}$ of $1\frac{3}{4} = 1$ (one seventh of $1\frac{3}{4}$ is a quarter, so $\frac{4}{7} = 1$); $3\frac{1}{2} + 1$ make $4\frac{1}{2}$.

Whenever you do a division of fractions sum it is helpful to check it back and ask yourself: have I found a sensible answer?

4.14 Exercises: division of fractions

1 Carry out the following divisions of fractions calculations.

(a) $\frac{2}{3} \div \frac{5}{9} =$ (b) $\frac{9}{10} \div \frac{3}{5} =$

(c) $\frac{7}{10} \div \frac{4}{5} =$ (d) $\frac{3}{8} \div \frac{9}{10} =$

(e) $\frac{11}{12} \div \frac{3}{8} =$ (f) $\frac{3}{4} \div \frac{9}{16} =$

(g) $\frac{5}{8} \div \frac{9}{10} =$ (h) $\frac{1}{10} \div \frac{3}{5} =$

(i) $\frac{1}{2} \div \frac{1}{8} =$ (j) $\frac{2}{3} \div \frac{7}{15} =$

2 (a) $1\frac{1}{4} \div \frac{3}{8} =$ (b) $1\frac{1}{2} \div \frac{7}{16} =$

(c) $2\frac{1}{2} \div 1\frac{1}{4} =$ (d) $2\frac{3}{4} \div 2\frac{1}{5} =$

(e) $3\frac{1}{5} \div 1\frac{1}{7} =$ (f) $4\frac{4}{5} \div 1\frac{3}{4} =$

(g) $3\frac{1}{3} \div 2\frac{1}{2} =$ (h) $2\frac{7}{8} \div 1\frac{11}{12} =$

(i) $1\frac{9}{10} \div 3\frac{1}{6} =$ (j) $1\frac{7}{8} \div 1\frac{1}{2} =$

4.15 More difficult fraction sums

Many fractions are very complex. They may well involve several or all of the different processes we have learned. We therefore have to have a rule that tells us which calculations to do first. Without the rule we could arrive at different answers. For example, suppose we have a calculation as follows:

$\frac{1}{2} + \frac{1}{4} \times 2$

If we do the *addition* part first:

$\frac{1}{2} + \frac{1}{4} \times 2$

$= \frac{3}{4_2} \times 2^1$

$= \frac{3}{2}$

$= 1\frac{1}{2}$

If we do the *multiplication* part first:

$\frac{1}{2} + \frac{1}{4_2} \times 2^1$

$= \frac{1}{2} + \frac{1}{2}$

$= 1$

To avoid this sort of situation we use a rule known as the BODMAS rule. BODMAS stands for the initial letters of the words 'brackets', 'of', 'division', 'multiplication', 'addition' and 'subtraction'. The rule says that we have to do the calculations in the following order: we have to do the *brackets* first, then *of* next; we do *division* next, then *multiplication*; we do *addition* before subtraction, so that we do *subtraction* last of all.

Now consider the first example, below:

$\frac{1}{2} + \frac{1}{2_1} \times \frac{2^1}{4}$ (we do the multiplication first, cancelling if we can)

$= \frac{1}{2} + \frac{1}{4}$

$= \frac{2+1}{4}$

$= \frac{3}{4}$

Consider the second example, below:

$1\frac{1}{2} - \frac{2}{3} \div \frac{7}{9}$ (do the division first; change the divisor upside down and multiply)

$= 1\frac{1}{2} - \frac{2}{3_1} \times \frac{9^3}{7}$ (cancelling by 3)

$= 1\frac{1}{2} - \frac{6}{7}$ (the common denominator is 14)

$= 1\frac{7-12}{14}$ (we have to change the 1 into 14 fourteenths before we can subtract 12 fourteenths)

$= \frac{9}{14}$

Consider the third example, below:

$(2\frac{1}{2} \times \frac{2}{3}) \div 1\frac{1}{4}$ (do the bracket first)

$= (\frac{5}{2_1} \times \frac{2^1}{3}) \div 1\frac{1}{4}$ (*note:* the part you are not using ($1\frac{1}{4}$) is simply brought down from line to line until required)

$= \frac{5}{3} \div \frac{5}{4}$ (change the divisor upside down and multiply)

$= \frac{5^1}{3} \times \frac{4}{5_1}$ (cancelling by 5)

$= \frac{4}{3}$

$= 1\frac{1}{3}$

4.16 Exercises: more complex fraction calculations

Work out the following fraction calculations, using the BODMAS rule.

1 (a) $\frac{2}{3} \times \frac{1}{2} + \frac{1}{5} =$

(b) $\frac{3}{8} + \frac{4}{9} \times \frac{3}{8} =$

(c) $\frac{3}{4} + \frac{4}{5} \times \frac{5}{8} =$

(d) $\frac{1}{6} \times \frac{2}{7} + \frac{3}{14} =$

(e) $\frac{5}{6} + \frac{1}{3} \times \frac{3}{8} =$

(f) $\frac{1}{3} + \frac{3}{10} \div \frac{2}{5} =$

(g) $\frac{1}{2} \div \frac{9}{10} + \frac{4}{7} =$

(h) $\frac{3}{28} + \frac{6}{7} \times \frac{1}{4} =$

(i) $\frac{1}{6} \times \frac{1}{4} + \frac{7}{12} =$

(j) $\frac{9}{14} \div \frac{3}{10} - \frac{10}{21} =$

2 (a) $\left(\frac{1}{3} + \frac{1}{2}\right) \times \frac{3}{4} =$

(b) $\frac{2}{3} + \frac{5}{6} \times \frac{1}{4} =$

(c) $\left(3\frac{2}{5} - \frac{1}{8}\right) \div \frac{3}{5} =$

(d) $3\frac{7}{12} - \frac{3}{4} \div \frac{3}{8} =$

(e) $\frac{2}{3} \times \frac{4}{5} \div \frac{1}{3} =$

(f) $\frac{4}{5} \div \left(\frac{7}{10} - \frac{1}{8}\right) =$

(g) $2\frac{3}{8} \div \left(\frac{7}{8} - \frac{3}{4}\right) =$

(h) $\left(3\frac{2}{7} \div 4\frac{3}{5}\right) + \left(3\frac{3}{10} \div 1\frac{5}{6}\right) =$

(i) $2\frac{1}{4} \times \left(2\frac{4}{5} - 1\frac{5}{6}\right) =$

(j) $\left(5\frac{2}{3} \div 3\frac{7}{9}\right) \times \left(4\frac{2}{5} + 2\frac{1}{10}\right) =$

5
Decimal Fractions

5.1 The decimal system

A decimal system is a system based on tens (from the Latin, *decimus*, meaning 'tenth'). We have already seen that we use a decimal system for ordinary numbers, units, tens, hundreds etc. It is also possible to use the system for fractions smaller than 1. When we do so, a dot or point is made on the paper to separate the whole number from the fractions. This point is called a **decimal point**. By international agreement the decimal point is now written on the line, not half the height of a number above the line. Consider the number:

$$888.888$$

This is read as: eight hundred and eighty eight point eight eight eight. We are familiar with the first part of this number, 888, but when we come to the decimal point we have fractions, eight tenths, eight hundredths and eight thousandths.

With decimal fractions we do not have halves, thirds or quarters as we do with vulgar fractions; all we have is tenths, hundredths, thousandths etc., and all other fractions have to be expressed in terms of these decimal fractions. We shall see later that this is not as difficult as it sounds; for example, $\frac{1}{2} = 0.5$ which is $\frac{5}{10}$ths, but it is certainly less convenient. This inconvenience is compensated for by the fact that addition, subtraction, multiplication and division are all very easy with decimal fractions.

Let us look at a few more numbers with decimal fractions:

(a) 5.7, or 5 point 7, means 5 whole units and 7 tenths.
(b) 0.157 means no units, 1 tenth, 5 hundredths and 7 thousandths.

(c) 27.65 means 2 tens, 7 units, 6 tenths and 5 hundredths.

Later we shall see how we use these decimal fractions. For the moment we need to learn how to manipulate them; in other words, how to use them for any arithmetical activity we need: addition, subtraction, multiplication etc.

5.2 Addition of decimals

If we wish to add decimals we will carry out the same processes as we did in Chapter 2, when adding ordinary numbers. For example $2.69 + 1.567 + 1.31$ is written down with the decimal points underneath one another.

$$
\begin{array}{r}
2.69 \\
1.567 \\
+\ 1.31 \\
\hline
\hline
\end{array}
$$

Notice that this automatically brings units under units, tenths under tenths, hundredths under hundredths etc. We can now add these up just as if they were whole numbers.

$$
\begin{array}{r}
2.69 \\
1.567 \\
+\ 1.31 \\
\hline
5.567 \\
\hline
\end{array}
$$
$$\scriptstyle 1\ 1$$

(a) The 7 thousandths is the only figure in this column, and consequently goes in the answer.
(b) $9 + 6 + 1$ hundredths = 16 hundredths. The 6 remains in the hundredths row, but the 10 hundredths become 1 tenth and is carried into the tenths row.
(c) $6 + 5 + 3 + 1$ (to carry) = 15 tenths. This is 5

tenths and 1 whole unit to be carried into the units row.

(d) $2 + 1 + 1$ (to carry) $= 5$ units.

5.3 Exercises: addition of decimals

Set down the following decimal sums and complete the additions.

1 (a)   17.25   (b)   192.6   (c)   42.756
      13.16   27.54   29.32
    + 18.25   + 33.82   + 185.616

(d) $32.54 + 371.65 + 42.65 =$

(e) $61.65 + 248.25 + 38.75 + 29.652 =$

(f) $78.325 + 736.84 + 496.17 + 27.25 =$

(g) $185.62 + 59.72 + 381.7259 =$

(h) $189.387 + 68.75 + 3.7656 =$

(i) $274.621 + 297.63 + 4.295 =$

(j) $149.56 + 3875.29 + 171.82 + 2965.35 =$

2 (a)   1 472.563 8   (b)   38.165 25
      2 475.629 4   149.723 85
    +   5.817 55   + 426.381 75

(c)   29.428 6
    138.725 4
  + 295.612 6

5.4 Subtraction of decimals

As you would expect, subtraction of decimals is no different from subtraction of whole numbers. Take the following example:

$$27.54 - 3.845 =$$

Set down the calculation with the decimal points under one another:

$$\begin{array}{r} 27.54 \\ - \ 3.845 \\ \hline 23.695 \end{array}$$

(a) The 5 thousandths has to be taken from the top line. As there are no thousandths there, we must take one of the 4 hundredths and turn it into 10 thousandths. So, 5 from $10 = 5$. Put 5 thousandths in the answer.

(b) Now we have to take 4 hundredths from 3 hundredths (one has been used already). We cannot do this so we must borrow a tenth and turn it into 10 hundredths. So, 4 from $13 = 9$. Put 9 in the hundredths row in the answer.

(c) We are now in the tenths row. We must take 8 tenths from 4 tenths (one has been used already). Again we cannot do this so must borrow. This time we borrow a whole 1 to make 10 tenths. So, 8 from $14 = 6$ tenths. Put 6 in the answer.

(d) Finally, 3 units from 6 units leaves 3. No tens from 2 tens leaves 2. The answer is therefore 23.695.

5.5 Exercises: subtraction of decimals

Set down these subtraction sums and find the differences in each case.

1 (a)   27.656   (b)   419.275   (c)   38.956
   −   3.235   −   27.256   − 19.894

(d) $42.63 - 8.75 =$

(e) $147.85 - 12.929 =$

(f) $249.625 - 134.878 =$

(g) $723.5 - 621.35 =$

(h) $816.94 - 72.656 =$

(i) $387.25 - 81.754 =$

(j) $125.9395 - 73.625 =$

2 (a)   275.621 3   (b)   49.562 87
   − 138.475   − 14.838 15

(c)   472.656 2   (d)   495.625
   −   19.813 8   − 27.387 5

(e)   287.387   (f)   385.827 5
   −   49.465 25   − 29.393 95

5.6 Multiplication of decimals

The underlying principle when multiplying decimals is that the multiplication is done exactly the same as with whole numbers, and the decimal point is only inserted at the end. Consider the simple example 1.6×1.2. Ignoring the decimal points completely (though we do usually put them in) we have:

$$\begin{array}{r} 16 \\ \times 12 \\ \hline \end{array} \quad \text{or} \quad \begin{array}{r} 1.6 \\ \times 1.2 \\ \hline \end{array} \quad \text{if we show the decimal points}$$

The answer is found by short multiplication: 12×16

$$\begin{array}{r} 1.6 \\ \times 1.2 \\ \hline 19\,2 \end{array}$$

We can now position the decimal point by the rule: *count up the figures after the decimal point in both the multiplier and the multiplicand. There will be the same number of figures after the decimal point in the answer.* In our example, as there is one figure after the decimal point in the multiplier and one figure after the decimal point in the multiplicand, making two figures in all, there will be two figures after the decimal point in the answer. The answer is therefore 1.92.

We can prove this is correct using vulgar fractions:

$$1.6 = \tfrac{16}{10} \qquad 1.2 = \tfrac{12}{10}$$

Multiplying $\tfrac{16}{10} \times \tfrac{12}{10} = \tfrac{192}{100} = \underline{1.92}$.

To take a further example, 2.756×3.4

$\quad$ 2.756 (set the sum down like an ordinary
$\qquad\quad$ multiplication sum, ignoring the
$\quad\underline{3.4}$ decimal points)
$\quad$ 11 024 (multiplying by 4)
$\quad\underline{82\,680}$ (multiplying by 30)
$\quad\underline{93\,704}$ (answer; but we have to insert the
$\qquad\qquad$ decimal point)

There are three figures after the decimal point in the multiplicand, and one figure after the decimal point in the multiplier. This makes four figures after the decimal point in the answer. The answer is therefore:

$$\underline{9.3704}$$

We can check this as before, using vulgar fractions, or we can do a rough estimate to see if the answer seems about correct.

rough estimate $\quad$ 2.756 is almost 3
$\qquad\qquad\qquad$ 3.4 is just over 3
$\qquad\qquad\qquad$ $3 \times 3 = 9$

Have we arrived at an answer somewhere near 9? Yes, we have. If we had arrived at an answer of 90, or 900, or .9, or .09 we would know we must have positioned the decimal point wrongly.

5.7 Exercises: multiplication of decimals

Multiply the following numbers, which all have decimal fractions.

1 (a) $1.3 \times 2.2 =$ $\qquad$ (b) $4.6 \times 5.3 =$
 (c) $7.12 \times 4.9 =$ $\qquad$ (d) $8.43 \times 2.7 =$
 (e) $16.75 \times 8.4 =$ $\qquad$ (f) $29.54 \times 3.2 =$
 (g) $141.65 \times 7.3 =$ $\qquad$ (h) $121.95 \times 1.35 =$
 (i) $217.94 \times 5.8 =$ $\qquad$ (j) $16.13 \times 9.75 =$

2 (a) $14.95 \times 1.3 =$ $\qquad$ (b) $25.63 \times 4.9 =$
 (c) $247.5 \times 9.8 =$ $\qquad$ (d) $37.81 \times 7.3 =$
 (e) $32.815 \times 9.5 =$ $\qquad$ (f) $29.28 \times 2.6 =$
 (g) $64.682 \times 2.79 =$ $\qquad$ (h) $14.18 \times 5.1 =$
 (i) $71.655 \times 1.38 =$ $\qquad$ (j) $27.63 \times 6.2 =$

5.8 Division of decimals

When we divide by decimal fractions a difficulty presents itself: it is not easy to place the decimal point. We can perhaps get a hint of the difficulty if we consider the following:

$$6 \div 3 = 2$$
$$6 \div 0.3 = \,?$$

Clearly, as 0.3 is only a tenth of 3, we must get an answer 10 times as big:

$$6 \div 0.3 = 20$$

We could prove this is the correct answer by multiplying back:

$\qquad\quad$ 0.3
$\qquad\underline{\times 20}$
$\qquad\quad\underline{6.0}$ (there is one figure after the deci-
$\qquad\qquad\quad$ mal point)

However, this is all a little confusing, what we need is a simple rule that we can always follow. The rule is:

(a) Make the divisor a whole number.
(b) What you did to the divisor you must now do to the dividend.
(c) Now divide in the ordinary way.

Taking our example, $6 \div 0.3$, *make the divisor a whole number.* To do this we have to push the number through the decimal point one place. This means of course we have multiplied it by 10, because in a decimal system the next place up is always ten times bigger. So, 0.3 becomes 3.

What you did to the divisor you must now do to the dividend. Since we multiplied 0.3 by 10 (moving it up one place), we must move 6 up one place as well. So, 6 becomes 60.

Now $6 \div 0.3$ becomes $60 \div 3 = \underline{\underline{20}}$

Let us take a more difficult example: $27.3 \div 0.91$. Make the divisor a whole number: 91. We moved .91 two decimal places. Do the same to 27.3 and it becomes 2730:

$$
\begin{array}{r}
30 \\
91{\overline{)2730}} \\
273 \\
\hline
\end{array}
$$

... the answer is $\underline{\underline{30}}$

5.9 Recurring numbers

In some division calculations with decimals, the answer may not have an ending. This would be true, for example, if we divide any of the integers from 1 to 10 (apart from 7) by the number 7. If, for example, we divide 2 by 7 we would arrive at the answer 0.285 714 285 714 2 etc. If we divide 10 by 3 we get 3.333 333 3 etc.

These numbers are said to be recurring numbers. Clearly there is no point in continuing to divide, for not only are we not adding to our knowledge but the figures are getting smaller every time we divide. The last 3 in the number shown above is three 10 millionths, which is not worth bothering with.

With recurring numbers we stop working and show that the number is recurring by putting a dot over the top. Thus 3.333 333 3 is written $3.\dot{3}$ (three point three recurring).

Where the repetition is of several figures, as in the case of $2 \div 7$ the answer is written: $0.\dot{2}85\,71\dot{4}$, as all the figures from 2 to 4 recur endlessly.

5.10 Answers correct to a given number of decimal places

Since division of decimal sums rarely work out exactly, we have to decide what degree of accuracy we require for an answer. Usually two places of decimals are enough, but we do want to get the answer as accurate as possible. Take the calculation:

$$27.595 \div 3.8 \quad \text{(answer correct to 2 decimal places)}$$

Rearranging, we have:

$$275.95 \div 38$$

$$
\begin{array}{r}
7.26 \\
38{\overline{)275.95}} \\
266 \\
\hline
99 \\
76 \\
\hline
235 \\
228 \\
\hline
70
\end{array}
\qquad
\begin{array}{r}
38 \\
\times\ 6 \\
\hline
228 \\
\hline
38 \\
\times\ 2 \\
\hline
76
\end{array}
\qquad
\begin{array}{r}
38 \\
\times\ 7 \\
\hline
266 \\
\hline
38 \\
\times\ 3 \\
\hline
114
\end{array}
$$

We want to get our answer correct to two decimal places. In the example above we have worked to two decimal places and have the answer 7.26. But is the 6 accurate? We can only tell if we work one more place. Bring down a 0 next to the 7 to give 70. We find that 38 into 70 goes once, so the next figure would be 1, i.e. 7.261. Since 1 in any column is less than half (5 in any column is half in a decimal system) we can forget the 1, and give the answer 7.26 (correct to two decimal places).

The rules about correcting up (or *rounding*) are as follows:

(a) If the next figure is 1, 2, 3 or 4, disregard it. So, 7.263 is 7.26.
(b) If the figure is a 5 and then continues, it is more than half. So are 6, 7, 8 and 9. All these are treated the same, we add on one to the figure in the second place. $7.268 = 7.27$; $7.266 = 7.27$.

(c) If a figure is exactly 5 (i.e., it does not continue any further) we round the figure in the second place to the nearest even number. So 7.265 = 7.26, but 7.275 = 7.28.

5.11 Exercises: rounding off

1 Round all these numbers off, correct to one decimal place.

(a) 27.14   (b) 27.15
(c) 27.63   (d) 27.69
(e) 27.559   (f) 27.58
(g) 27.49   (h) 27.31
(i) 27.055   (j) 27.05

2 Round all these numbers off, correct to three decimal places.

(a) 2.9574   (b) 2.9577
(c) 2.9575   (d) 2.957 56
(e) 3.8126   (f) 3.8127

(g) 3.8124   (h) 3.8125
(i) 3.9786   (j) 3.9784

5.12 Exercises: division of decimals

1 Do these division sums. (Answer correct to one decimal place, if necessary.)

(a) $15.75 \div 2.1 =$ (b) $13.95 \div 3.2 =$
(c) $14.75 \div 0.22 =$ (d) $25.65 \div 4.7 =$
(e) $32.54 \div 1.6 =$ (f) $725.5 \div 1.7 =$
(g) $49.69 \div 2.3 =$ (h) $28.64 \div 3.2 =$
(i) $721.6 \div 4.5 =$ (j) $81.75 \div 2.9 =$

2 Do these division sums. (Answer correct to two decimal places.)

(a) $186.16 \div 3.5 =$ (b) $326.25 \div 4.2 =$
(c) $237.75 \div 0.021 =$ (d) $425.31 \div 3.8 =$
(e) $325.3 \div 0.36 =$ (f) $72.561 \div 2.6 =$
(g) $1426.85 \div 0.54 =$ (h) $45.95 \div 1.45 =$
(i) $2495.42 \div 0.12 =$ (j) $16.62 \div 0.27 =$

6

Money

6.1 Decimal coinage

The coinage of the United Kingdom is now completely decimalised. The last non-decimal coin (the halfpenny) was withdrawn in 1984 and the coinage now consists of the £1, 50 pence, 20 pence, 10 pence, 5 pence, 2 pence and 1 penny coins. As a result of the decimalisation of our currency, calculations in money are now very easy: they are exactly the same as other calculations in decimals. The vast majority of business calculations are concerned with money, and it is essential that you are thoroughly familiar with the four basic rules: addition, subtraction, multiplication and division of money.

There are certain rules about writing down sums of money. For all sums of money larger than £1 it is necessary to use the £ sign, followed by the sum of money. Thus £1.25, £13.87 and £127.98 are correctly written. It is wrong to put p for pence at the end: £127.98p is incorrect.

For sums less than £1 we can use the same notation, but put a 0 in the £ position, i.e. £0.35, £0.72 etc. It is also correct to leave out the £ sign and just write the pence. Thus 35p, 72p etc. is acceptable, but £0.35p is not acceptable.

When writing cheques, the written amount must have the word 'pounds' in full. It would be incorrect to write:

Pay T. Jones
   One hundred and eight 37   £108.37

We must write:
Pay T. Jones
   One hundred and eight pounds 37   £108.37

Notice that words do not have to be written for pence, so 'One hundred and eight pounds thirty seven pence' is not necessary, though the bank would accept the cheque as valid.

6.2 Addition and subtraction of money

As with decimals, we keep the decimal points underneath one another. This brings all the other figures in their correct places: units under units, tens under tens, etc. Consider the following examples:

Add up £3.51, £17.24, £149.35 and £68.99. Setting the sum down we have:

$$
\begin{array}{r}
£ \\
3.51 \\
17.24 \\
149.35 \\
+ \ 68.99 \\
\hline
\text{Answer} \quad £239.09 \\
\hline
{\scriptstyle 1\,2\,2\,1}
\end{array}
$$

Subtract £39.75 from £894.29. Setting this down we have:

$$
\begin{array}{r}
£ \\
894.29 \\
- 39.75 \\
\hline
£854.54 \\
\hline
\end{array}
$$

6.3 Exercises: addition and subtraction of money

1 (a) Add £2.41, £7.91, £9.35 and £4.01
  (b) Add £3.70, £5.64, £4.31 and £16.17
  (c) Add £5.15, £9.02, £14.29 and £17.96
  (d) Add £6.18, £2.51, £19.20 and £14.40
  (e) Add £1.16, £4.39, £11.77 and £18.11

(f) Add £5.43, £8.13, £26.77 and £31.15

(g)   £   (h)   £
       1 956.71   34.60
        492.35   1 154.32
        422.95   578.29
     + 1 869.37   + 3 333.45
     ══════════   ══════════

(i)   £   (j)   £
        383.67   2 720.78
       2 912.86   2 652.12
        441.10   978.44
     + 1 586.77   + 2 396.55
     ══════════   ══════════

2 (a) Subtract £3.60 from £14.31
  (b) Subtract £9.26 from £95.58
  (c) Subtract £15.96 from £125.42
  (d) Subtract £15.36 from £87.11
  (e) Subtract £31.10 from £965.49
  (f) Subtract £56.91 from £363.43
  (g) Subtract £1759.74 from £3862.59
  (h) Subtract £1786.58 from £12 868.25
  (i) Subtract £2356.56 from £8279.37
  (j) Subtract £3897.72 from £13 978.54

3 Here are the daily takings of two departments
  of a confectioner–newsagent. Set this down on
  paper and find the daily takings for the shop,
  the weekly takings for each department and the
  weekly takings of the shop.

Day	Confectionery (£)	News-agency (£)	Total takings (£)
Monday	254.67	195.12	
Tuesday	377.82	187.27	
Wednesday	236.78	148.61	
Thursday	164.73	75.40	
Friday	429.51	244.69	
Saturday	354.79	363.34	
Totals			

4 In a sale, a firm reduces items to clear as shown
  below. In each case find the sale price.

  (a) Price 56p; reduction 19p
  (b) Price £8.92; reduction £1.75
  (c) Price £9.78; reduction £1.55
  (d) Price £15.39; reduction £2.11

(e) Price £11.28; reduction £3.78
(f) Price £200; reduction £54.50
(g) Price £136.50; reduction £25.50
(h) Price £245; reduction £38.50
(i) Price £144.75; reduction £32.25
(j) Price £325; reduction £65.50

5 A book-keeper is told that all settled accounts
  are subject to a discount if paid within 7 days.
  The book-keeper makes a practice of taking
  this discount by settling promptly. What will be
  the value of the cheques written to settle the
  following debts?

  (a) £34.62; discount £0.87
  (b) £24.30; discount £1.22
  (c) £567.92; discount £28.40
  (d) £341.91; discount £17.10
  (e) £256.72; discount £25.67
  (f) £4569.70; discount £114.24
  (g) £385.75; discount £19.29
  (h) £2500.00; discount £62.50
  (i) £426.25; discount £10.66
  (j) £3575.50; discount £268.16

6.4 Multiplication of money

Multiplication of money is exactly the same as
multiplication of decimals. As almost every invoice that is written or typed involves some
element of multiplication, it is one of the commonest activities in business. An invoice is a
business document made out when one person
sells goods to another. A typical line on an
invoice might read:

Number	Description	Price	Value
3	9.5 cm left-handed-thread bolts	£1.95	£5.85

Such small multiplication sums, $3 \times £1.95$
= £5.85, occur endlessly in business. Consider the
following multiplication sums.

Example: (a) What will be the total cost of 7 items
at £4.35 each?

```
         £
       4.35
       × 7
     ──────
     £30.45
     ══════
```

Example: (b) What will be the total wages bill for 326 employees earning £138.50 each? In addition to wages the employer must pay £8.76 per employee in National Insurance charges.

Total charges per employee = £138.50 + £8.76
= £147.26

$$
\begin{array}{r}
£ \\
147.26 \\
\times\,326 \\
\hline
883\,56 \quad (\times 6)\\
2\,945\,20 \quad (\times 20)\\
44\,178\,00 \quad (\times 300)\\
\hline
48\,006\,76 \\
\hline
\end{array}
$$

= £48 006.76

Note: There are two figures after the decimal point in both the multiplier and the multiplicand; consequently there are two figures after the decimal point in the answer.

6.5 Exercises: multiplication of money

1 (a) £2.75 × 8 =   (b) £3.65 × 9 =
  (c) £42.35 × 4 =   (d) £72.65 × 5 =
  (e) £625.84 × 12 =   (f) £736.45 × 7 =
  (g) £1264.35 × 15 =   (h) £2384.71 × 16 =
  (i) £225.48 × 134 =   (j) £175.65 × 145 =

2 What will be the value of this invoice from a decorator's shop?

    16 rolls wallpaper at £3.85 per roll
    3 litres white paint at £2.76 per litre
    1 paint-brush £4.56
    2 bottles paint-thinner at 65p per bottle

3 A college buys 48 calculators for examination purposes at £11.78 per calculator. What is the total bill?

4 Eleven technicians at a television company are paid £15735 per year each. What is the total wage bill if, in addition, £11.55 is payable *per week* (52 weeks) for National Insurance for each technician?

5 A computer technician who earns £162.35 per week is offered a position in a rival organisation at £9500 a year. Will she be financially better placed if she changes employment? By how much? (Take 1 year to equal 52 weeks.)

6.6 Division of money

Division of money is a process of sharing money among a number of people or projects entitled to it. It frequently occurs in such branches of business life as solicitors' activities to settle wills and intestacies (where people die without leaving a will). Similarly, when a business goes bankrupt and ceases to trade, the creditors share up what can be realised from the sale of the collapsed business's assets.

Division of money is exactly the same as division of decimals, except that we cannot proceed further than pence will allow; that is, our answer must be correct to two decimal places.

Example: (a) Share up £10 000 equally among 7 children named in the will of an aunt.

$$
\begin{array}{r}
£ \\
7)\overline{10000} \\
\hline
1428.571
\end{array}
$$

They will each receive £1428.57 (actually, there will be a remainder of 1p).

Example: (b) The assets of a company going into voluntary liquidation (ceasing to trade) realise £450 792. There are 186 shares in the company. What will each share be entitled to receive? Mrs Arkwright has 28 shares. What will she receive altogether?

$$
\begin{array}{r}
£ \\
2423.61 \\
186)\overline{450792.00} \\
372 \\
\hline
787 \\
744 \\
\hline
439 \\
372 \\
\hline
672 \\
558 \\
\hline
1140 \\
1116 \\
\hline
240 \\
186 \\
\hline
54
\end{array}
$$

$$
\begin{array}{r}
186 \\
\times 2 \\
\hline
372 \\
186 \\
\times 3 \\
\hline
558 \\
186 \\
\times 6 \\
\hline
1116
\end{array}
\qquad
\begin{array}{r}
186 \\
\times 4 \\
\hline
744 \\
186 \\
\times 5 \\
\hline
930
\end{array}
$$

Each share receives £2423.61. There is 54p left over. Mrs Arkwright will receive:

```
               £
          2 423.61
            × 28
        19 388 88
        48 472 20
       £67 861 08
```

£67 861.08 Answer

6.7 Exercises: division of money

1 Do the following division calculations.
   (a) £10.64 ÷ 7 =   (b) £29.75 ÷ 5 =
   (c) £287.32 ÷ 4 =   (d) £462.78 ÷ 8 =
   (e) £8565 ÷ 13 =   (f) £5992.26 ÷ 14 =
   (g) £12 775 ÷ 15 =   (h) £5198.34 ÷ 23 =
   (i) £13 826 ÷ 28 =   (j) £77 856.50 ÷ 36 =

2 Commission of £3892 is to be shared equally between 17 members of a sales organisation. The money is to be shared correct to the nearest pound, any balance going to charity. (a) How much will each member receive? (b) How much will go to charity?

3 An invoice reads: '25 calculators; total £293.75'. What was the price of each calculator?

4 A company is wound up voluntarily, and its assets realise £391 560. There are 1560 shares, of which 148 are held by Mrs Jones. (a) What is each share entitled to? (b) How much will Mrs Jones receive?

5 A father declares in his will that his eldest son is to have 3 shares in his estate, his eldest daughter 2 shares, and his other six children 1 share each. The estate is valued at £1 572 362. What will the eldest son receive?

7

Percentages

7.1 What are percentages?

Percentage means 'out of a hundred', and percentages are proportional parts of 100. So 37 per cent means thirty-seven parts out of a hundred, and 10 per cent means ten parts out of a hundred. The sign for percentage is %, so we write 1%, 2%, 3% etc. If, we say that an answer is 100 per cent right it means it is completely correct, because a hundred parts out of 100 are correct.

Percentages are widely used in business calculations. For example, interest rates are usually expressed in percentages. You will probably have seen on television or in the press that the building societies have raised or lowered their percentage interest rates for mortgages. Similarly, when we save money, if we deposit it in a bank, post office or building society the rates of interest quoted are percentages.

Rates of inflation showing how much money has fallen in value over the year are also examples of percentages. Wages increases are often negotiated as a percentage of current income. Many salespeople receive bonuses as a percentage of their total sales. If you go to sales in shops, you will often find that the prices have been reduced by a certain percentage of the original price. Similarly, price increases of many products are expressed in percentages.

The simplest calculations connected with percentages require us to work out simple problems such as:

What is 35% of 5800 tonnes?

This is the same as asking: what is $\frac{35}{100}$ of 5800 tonnes?

$$\frac{35}{100} \times 58\emptyset\emptyset \text{ tonnes}$$
$$\text{(cancelling by 100)}$$
$$= 35 \times 58 \text{ tonnes}$$
$$= \underline{2030 \text{ tonnes}}$$

$$
\begin{array}{r}
35 \\
\times 58 \\
\hline
280 \\
1750 \\
\hline
2030 \text{ tonnes}
\end{array}
$$

Similarly, what is 63% of £2750?

$$\frac{63}{100} \times £27\overset{55}{\underset{2}{5\emptyset}}\emptyset \qquad \text{(Cancelling by 10 and then by 5)}$$

$$= \frac{£3465}{2}$$
$$= £1732.50$$

$$
\begin{array}{r}
63 \\
\times 55 \\
\hline
315 \\
3150 \\
\hline
3465
\end{array}
$$

In each case you simply replace the % sign with 'fraction over 100'. For example, 17% becomes $\frac{17}{100}$, 19% becomes $\frac{19}{100}$, etc.

Before trying some calculations of this sort, there are certain well known groups of percentages we need to know. The most important groups are as follows:

(a) The halves, quarters and eighths group.
(b) The tenths and fifths group.
(c) The thirds group.

$\frac{1}{2} = 50\%$	$\frac{1}{8} = 12\frac{1}{2}\%$	$\frac{1}{3} = 33\frac{1}{3}\%$
$\frac{1}{4} = 25\%$	$\frac{3}{8} = 37\frac{1}{2}\%$	$\frac{2}{3} = 66\frac{2}{3}\%$
$\frac{3}{4} = 75\%$	$\frac{5}{8} = 62\frac{1}{2}\%$	
	$\frac{7}{8} = 87\frac{1}{2}\%$	

$\frac{1}{10}\% = 10\%$ $\frac{2}{10} = \frac{1}{5} = 20\%$
$\frac{3}{10} = 30\%$ $\frac{4}{10} = \frac{2}{5} = 40\%$
$\frac{5}{10} = \frac{1}{2} = 50\%$, of course $\frac{6}{10} = \frac{3}{5} = 60\%$
$\frac{7}{10} = 70\%$ $\frac{8}{10} = \frac{4}{5} = 80\%$
$\frac{9}{10} = 90\%$

Other useful percentages are $\frac{1}{20} = 5\%$; $\frac{1}{40} = 2\frac{1}{2}\%$; $\frac{1}{80} = 1\frac{1}{4}\%$.

7.2 Exercises: simple percentage calculations

1 A shopkeeper reduces all prices by 10 per cent for a sale. What will be the reduction on items formerly priced at:

(a) £100	(b) £10
(c) £1	(d) £50
(e) £25	(f) £20
(g) £17	(h) £8.50
(i) £5.50	(j) £3.50

2 A shopkeeper reduces all prices by 25% in a sale. What will he now charge for items formerly costing:

(a) £40	(b) £36
(c) £24	(d) £12.60
(e) £14.80	(f) £6.20
(g) £7.20	(h) £84
(i) £55	(j) £35

3 Calculate the following. (Answer correct to the nearest penny where necessary.)

(a) 40% of £200	(b) 30% of £575
(c) 25% of £445	(d) 50% of £8.26
(e) 75% of £3275	(f) 10% of £4275
(g) $87\frac{1}{2}$% of £625	(h) $33\frac{1}{3}$% of £1872
(i) 42% of £840	(j) 47% of £5850

7.3 Changing percentages to fractions, and fractions to percentages

As a percentage is only a special kind of fraction (one with a denominator of 100), we frequently need to change percentages to fractions and vice versa. Both these procedures are quite simple and we should become thoroughly familiar with them.

To change percentages to fractions

(a) Write down the percentage as a fraction with 100 as the denominator.
(b) Cancel if you can, to reduce the fraction to its lowest terms.

$25\% = \frac{25}{100} = \frac{1}{4}$ (cancelling by 25)

$38\% = \frac{38}{100} = \frac{19}{50}$ (cancelling by 2)

$20\% = \frac{20}{100} = \frac{1}{5}$ (cancelling by 10 and then by 2)

If the percentage has a fraction in it, we have a little problem to overcome:

$$22\frac{1}{2}\% = \frac{45}{200} = \frac{9}{40}$$

(*Note*: $22\frac{1}{2} = \frac{45}{2}$, therefore $\frac{22\frac{1}{2}}{100} = \frac{45}{200}$.)

If a percentage is more than 100%, as for example 150% or 275% the fraction will finish up as a mixed number. For example:

$150\% = \frac{\overset{3}{\cancel{150}}}{\underset{2}{\cancel{100}}}$ (cancelling by 10 and 5)

$= 1\frac{1}{2}$

To change fractions to percentages

Here the rules are quite simple. To change anything to a percentage we simply multiply it by 100.

If, for example, we wish to change $\frac{1}{2}$, $\frac{3}{4}$, $\frac{5}{8}$, $\frac{7}{20}$ and $\frac{5}{6}$ to percentages:

(a) Set down the fraction.
(b) Multiply by 100.
(c) Cancel if you can, and then multiply out.
(d) The answer is in per cent.

$\frac{1}{2}$ as a percentage

$= \frac{1}{\cancel{2}_1} \times \overset{50}{\cancel{100}} = 50\%$ (cancelling by two)

$\frac{3}{4}$ as a percentage

$= \frac{3}{\cancel{4}_1} \times \overset{25}{\cancel{100}} = 75\%$ (cancelling by 4)

$\frac{5}{8}$ as a percentage

$= \frac{5}{\cancel{8}_2} \times \overset{25}{\cancel{100}} = \frac{125}{2} = 62\frac{1}{2}\%$

$\frac{7}{20}$ as a percentage

$= \frac{7}{\cancel{20}_1} \times \overset{5}{\cancel{100}} = 35\%$ (cancelling by 10 and then by 2)

$\frac{5}{6}$ as a percentage

$= \frac{5}{\cancel{6}_3} \times \overset{50}{\cancel{100}}$ (cancelling by 2)

$= \frac{250}{3}$

$= 83\frac{1}{3}\%$

If a mixed number is turned to a percentage, the percentage will be greater than 100. For example:

$2\frac{1}{2}$ as a percentage $= 2\frac{1}{2} \times 100$

$= \frac{5}{\cancel{2}_1} \times \overset{50}{\cancel{100}}$ (cancelling by 2)

$= 250\%$

7.4 Exercises: changing percentages to fractions, and fractions to percentages

1 Change the following percentages to fractions in their lowest terms.

(a) 70%　　(b) 50%　　(c) 23%　　(d) 94%
(e) 66%　　(f) 25%　　(g) $42\frac{1}{2}$%　　(h) $81\frac{1}{4}$%
(i) $47\frac{1}{2}$%　　(j) 95%　　(k) $77\frac{1}{2}$%　　(l) $66\frac{2}{3}$%

2 Change the following percentages to fractions in their lowest terms.

(a) 45%　　(b) $67\frac{1}{2}$%　　(c) 85%　　(d) 54%
(e) $71\frac{1}{4}$%　　(f) $33\frac{1}{3}$%　　(g) $83\frac{3}{4}$%　　(h) $96\frac{1}{4}$%
(i) 55%　　(j) $72\frac{1}{2}$%　　(k) 80%　　(l) 28%

3 Change the following fractions to percentages. (Answer correct to one decimal place where necessary.)

(a) $\frac{3}{4}$　　(b) $\frac{1}{2}$　　(c) $\frac{3}{8}$　　(d) $\frac{5}{8}$
(e) $\frac{3}{5}$　　(f) $\frac{2}{5}$　　(g) $\frac{17}{20}$　　(h) $\frac{3}{20}$
(i) $\frac{1}{3}$　　(j) $\frac{2}{3}$　　(k) $\frac{1}{7}$　　(l) $\frac{3}{7}$

4 Change the following mixed numbers to percentages.

(a) $3\frac{4}{5}$　　(b) $2\frac{1}{2}$　　(c) $4\frac{7}{8}$　　(d) $5\frac{7}{20}$
(e) $6\frac{3}{4}$　　(f) $1\frac{4}{5}$　　(g) $3\frac{2}{5}$　　(h) $2\frac{7}{8}$
(i) $7\frac{7}{25}$　　(j) $4\frac{2}{3}$　　(k) $5\frac{5}{8}$　　(l) $4\frac{1}{10}$

7.5 Changing percentages to decimals, and decimals to percentages

Just as we can convert percentages to fractions, and fractions to percentages, so we can change percentages to decimals, and decimals to percentages. These are very simple conversions.

To change percentages to decimals

(a) Set down the percentage.
(b) Divide it by 100. (This means we have to push it through the decimal point two places to the right.)

If, for example, we wish to change 72%, 45% and 150% to decimals:

$$72 \div 100 = 0.72$$
$$45 \div 100 = 0.45$$
$$150 \div 100 = 1.5$$

To change decimals to percentages

(a) Set down the decimal.
(b) Multiply it by 100. (This means we have to push the number through the decimal point two places to the left.)

If, for example, we wish to change 0.87, 0.145 and 1.0565 to percentages:

$$0.87 \times 100 = 87\%$$
$$0.145 \times 100 = 14.5\%$$
$$1.0565 \times 100 = 105.65\%$$

7.6 Exercises: Converting percentages to decimals, and decimals to percentages

1 Change the following percentages to decimals.

(a) 36%　　(b) 48%　　(c) 86%　　(d) 36.5%
(e) 72%　　(f) 92%　　(g) 2.5%　　(h) 48.75%
(i) 144%　　(j) 150%　　(k) 225%　　(l) 590%
(m) 85.5%　(n) 66.6%　(o) 8.3%　　(p) 27.25%

2 Change the following decimals to percentages.

(a) 0.46　　(b) 0.87　　(c) 0.54　　(d) 0.63
(e) 0.91　　(f) 0.35　　(g) 0.72　　(h) 0.48
(i) 0.65　　(j) 0.507　　(k) 0.743　　(l) 0.869
(m) 4.25　　(n) 3.875　　(o) 4.25　　(p) 0.85

7.7 Other examples of percentages

Value Added Tax

In the United Kingdom, value added tax (VAT) is levied as a percentage on the cost of all goods, except for a few special items which are said to be zero rated. Let us take some examples.

Example: (a) Value added tax is 15% and this is to be added to the price of a piece of furniture. The firm manufactures the item to sell at £300. What would be the VAT inclusive charge? In this case, we would have to add 15% of £300:

Price = £300 + (15% of £300)
　　　= £300 + ($\frac{15}{100} \times £300$) (cancelling by 100)
　　　= £300 + £45
　　　= £345

Example: (b) What is the VAT on a motor vehicle manufactured to sell at £4730, and what will the selling price be?

$$VAT = 15\% \times £4730$$
$$= \tfrac{15}{100} \times £4730$$
$$= 15 \times £47.3$$

$$\begin{array}{r} 47.3 \\ \times\ 15 \\ \hline 2365 \\ 4730 \\ \hline 709.5 \end{array}$$

Therefore selling price = £4730 + £709.5
$$= £5439.50$$

Discounts

In a great many business activities, but particularly in wholesale and retail trade, discounts are deducted at a percentage rate. For example, trade customers are usually given a reduction called **trade discount**. This is usually a large discount, and can be as much as 55%. This is to enable trade customers to make a profit. Slow-selling items carry a large trade discount, while items that turn over rapidly do not command such a large discount.

Other customers are often given a much smaller discount, often about 5%, called **cash discount** if they pay promptly for goods.

Consider the following examples.

Example: (a) A motorcycle dealer is given a 40% trade discount on a motorcycle selling at £780. (a) What will be the discount given to the trader? (b) What will he pay for the motorcycle?

$$Discount = \tfrac{\cancel{40}^{2}}{\cancel{100}_{5}} \times £\cancel{780}^{156} \text{ (cancelling by 10, 5 and 2)}$$
$$= £312$$

Price of motorcycle = £780 − £312
$$= £468$$

Example: (b) A customer who buys a colour television set for £312.50 is given a 5% cash discount. How much will she actually pay? (Answer correct to nearest penny.)

Discount $= \tfrac{5}{100} \times £312.50$
$= 5 \times 3.125$ (moving the number through the decimal point two places)
$= 15.625$
$= £15.62$

Price paid = £312.50 − £15.62
$= £296.88$

7.8 Exercises: VAT and discounts

1 What will a retailer need to charge for goods costing as shown below, if VAT at 15% must be added? (Answer correct to nearest penny where necessary.)

(a) £100 (b) £200
(c) £500 (d) £30
(e) £65   (f) £48
(g) £24   (h) £12.50
(i) £8.60 (j) £5.35

2 Work out the following trade discounts on the items listed below.
(a) A refrigerator costing £185 on which the discount is 40%.
(b) A gas cooker costing £235 on which the discount is 35%.
(c) A motor vehicle retailing at £5250 on which the trade discount is 20%.
(d) A consignment of wallpaper valued at £850 on which the trade discount is 55%.
(e) A table and 6 chairs valued at £1850 on which the discount is $37\tfrac{1}{2}\%$.

3 Work out the cash discounts at the % rate shown on the prices listed below. (Calculations to the nearest penny where necessary.)

(a) £27; 5% discount.
(b) £800; 5% discount.
(c) £35; $2\tfrac{1}{2}\%$ discount.
(d) £640; 10% discount.
(e) £84; 5% discount.
(f) £720; $2\tfrac{1}{2}\%$ discount.
(g) £165; $2\tfrac{1}{2}\%$ discount.
(h) £5; $2\tfrac{1}{2}\%$ discount.
(i) £80; $1\tfrac{1}{4}\%$ discount.
(j) £4.80; $2\tfrac{1}{2}\%$ discount.

4 The manager of a garden centre orders goods at a catalogue price of £425. He is given a 35% trade discount on the invoice, and is then allowed to deduct $2\frac{1}{2}$% from the final (i.e. net) invoice price if he pays cash within 7 days. What is the prompt cash price? (Answer correct to the nearest penny.)

5 A furniture dealer orders furniture at a catalogue price of £1240. He is given a trade discount of 45% on the invoice, and a settlement discount of 5% off the final invoice price if he pays within 15 days. What will he finally pay for these goods if he takes both discounts?

6 A garage proprietor orders spare parts at a catalogue price of £375. He is given a trade discount of 35%, and then a cash discount of $2\frac{1}{2}$% on the final invoice price. What does he pay in the end for these goods? (Answer correct to the nearest penny.)

8
Metric Weights and Measures

8.1 The metric system

The metric system of weights and measures is gradually replacing the traditional English measures, which are called imperial measures. The metric system is more scientific, more easily manipulated mathematically, and is now used all over the world. The name of the system is the 'SI units system', which stands for the French words *Système International d'Units*: the International System of Units (of measurement).

The four systems of measures are called length, weight, capacity and time. Of these four sets of measures, only time is exactly the same as the old imperial system (because, of course, time is based upon the movement of the earth around the sun and is a very ancient measure indeed). The other metric units are the metre (length), the gram (weight) and the litre (capacity).

8.2 The metric tables

The four metric tables are shown below, with the old imperial tables below in each case. Note that the SI names can be shortened to symbols; for instance, metre becomes m and millimetre becomes mm. As these are symbols (signs only) they do not have plurals, so it is wrong to write mms for millimetres. The symbol mm is all that is required. No abbreviation points are used on symbols, so 'mm.' is incorrect.

Table of length		*Length in symbol form*
10 millimetres	= 1 centimetre	10 mm = 1 cm
10 centimetres	= 1 decimetre	10 cm = 1 dm
10 decimetres	= 1 metre	10 dm = 1 m
10 metres	= 1 decametre	10 m = 1 dam
10 decametres	= 1 hectometre	10 dam = 1 hm
10 hectometres	= 1 kilometre	10 hm = 1 km

(*Note*: dam is used for decametre to distinguish it from dm, which means decimetre.)

Imperial table of length

12 inches	=	1 foot
3 feet	=	1 yard
22 yards	=	1 chain
10 chains	=	1 furlong
8 furlongs	=	1 mile

During the change-over period from imperial measures to metric measures the following links may be helpful; but ideally we should abandon the old, inconvenient, imperial measures and think of metric units.

Links with the metric system

1 metre = 39.37 inches
8 kilometres = 5 miles (approximately)

Table of weight

10 milligrams	= 1 centigram	10 mg	= 1 cg
10 centigrams	= 1 decigram	10 cg	= 1 dg
10 decigrams	= 1 gram	10 dg	= 1 g
10 grams	= 1 decagram	10 g	= 1 dag
10 decagrams	= 1 hectogram	10 dag	= 1 hg
10 hectograms	= 1 kilogram	10 hg	= 1 kg
1000 kilograms	= 1 metric tonne	1000 kg	= 1 tonne

(*Note*: dag is used to distinguish decagrams from decigrams.)

Imperial table of weight

16 ounces	=	1 pound (1 lb)
14 pounds	=	1 stone
2 stones	=	1 quarter
4 quarters	=	1 hundredweight (cwt)
20 cwt	=	1 ton

Links with the metric system

1 kg = 2.205 pounds
1 tonne = 1 ton (very approximately)

Table of capacity

10 millilitres	= 1 centilitre	10 ml	= 1 cl
10 centilitres	= 1 decilitre	10 cl	= 1 dl
10 decilitres	= 1 litre	10 dl	= 1 litre
10 litres	= 1 decalitre	10 litres	= 1 dal
10 decalitres	= 1 hectolitre	10 dal	= 1 hl
10 hectolitres	= 1 kilolitre	10 hl	= 1 kl

(*Note*: As the symbol l is indistinguishable from the number 1, the SI system says that the symbol should not be used if it may cause confusion, and the full word 'litre' should be written out.)

Imperial table of capacity

4 gills	=	1 pint
2 pints	=	1 quart
4 quarts	=	1 gallon
2 gallons	=	1 peck
4 pecks	=	1 bushell
8 bushells	=	1 quarter

Link with the metric system

1 litre = 1.760 pints

Table of time

60 seconds	=	1 minute
60 minutes	=	1 hour
24 hours	=	1 day
7 days	=	1 week
4 weeks	=	1 month (but it varies)
365 days	=	1 year
366 days	=	1 leap year

8.3 Calculations with SI units

Because of their decimal nature, all calculations with SI units are very easy. It is best to look at them in columnar form:

km	hm	dam	m	dm	cm	mm
1	4	3	7.	5	2	9

Although rather widely spaced out because there is more than one letter in the column headings, we can see that if a decimal point is put in where the basic unit (in this case, the metre) occurs, we have a simple decimal layout, with units, tens, hundreds and thousands of metres on the left-hand side and tenths, hundredths and thousandths on the right-hand side of the decimal point.

There is little point in practising addition, subtraction, multiplication and division of metric measures, as they are so similar to these processes in both decimals and money. Instead we will consider them in problem form in the set of exercises in Section 8.4 below.

A word about problems. In fact, they are much easier than many sums set down mechanically in the earlier part of this book. What you do is read the question, decide what is necessary to do, and then do it. Consider the following examples.

Example: (a) A cyclist is to make a round trip. From A to B is 34.6 kilometres, from B to C is 17.9 kilometres, from C to D is 23.8 kilometres and from D to A again is 7.8 kilometres. How far does he cycle altogether? Clearly this is a simple addition sum.

$$
\begin{array}{r}
\text{km} \\
34.6 \\
17.9 \\
23.8 \\
\underline{7.8} \\
\underline{84.1\,\text{km}}
\end{array}
$$

Example: (b) A tea importer makes up tea in $\frac{1}{4}$-kg and $\frac{1}{2}$-kg packets. How many small packets can be made up from 5000 kg if he intends to make only 1440 half-kilogram packets?

In this calculation we have to work out how many kilograms 1440 packets will need, take this from 5000 kg, and then multiply by 4 to find how many quarter-kilogram packets can be made up:

$$
\begin{array}{r}
2)\overline{1440} \\
\underline{720}\,\text{kg} \\
5000 \\
\underline{-720} \\
4280\,\text{kg} \\
\underline{\times 4} \\
\underline{17120\ \tfrac{1}{4}\text{-kg packets}}
\end{array}
$$

8.4 Exercises: calculations with SI units

1 A lorry makes four return journeys from Manchester to Newcastle on Tyne, a distance of 205 kilometres. (a) How far does it travel

altogether? (b) What is the cost at 13.6p per kilometre?

2 A commercial traveller charges his employer for the following distances travelled in a week.

Monday	90 km	Thursday	365 km
Tuesday	213 km	Friday	26 km
Wednesday	21 km	Saturday	74 km

He is allowed to claim 17p for each kilometre. What will be the amount of his travel claim for the week?

3 A cycle club plans a weekend tour including the following distances. A to B 94.6 km, B to C 37.4 km, C to D 115.5 km, D to A 46.2 km. What is the total distance of the tour?

4 An aircraft flies the following distances at a fuel cost of 41.5p per kilometre. Calculate the total fuel bill.

Sunday	3784 km	Thursday	3222 km
Monday	3012 km	Friday	6678 km
Tuesday	5613 km	Saturday	9896 km
Wednesday	9967 km		

5 A metric tonne of sugar (1000 kg) is made up into packets containing 200 grams and 100 grams. There were 660 of the larger packets and the rest were small. How many small packets were there?

6 How many packets of long-grain rice can be made up from 2000 kg if each packet contains 454 grams? What quantity will be left over?

7 How many cartons of currants can be filled from a container holding 24 metric tonnes, if each carton holds 200 grams of fruit?

8 A supermarket retails potatoes in bags containing $2\frac{1}{2}$ kg and 1 kg. A grower supplies 25 tonnes. 2200 of the larger bags are made up, and the rest of the potatoes are put into 1 kg bags. How many of these are there?

9 Milk lorries bringing milk in from farms to a bottling plant carry 31 000 litres. The milk from nine such lorries is made up into containers holding 2 litres and $\frac{1}{2}$ litre. If there are 45 000 two-litre containers how many half-litre cartons are made up?

10 From a vat of wine holding 3000 litres, bulk supplies are drawn off as follows: 250 litres, 360 litres, 900 litres and 1400 litres. What quantity is wasted, being considered unsaleable?

8.5 Manipulating SI units

One feature of metric units which we must be familiar with is their ability to be changed into different denominations simply by moving them through the decimal point. For example:

$$1 \text{ metre} = 10 \text{ dm} = 100 \text{ cm} = 1000 \text{ mm}$$
and
$$1 \text{ metre} = 0.1 \text{ dam} = 0.01 \text{ hm} = 0.001 \text{ km}$$

Put another way, a distance of 27.15 metres can be re-written as follows:

27.15	metres
2.715	decametres
0.2715	hectometres
0.02715	kilometres
or	
271.5	decimetres
2715	centimetres
27150	millimetres

Consider the following example:

Change each of the weights given in grams below, first to kilograms (kg), and then to milligrams (mg).

275 grams
3275.5 grams

Changing these to kilograms we can see that 275 grams is less than 1 kilogram (1000 g). We must push the number three places to the right through the decimal point, because 1000 grams = 1 kg. Therefore:

$$275 \text{ grams} = 0.275 \text{ kg}$$
$$3275.5 \text{ grams} = 3.2755 \text{ kg}$$

Changing the same weights to milligrams we must move the number through the decimal point three places the other way, to the left, since every gram is worth 1000 mg.

Therefore:

$$275 \text{ grams} = 275 000 \text{ mg}$$
$$3275.5 \text{ grams} = 3 275 500 \text{ mg}$$

8.6 Exercises: manipulating SI units

1 Change each of the lengths given in metres below, first to kilometres (km), and then to centimetres (cm).

(a) 3218 metres   (b) 4852 metres
(c) 5892.3 metres   (d) 6384.25 metres
(e) 85 167.589 metres   (f) 678.219 metres

2 Change each of the weights given in grams below, first to kilograms (kg), and then to milligrams (mg).

(a) 93 781 grams   (b) 7312.9 grams
(c) 5683.246 grams   (d) 4593.668 grams
(e) 76 543.2 grams   (f) 216 712.458 grams

3 Change each of the capacities given in litres below, first to millilitres (ml), and then to decilitres (dl).

(a) 3.6 litres   (b) 9.3 litres
(c) 58.9 litres   (d) 41.7 litres
(e) 9.322 litres   (f) 6.313 litres

8.7 Inclusive days

We frequently meet references in business life to 'inclusive' days. This usually occurs with regard to travelling and vacational residence at hotels, guest-houses etc. To say 'I shall be staying from the third to the sixth inclusive' means that you require accommodation on the 3rd, 4th, 5th and 6th; that is, for four days—although from 3rd to 6th seems to indicate only three days.

The rule for calculating inclusive days is to deduct the first day from the last day, and then add one. Thus $(6 - 3) + 1 = 4$ days. So 'from 17th–29th inclusive' means $(29 - 17) + 1 = 13$ days.

If we go through the end of the month we require to take special care. For example, 'from 17th March to the 4th April' is calculated as follows:

$$
\begin{aligned}
\text{days in March } (31 - 17) &= 14 \\
\text{add 4 days in April} &= 4 \\
\text{add } 1 &= \underline{1} \\
&\ \underline{19 \text{ days}}
\end{aligned}
$$

8.8 Exercises: inclusive days

1 How many days from 13th to 25th July inclusive?
2 How many days from 3rd to 28th May inclusive?
3 How many days from 27th July to 17th August inclusive?
4 How many days from 15th December to 16th January inclusive?
5 How many days from March 4th to May 5th inclusive?
6 How many days from August 27th to 25th October inclusive?

9

Ratios, Proportions and Approximations

9.1 Simple ratios

A ratio is a way of making comparisons. For example, we might want to compare the profits of two different departments. If one department 'A' had made £50 000 whilst the other 'B' had made £25 000 we could say that the profits were in the ratio of 50 000 to 25 000. We would usually put this into its simplest form by cancelling down. In this case we would divide both parts by 1000, and then by 25. We could therefore say that the profits were in the ratio of 2 to 1. Set down in mathematical form we have:

$$£50\,000 : £25\,000$$
$$= \quad 50\,000 : 25\,000$$
$$= \quad 50 : 25$$
$$= \quad 2 : 1$$

(a) A colon is used to separate the two things we are comparing.
(b) When we start to cancel, the first things we can cancel from both sides are the units that are being used; in this case, £ (pounds sterling). Our ratio therefore finishes up as a numerical comparison, not in any particular units.
(c) After cancelling to the lowest terms the final result is 2:1. This is read 'as two is to one'. We would therefore compare the two sets of profits by saying 'A's profits are to B's profits as two is to one'.
This is written:

$$A : B :: 2 : 1$$
$$A \text{ is to } B \text{ as } 2 \text{ is to } 1$$

Ratios where the units are different

Part of the example given above was the cancelling out of the units, to reduce the ratio to a comparison of two numbers only. As with all cancelling we can only cancel if we divide both parts by the same thing. Suppose we wish to compare weights of 20 tonnes and 200 kilograms.

$$20 \text{ tonnes} : 200 \text{ kg}$$

Clearly we cannot cancel these until we turn both pieces of information to the same units. It will therefore be best to use kilograms, the smaller unit. As 1 tonne = 1000 kg, we have:

$$20\,000 \text{ kg} : 200 \text{ kg}$$
$$= \quad 20\,000 : 200$$
$$= \quad 200 : 2$$
$$= \quad 100 : 1$$

Example: (a) Compare £1500 and £300

$$\overset{5}{\cancel{£1500}} : \overset{1}{\cancel{£300}} \quad \text{(cancelling £, 100 and 3)}$$
$$= 5 : 1$$

Example: (b) Compare £2400 and 80p

$$£2400 : 80\text{p}$$
$$= \quad 240\,000 : 80 \quad \text{(changing £2400 to pence and cancelling pence)}$$
$$= \quad 3000 : 1 \quad \text{(cancelling by 10 and then 8)}$$

Example: (c) Compare 500 kilometres and 800 metres

$$500 \text{ km} : 800 \text{ m}$$
$$= 500\,000 : 800 \quad \text{(changing 500 kilometres to metres and cancelling metres)}$$
$$= 5000 : 8 \quad \text{(cancelling by 100)}$$
$$= 625 : 1 \quad \text{(cancelling by 8)}$$

Ratios which only cancel as far as small whole numbers

Sometimes a ratio only reduces to small whole numbers, for example 25:40 reduces to 5:8.

Sometimes this is easily understood, for example the ratio 2:3. Where the numbers are more awkward it is usual to reduce one of the numbers to 1, so that the other side becomes a decimal fraction or a mixed number.

$$2:3$$
$$= 1:1\tfrac{1}{2} \quad \text{or} \quad 1:1.5$$

To reduce one side to unity (that is, to 1) we had to divide by 2. What we do to one side we must do to the other, so 3 is reduced to $1\tfrac{1}{2}$. Of course 1:1.5 is equally correct.

Similarly 5:8
$$= 1:1.6 \quad \text{(dividing both sides by 5)}$$

Example: (a) Compare 35:80

$$35:80$$
$$= 7:16 \quad \text{(cancelling by 5)}$$
$$= 1:2.2857$$
$$= 1:2.3 \quad \text{(correct to 1 decimal place)}$$

Example: (b) Compare 1200 m:3.5 km

$$1200\,\text{m}:3.5\,\text{km}$$
$$= 1200:3500$$
$$= 12:35$$
$$= 1:2.9 \quad \text{(correct to 1 decimal place)}$$

Example: (c) Compare 48 mins:5 hours

$$48\,\text{mins}:5\,\text{hours}$$
$$= 48:300$$
$$= 4:25$$
$$= 1:6.25$$

9.2 Exercises: simple ratios

1 Express the following ratios as simply as possible.

(a) £10 to £150
(b) £25 to £175
(c) £25 to £75
(d) £16 to £32
(e) 40 m to 400 m
(f) 125 km to 375 km
(g) 36 cm to 108 cm
(h) 24 cm to 48 cm
(i) 28 tonnes to 7 tonnes
(j) 500 litres to 25 litres

2 Express the following ratios as simply as possible. Both parts of the ratio must be in the same units before cancelling can begin.

(a) 120 m to 2 km
(b) 20 m to 2 km
(c) 25 pence to £75
(d) 18 cm to 1.26 m
(e) 7 minutes to 35 seconds
(f) 10 millilitres to 3 litres
(g) $2\tfrac{1}{2}$ days to 45 minutes
(h) 15 minutes to $3\tfrac{3}{4}$ hours
(i) 5 millilitres to 25 litres
(j) 12.5 pence to £50

3 Express the following ratios as simply as possible in the form 1:?. If necessary, give the answer correct to 1 decimal place.

(a) 15 m:80 m
(b) 27 grams:9 kg
(c) £35:£80
(d) 26 litres:1 hectolitre
(e) 12 minutes to $2\tfrac{3}{4}$ hours
(f) 36 pence:£5
(g) 20 seconds to 55 seconds
(h) 14 m:180 decametres
(i) 3 millilitres to 2 litres
(j) $3\tfrac{1}{2}$ hours:5 days

4 Department A makes 10 defective units out of 5000. Department B makes 18 defective items out of a total output of 54 000. Which department is the most efficient from the production point of view, if we compare these rates of failure?

5 Although in the years 19.1 and 19.2 output did not vary in a particular factory, costs rose from £24 000 to £29 500. What is the ratio of these costs? Give your answer in the form 1:?. (Give the answer correct to 2 decimal places.)

9.3 Proportional parts

We often use proportions in business or domestic life. For example, if four people share a flat, they may share the expenses equally. They may, however, share on a proportionate basis. For example, the people with larger rooms might pay more than others. They might share on the basis 4, 3, 2, 1. In this case, there would be 10 shares altogether. If the expenses came to £100 per week, then the person enjoying the largest share of the house would pay $\frac{4}{10}$, the next $\frac{3}{10}$, the next $\frac{2}{10}$ and the last $\frac{1}{10}$.

Cancelling where we can, we could thus say $\frac{2}{5}$, $\frac{3}{10}$, $\frac{1}{5}$ and $\frac{1}{10}$. The calculation would be:

$$\frac{2}{5} \times £100 = £40$$
$$\frac{3}{10} \times £100 = £30$$
$$\frac{1}{5} \times £100 = £20$$
$$\frac{1}{10} \times £100 = £10$$
$$\overline{£100}$$

In business, partners may share equally, or may share in proportion to the capital they have contributed. In companies, shareholders receive profits in proportion to their shareholdings. If there were a thousand shares in a company, and Mr Jones had 500 shares, Mr Smith 250, Mr Brown 200 and Mr Green 50, they would share profits in the proportions 500:250:200:50. Cancelling by 50 this becomes 10:5:4:1, a total of 20 parts. Suppose the profits were £48 000. The division between the shareholders would be:

$$\text{Mr Jones} \quad \frac{10}{20} = \frac{1}{2} = £24\,000$$
$$\text{Mr Smith} \quad \frac{5}{20} = \frac{1}{4} = £12\,000$$
$$\text{Mr Brown} \quad \frac{4}{20} = \frac{1}{5} = £9\,600$$
$$\text{Mr Green} \quad \frac{1}{20} = £2\,400$$
$$\overline{£48\,000}$$

9.4 Exercises: proportional parts

1 A solicitor specialising in wills has to share out the amounts of money shown below in the proportions shown. How much will the parties in each case receive?

(a) £6250 in the proportions of 7:3
(b) £12 600 in the proportions of 2:1
(c) £18 508 in the proportions of 3:2:2
(d) £4050 in the proportions of 3:1:1
(e) £15 500 in the proportions of 3:2
(f) £8600 in the proportions of 4:3:2:1
(g) £6327 in the proportions of 4:3:2
(h) £15 360 in the proportions of 5:4:3
(i) £9891 in the proportions of 4:2:1
(j) £18 992 in the proportions of 7:6:3

2 Share the following stocks of goods between wholesalers in the proportions shown.

(a) 952 kg dried fruit in the proportions of 4:3
(b) 1575 kg butter in the proportions of 2:1
(c) 6252 kg cheese in the proportions of 3:2:1
(d) 6000 tonnes wheat in the proportions of 5:4:3
(e) 5278 tonnes barley in the proportions of 5:5:4
(f) 2565 tonnes oats in the proportions of 2:2:1
(g) 5649 litres wine in the proportions of 3:3:1
(h) 4400 litres whisky in the proportions of 5:2:1
(i) 15 600 litres milk in the proportions of 7:3:2
(j) 260 000 eggs in the proportions of 4:4:5

9.5 Direct and inverse proportion

In many situations in business the sums payable vary in direct proportion to one another. Thus a person who buys 2 refrigerators would expect to pay twice as much as a person buying only 1 refrigerator. If I employ 20 people of similar ability I expect my wage bill to be 20 times larger than if I have only 1 employee.

In other situations the variation may be inverse. For example, if 100 men can construct an oil pipeline in 60 days, we expect the time to be reduced if the number of men is increased. If we double the labour force we expect the time taken to be halved. If we treble the labour force we expect to take $\frac{1}{3}$ of the time. The name 'inverse variation' comes from the fact that $\frac{1}{3}$ is 3 inverted. Similarly, 4 when inverted (put as the denominator instead of the numerator of a fraction) is $\frac{1}{4}$.

These direct and inverse proportion calculations are done as 'three-line sums' (sometimes called the unitary method, because the middle line of a three-line sum is always what 1 item would cost, or take the time to perform etc.). The actual calculation is always postponed until the third line, because we may be able to simplify the calculation by cancelling. Consider the following examples.

Example: (a) If 6 books cost £37.50, what will 27 cost?

Line 1   6 books cost   £37.50
                   (what we know to begin with)

Line 2   1 book   costs $\dfrac{£37.50}{6}$ (what 1 costs)

Line 3   27 books cost $\dfrac{£37.50}{6} \times 27$

(what we are asked to find)

We can now do the calculation:

$$\dfrac{£37.50}{\cancel{6}\,_2} \times \cancel{27}\,^9 \quad \text{(cancelling by 3)}$$

$$= \dfrac{£337.50}{2}$$

$$= \underline{\underline{£168.75}}$$

Example: (b) Accommodation at a conference centre for 12 students costs £720 for 3 days. What will it cost at the same rate for 15 days?

Line 1   cost for 3 days = £720

Line 2   cost for 1 day = $\dfrac{£720}{3}$

Line 3   cost for 15 days = $\dfrac{£720}{\cancel{3}\,_1} \times \cancel{15}\,^5$

$$= \underline{\underline{£3600}}$$

Example: (c) If 240 men can build an aerodrome in 180 days, how long will it take 600 men?

240 men take 180 days

1 man takes 180 × 240 days

(he takes 240 times as long)

600 men take $\dfrac{180 \times \cancel{240}\,^4}{\cancel{600}\,_1}$ days

(they take *less* time)

$$= \underline{\underline{72 \text{ days}}}$$

(cancelling by 10, 10 and 6)

9.6 Exercises: direct and inverse proportion

1 Work out the answers to these simple proportion sums.

(a) 2 cost 8p. How much for 6?

(b) 3 cost 9p. How much for 5?

(c) 7 cost 14p. How much for 9?

(d) 5 cost 20p. How much for 3?

(e) 17 cost 51p. How much for 32?

(f) 13 cost 26p. How much for 8?

(g) 4 cost £73. How much for 20?

(h) 12 cost £186. How much for 16?

(i) 18 cost £98. How much for 27?

(j) 15 cost £72. How much for 25?

2 Work out the answers to these 3-line sums (unitary method).

(a) If 8 'Hover-collect' mowing machines for a sports complex cost altogether £380, what will 5 cost?

(b) If 4 cameras cost £240, what will 12 cost?

(c) If 5 spin dryers cost £480, what will 11 cost?

(d) If 9 theatre tickets cost £58.50, what will 12 cost?

(e) A guest house charges £126 per week, what will the charge be for 5 days at the same rate?

(f) A coach trip for a journey of 90 kilometres costs £3.96. What will it cost at the same rate for a journey of 165 kilometres?

(g) A berth on a liner travelling 3500 kilometres costs £656.80. What will it cost at the same rate for a journey of 6300 kilometres?

(h) Renting a holiday car costs £112 per week. What will the charge be for 3 days at the same rate?

3 If 15 men take 165 days to perform a set task, how long would (a) 5 men, and (b) 50 men take to do the work?

4 A trench can be dug by 7 mechanical navvies in 3 days. How long would 5 machines take?

5 A team of 1400 men can construct an airport in 165 days. A national event which is to occur in 146 days time will be greatly assisted if the airport can be ready 14 days earlier. How many men should be put on the construction project to complete the airport in time?

9.7 Approximations

Many business calculations are approximations. This will often be true of measurements of length, or of weights. How accurate we require our calculations to be depends very much upon the purpose. For example, some engineers may wish to measure to the hundredth part of a millimetre for their machine parts. Businessmen, when considering the space in a factory or an office, would usually be content with far less accurate measurements.

Similarly with weights: if we are dealing with very precious metals or poisonous chemicals, we may need to be accurate to a very small part of a gram. When buying or selling coal or cement, we may be content to have the weights' measurements to the nearest kilogram.

We use approximations for many purposes. A businessman wishing to know the total number of people owning washing machines or television sets would probably be content to know the figure to the nearest thousand. An advertiser might be satisfied to know to the nearest 10 thousand how many people saw a particular advertisement. Transport firms wanting to know how many people are likely to use a new bus service, may wish to know the figures slightly more accurately, but would still be pleased if they could know the figures within perhaps one hundred.

In statistics (see Chapter 26) we call this process of approximating answers 'rounding'. We round the figures off to the nearest 1000, or 100, by adjusting the small number at the end in the same way as we do in decimals to give an answer correct to a given number of decimal places. To illustrate rounding, consider the population of the countries below:

Country (A)	55 151 131
Country (B)	24 275 836
Country (C)	28 397 500
Country (D)	17 236 500

When rounding these figures to the nearest 1000 we have:

Country	Population (thousands)	
(A)	55 151	(the 131 is less than half a thousand and is disregarded)
(B)	24 276	(the 836 is more than 500 and an extra thousand is counted)
(C)	28 398	(the 500 obeys the rule of rounding to the nearest *even* number)
(D)	17 236	(the 500 obeys the rule above, and we round down to the even number)

9.8 Significant figures

Frequently in business calculations we use the phrase 'significant figures'. Suppose that the population of the United Kingdom is given as 55 651 131. All these figures are significant, that is they mean something. The figure 3 is 3 tens = 30, and the first 5 is tens of millions, i.e. 50 millions. If we give the population to the nearest thousand it becomes 55 651 000. The three 0s are insignificant (that is, we do not really know what the hundreds, tens and units figures are), so we only have 5 significant figures. The 0s are not significant, although it is possible to have a significant 0, as in the number 50 627 000. The first 0, meaning no millions, is significant here.

In certain circumstances it might be sufficient to give the population to the nearest million. In this case 55 651 000 becomes 56 millions, and we have only two significant figures.

Figures from computers and calculators

The development of computers and calculators has meant that it is easier to do many calculations than in the past. However, producing more significant figures than are necessary for our purpose, will involve us in more labour and often more errors. As we stress throughout this book, it is nearly always helpful to do a rough check. Suppose we want to multiply 22.4×21.1. The first step would be to do a rough check 20×20. This is 400. Therefore, we would expect our answer to be rather larger than 400. If we then do the calculation, we will find that our answer is 472.64. If we wish our answer to be correct to four significant figures, the answer would be 472.6. If we need our answer to be correct to three significant figures the answer would be 473. This is in accordance with the rules for 'rounding' explained above.

How many significant figures do we need?

This will depend very much upon the purposes for which we need the calculations. For example, in most business calculations we would ignore fractions of a penny. Therefore, if we were calculating wages, we would want to know the answer correct to the nearest penny. Some firms have decided, when they are dealing with customers who have large accounts, they will have an agreement that all bills will be to the nearest pound. This saves them time on calculations and makes book-keeping easier.

9.9 Problems in ratio and proportion

Many elementary examination questions involve simple problems in ratio and proportion. All such problems are tests in simple logic. We read the question, use our background knowledge on ratio and proportion, and arrive at a sensible method to solve the problem. Consider the following examples:

Example: (a) The proceeds of a charity collection are shared among three charities so that A gets twice as much as B which gets three times as much as C. How much does each charity receive, if the total collection was £7280?

The charity C gets the lowest
share, which we will
call   1 share
B gets three times as
much as C, so B gets   3 shares
A gets twice as much
as B   6 shares
                            10 shares in all

$\therefore$ £7280 ÷ 10 = £728 per share

The result:

A gets £4368, B gets £2184, and C gets £728

(*Check:* £4368 + £2184 + £728 = £7280)

Example: (b) A will states that 7 nephews and 5 nieces are to share in an inheritance, so that each niece gets twice as much as each nephew. If the total inheritance is £25500, how much will each nephew and each niece receive?

Give each nephew 1 share = 7 shares
Give each niece 2 shares = 10 shares
                          17 shares

$$\begin{array}{r} \text{£} \\ 1500 \text{ per share} \\ 17\overline{)25\,500} \\ \underline{17} \\ 85 \\ \underline{85} \end{array}$$

$\therefore$ Each niece receives £3000 and

each nephew £1500

(*Check:* (5 × £3000) + (7 × £1500) =
£15 000 + £10 500 = £25 500)

9.10 Exercises: problems in ratio and proportion

1 The proceeds of a charitable collection are shared out among 3 charities A, B and C in such a way that B has three times as much as A which has three times as much as C. What will each receive if the total collection is £6955?
2 A football pools win of £3850 is shared out among 4 people W, X, Y and Z so that Z gets three times as much as X, who gets the same as Y while W gets twice as much as X. What will each receive?
3 Blankets are shared amongst 3 disaster-hit villages in a relief campaign, pro rata to the number of families. In village A there are 35 families, in village B there are 23 families and in village C there are 14 families. The relief column brings in 288 blankets. How many should each village receive?
4 The marks in an examination total 100. They are distributed between three compulsory questions that have a total of 60 marks, and eight optional questions of which the student has to answer only 5. The first compulsory question earns twice as many marks as each of the other two. The optional questions all have equal marks. How many marks for (a) compulsory question 1, (b) compulsory question 2, and (c) each of the optional questions.
5 Divide £369 between A, B and C so that A has

three times as much as B who has half as much as C. How much does each receive?

6 Theatre tickets are priced as follows. The gallery seats cost £2, circle seats are three times the gallery price, and stall seats are half as much again as the circle. (a) What is the ratio between the prices? (b) If equal numbers of seats are sold at each price, what are the takings on each class of seat if the total takings at a performance are £3910?

7 Theatre tickets are priced as follows. The best stalls are £10, circle seats are half that, and gallery seats half the circle price. Each part of the house has the same number of seats. A full house takes £3255. (a) How much of this is for stall seats? (b) How many stall seats are there?

8 Cinema tickets sell at two prices. The lower price is three-fifths of the higher price. There are equal numbers of seats at the two prices: 325 of each. A full house earns total takings of £910. (a) What are the total takings on the cheaper priced seats? (b) What is the cost of each seat, at each price?

10

Averages

10.1 Introduction to averages

An average is a measure of centrality. It takes up a central position among the figures (data) from which it is devised, and therefore is representative of all the data.

Consider a batsman in a cricket match who in one innings scores 100 runs (a century) and in the next innings scores only 4 runs. Which of these figures really represents his ability as a batsman? The answer is neither 100 nor 4; his general ability is best represented by an average score. If the two scores are spread evenly over the two innings:

$$\frac{100 + 4}{2} = \frac{104}{2} = 52 \text{ runs}$$

we arrive at an average, central figure of 52 runs. If we send him in to bat we can hope that he will make 52 runs, because this is an average effort for him.

To find a simple average, we add up the data available and divide by the number of pieces of data we have used. Let us find the average scores of three cricketers whose results so far this season are as follows:

  A has scored 27, 32, 5, 0, 4 (5 innings)
  B has scored 36, 42, 71, 31, 0, 0, 5, 164 (8 innings)
  C has scored 48, 21, 49, 52, 3, 0, 115, 4, 7, 121 (10 innings)

  The average scores are:

  A has scored $\frac{68}{5}$ = 13.6 runs on average
  B has scored $\frac{349}{8}$ = 43.625 runs on average
  C has scored $\frac{420}{10}$ = 42 runs on average

We usually only calculate cricket averages correct to one decimal place, so the results are 13.6, 43.6 and 42. Batsman B has the best average.

In the business world, averages are important. Firms frequently need to know their average costs. For example, transport firms will try to work out the average number of kilometres their vehicles travel per litre of fuel. They will also work out the average number of kilometres driven during the day. Since the introduction of the tachograph they can obtain many other useful averages, such as the average speed of their vehicles and the average break time taken by drivers. In another area, motor vehicle designers usually design their cars for the average person. They only take account of different sized people in certain areas such as the adjustment of the driver's seat to allow for tall and short people.

Many students will know the problems faced in shopping for clothes by people who are not stock size. The choice of those with very small frames or very large frames is limited, whereas those who are close to average size have a wide selection of garments.

10.2 Averages in statistics

The chief use of averages is in the study of statistics, and Chapters 26 to 29, below, give a brief introduction to this subject. The general term for averages in statistics is 'mean', which means 'a central position'. There are four of these averages in common use: the arithmetic mean, the geometric mean, the median and the mode. They have their different uses, but we will not bother with them here. They are discussed more fully in Chapter 29.

10.3 Simple averages

As explained above, the rule for finding a simple average is: *add up the pieces of data supplied, then divide by the number of pieces of data.*

Example: (a) Find the average number of pupils in six universities, A to F, which have the following enrolments:

A	13 227
B	11 368
C	8 462
D	12 835
E	9 275
F	6 372
	61 539

6)61 539

10 256.5   average enrolment

As it is unusual to enrol half a student, we could give this answer correct to the nearest whole number: 10 256 students.

Average of large numbers

We can sometimes save effort when finding the average of large numbers by ignoring most of each number until the end of the calculation, when we restore it. Thus, to find the average of 10 017, 10 024 and 10 055 we can ignore the 10 000 for calculation purposes, and simply find the average of 17, 24 and 55 = $\frac{96}{3}$ = 32. Restoring the 10 000 (which of course appears in every one of the three numbers given), we have 10 032 as the average.

Note: A useful check on averages: the average being a 'central' figure, there should be an equal number of items above and below average if the answer we have found is correct. To check this in the example just used:

10 032 is the average

Below average
10 017 = 15 below average
10 024 = _8 below average
        23

Above average
10 055 = 23 above average

Our answer is correct because the numbers below average are altogether 23 below the centre, and the number above average is 23 above the centre.

With some large numbers it may not be easy to pick a round number to disregard, like the 10 000 we disregarded in the last examples. In this case we can discard any number we like. Consider the following example.

Example: (b) Find the average of 2386, 2392, 2410 and 2524.

We could disregard 2380. The numbers then become:

6, 12, 30 and 144

$6 + 12 + 30 + 144 = \frac{192}{4} = 48$

Restoring the 2380 we have:

2380 + 48 = 2428 average

Check:
Numbers below average 2386 = 42 below average
2392 = 36 below average
2410 = 18 below average
        96 below average

Numbers above average 2524 = 96 above average.

As we have an equal amount above and below average, our answer is correct.

10.4 Exercises: simple averages

1 Find the average of each of the following groups of data.

(a) 6, 9, 12 (b) 3, 6, 15
(c) 5, 7, 8, 12 (d) 8, 10, 12, 18
(e) 10, 14, 18, 22 (f) 5, 6, 8, 12, 14
(g) 5, 8, 9, 10, 18 (h) 4, 5, 9, 13, 16, 19
(i) 340, 620, 720 (j) 560, 840, 911, 1301

2 Find the average of each of the following groups of data.

(a) 16 kg, 21 kg, 40 kg, 75 kg
(b) 30 kg, 55 kg, 21 kg, 46 kg, 58 kg
(c) 20 hrs 15 mins, 17 hrs 29 mins, 18 hrs 36 mins, 19 hrs 50 mins
(d) 546 litres, 329 litres, 726 litres, 452 litres, 636 litres, 377 litres
(e) 38.5 m, 42.6 m, 71.3 m, 84.5 m, 46.3 m, 72.5 m, 21.6 m
(f) 32.7 tonnes, 46.8 tonnes, 15.5 tonnes, 17.9 tonnes, 31.6 tonnes

3 Using the short-cut method shown above find the average of the following large numbers.

(a) 7004, 7008, 7015
(b) 24 301, 24 303, 24 304, 24 308
(c) 50 150, 50 250, 50 500
(d) 49 712, 49 722, 49 736, 49 750
(e) 16 858, 16 859, 16 879, 16 921 16 923

4 Find the average of the following sets of numbers.

(a) 4.5, 4.9, 4.7, 4.6, 4.8
(b) 5.63, 7.54, 7.78, 6.21, 5.34
(c) 17.4, 18.2, 19.3, 16.5, 15.8, 16.9
(d) 32.4, 34.6, 33.2, 35.7, 36.6, 39.8, 42.5
(e) 19.25, 20.2, 19.89, 20.34, 19.92

10.5 Weighted averages

Many calculations involving averages are affected by a process known as 'weighting'. The word 'weighting' in this connection means 'influence'. Just as we might say, with regard to an office, that the manager's opinion carries more weight, or wields more influence, than others. Weighted averages are widely used in statistics, and are referred to again in Chapter 29. Consider the following cases.

Example: (a) A football team plays in 5 matches, scoring goals as follows: 3, 2, 0, 1, 4. Find the average number of goals.

This is a simple average

$$\frac{3+2+0+1+4}{5} = \frac{10}{5}$$

$$= 2 \text{ goals on average}$$

Example: (b) A football team plays in 11 matches, scoring 3 goals in 2 matches, 2 goals in 4 matches, 1 goal in 3 matches and 0 goals in 2 matches. Find the average number of goals.

This is a weighted average. We could set it down in columnar form, as follows:

Number of goals	Weighting (i.e. frequency)		Total goals
3	×	2	= 6
2	×	4	= 8
1	×	3	= 3
0	×	2	= 0
		11	17

$$\text{Average} = \frac{\text{number of goals}}{\text{total matches}} \quad \text{(total weighting)}$$

$$= \frac{17}{11} = 1.54 = 1.5 \text{ (correct to one decimal place)}$$

Example: (c) A class of students includes 16 students aged 19 years, 11 aged 20, 2 aged 21 and 3 aged 22. Three other students were aged 27, 31 and 43 respectively. What is the average age?

Age in years	Weighting	Products (age × weight)
19	16	304
20	11	220
21	2	42
22	3	66
27	1	27
31	1	31
43	1	43
	35	733

$$\text{Average} = \frac{733}{35} = 35\overline{)733} \quad 20.94$$

$$\frac{70}{330}$$
$$\frac{315}{150}$$
$$\frac{140}{10}$$

= 20.9 years (correct to one decimal place)

10.6 Exercises: weighted averages

1 Find the average height of 15 recruits measured as follows: 3 recruits height 162 cm, 5 recruits height 164 cm, 1 recruit height 168 cm, 2 recruits height 169 cm, 2 recruits height 171 cm and 2 recruits height 172 cm. (Answer correct to one decimal place of a centimetre.)

2 Parcels are posted as follows: 1.25 kg (1 parcel), 1.75 kg (3 parcels), 2.25 kg (5 parcels). What is the average weight? (Answer correct to two decimal places of a kilogram.)

3 A wages office makes up wage packets as

follows: 4 supervisors get £194.00 each, 15 skilled tradesmen get £178.00 each, 12 semi-skilled men get £105.00 each, 4 apprentices get £67.00. Work out the average wage. (Answer correct to the nearest penny.)

4 A shipping office deals with 4 crates weighing 51.8 kg and 12 crates weighing 28.8 kg. What is the average weight? (Answer to the nearest kilogram.)

5 In an examination taken by 35 students, 5 students scored 82%, 3 scored 79%, 2 scored 76%, 4 scored 72%, 1 scored 71%, 3 scored 66%, 3 scored 61%, 1 scored 59%, 1 scored 57%, 4 scored 52%, 1 scored 49%, 3 scored 44% and 4 scored 39%. What was the average score? (Answer correct to one decimal place.)

11

Simple Pricing and Costing Calculations

11.1 Simple price calculations

In these days of electronic calculators and electronic tills, even the most difficult price calculations are relatively simple, but it is important to be able to do simple money calculations on a scrap of paper. For elementary examinations it is usual to prohibit the use of calculators, and thus to ensure that candidates can actually do simple calculations without these electronic aids.

A **bill** is an abbreviated invoice, given in shops to the customer as evidence of the goods supplied, and as a receipt for the cash paid. Of course, we do not always ask for a bill, for example when we purchase a bar of chocolate or a packet of cigarettes, but if we purchase items for business use it is customary to ask for a bill. We shall see later in Chapter 22 that such bills are often called petty cash vouchers, because they are used to reclaim the money spent from the petty cashier.

Many simple bill calculations can be done mentally, as shown in the following examples.

Example: (a) The price of 5 paperback books at £1.95 each.

$$£1.95 \text{ is } £2 \text{ less } 5 \text{ pence}$$
$$5 \times £2 = £10$$
$$\text{less } 5 \times 5 = \underline{\quad 0.25}$$
$$\text{answer} = \underline{\underline{£ \ 9.75}}$$

Alternatively, we could have multiplied £1.95 by 5 to reach the same answer.

Example: (b) The price of 4 reams of duplicating paper at £2.25 per ream.

$$£2.25 = £2\tfrac{1}{4}$$
$$4 \times 2\tfrac{1}{4} = \underline{\underline{£9}}$$

Example: (c) The total cost of 4 rising hinges at £1.55 each, twelve 4″ door hinges at 98p each, and 36 screws at 45p per dozen.

	£
4 rising hinges at £1.55 each =	6.20
12 4″ door hinges at 98p each =	11.76
36 screws at 45p per dozen =	1.35
	£19.31

Where a bill has several items, each item must be calculated and then a total arrived at.

11.2 Exercises: simple bills

1 Calculate the following prices.

   (a) 4 packets detergent at 61p each.
   (b) 3 packets of sweets at 59p per packet
   (c) 5 calculators at £25.50 each
   (d) 3 radial tyres at £15.60 each
   (e) 6 packets of frozen fish at 84p per packet
   (f) 8 office diaries at £2.95 each
   (g) 7 pot plants at 77p each
   (h) 12 m² of floor covering at £6.55 per square metre
   (i) 9 bed covers at £15.70 each
   (j) 12 saucepans at £3.45 each

2 Calculate the total charge on the following bills.

   (a) 6 reams of paper at £2.95 per ream,
      4 packets envelopes at 56p per packet, and
      1 packet carbon paper at £1.55.
   (b) 4 window catches at 63p each,
      3 door handles at £2.75p each, and
      2 packets wood screws at 92p per packet.
   (c) 4 brush and comb sets at £4.45 per set,
      4 electric shavers at £11.55 each, and
      2 vanity bags at £5.75 each.

(d) 4 copies of a concise dictionary at £2.65 each,
3 copies of *Roget's Thesaurus of Words and Phrases* at £4.99 each, and
2 copies of *Illustrated Encyclopaedia* at £2.40 each.

(e) 3 cardigans at £10.50 each,
2 leather jackets at £90.75 each,
1 pair of leather shoes at £22.40 per pair, and
4 pairs of socks at £1.95 per pair.

11.3 Simple costing activities

Many firms are interested in pricing not from the simple viewpoint of a bill, but from the point of view of the price to be charged for a particular good or service, so as to recover costs and yield a reasonable margin of profit. This involves us in an activity called **costing**.

Costing is a subject for study in its own right, as there are many types of costing activities. We can have **job costing** (finding the cost of a particular job), and **contract costing** (finding the cost of a complete contract, such as building a motorway or a bridge or a tunnel). Many firms use **process costing**, if they have continuous processes like oil refining or cement manufacture going on 24 hours a day, seven days a week. Let us consider a simple case of job costing, in the example below.

Example: A firm is asked to manufacture a gang-plank for use in boarding a ship. The costs are estimated as follows.

Raw materials:	sheet steel £18; steel rod £24; oak panels £16; paint etc. £12.
Labour:	machine shop 38 hours at £3.20 per hour. Fabrication shop 20 hours at £2.40 per hour. Paint shop 8 hours at £2.25 per hour.
Overheads:	these are estimated at £220 for general overhead. In addition to this, the stores (raw materials) and each of the three other shops are entitled to add 15% to their charges for 'shop overheads'.

What will be the total price for the job if 20% is added to the total cost for profit margin? (Answer to the nearest £1.)

The calculations are as follows:

		£
Raw materials	Sheet steel	18
	Steel rod	24
	Oak panels	16
	Paint	12
		70
Stores overhead 15%		10.50
		£80.50

$(£7 = 10\%\ £3.50 = 5\%)$

Other shops

	Machine shop	Fabrication shop	Paint shop
	£3.20	£2.40	£2.25
	× 38	× 20	× 8
	25.60	48.00	18.00
	96.00 10%	4.80 10%	1.80
	—— 5%	2.40 5%	0.90
	121.60		
Overheads 10%	12.16	£55.20	£20.70
5%	6.08		
	£139.84		

	£	
Total cost	80.50	Raw materials
	139.84	Machine shop
	55.20	Fabrication shop
	20.70	Paint shop
	220.00	General overhead
	516.24	
Add 20% profit $(=\frac{1}{5})$	103.248	
	£619.488	

Answer correct to nearest £1 = £619 for the job.

In some cases, a job like the one considered above might present an opportunity for further sales to other shipowners. It might be worth setting up a production line to manufacture this type of equipment as a 'stock' item, available to any customer who cares to ask for it. Usually making several similar items will mean reductions in costs, and we may be able to charge a more reasonable price (say, £500) for the stock item.

Similarly, prices are often quoted at a standard

rate for such things as road haulage (so much per tonne-kilometre). Thus if we charge 5p per tonne-kilometre for loads of 30 tonnes, this works out at £1.50 per kilometre for the load. To carry 30 tonnes 200 kilometres will therefore cost $200 \times £1.50 = £300$.

11.4 Exercises: simple costing activities

1 What will be the charge for each of the following orders for standard components in use in shipbuilding?

(a) 124 cabin doors at £7.56 per door
(b) 80 bell pushers at £2.35 each
(c) 124 bunk beds at £38.50 each
(d) 64 cabin refrigerators at £83.60 each
(e) 42 electric fans at £27.56 each

2 Find the transport charges for each of the following lorry loads at the quoted rates per tonne.

(a) 44 tonnes at £4.55 per tonne for the journey concerned
(b) 38 tonnes at £3.80 per tonne for the journey concerned
(c) 30 tonnes at £2.20 per tonne for the journey concerned
(d) 44 tonnes at £1.99 per tonne for the journey concerned
(e) 21 tonnes at £5.80 per tonne for the journey concerned

3 An accountant requires all jobs to be costed using a special form, which is reproduced in Figure 11.1 below. Using the format shown, find the price charged to each customer in the examples (a) to (e) below. Be careful to add on the various overheads and the profit margin as shown in Figure 11.1.

(a) Mr A. Fields. Raw materials: timber £28.50; 2 doors at £32.50 each; window frame £38.25; small fittings £18.50. Factory labour costs: carpentry shop 16 hours at £3.25 per hour; painters 7 hours at £2.25 per hour.

Figure 11.1 An estimate sheet for pricing jobs

Customer's name _____ Ref. No._____

(a) Raw Materials 1. _____ £
                     2. _____
                     3. _____
                     4. _____

        Total _____
        Stores overhead (25%) _____

(b) Factory labour costs 1. _____
                        2. _____
                        3. _____

Total _____
Factory overhead (25%) _____

                    Total factory cost _____

General overhead (50%) _____

                    Total cost _____

Profit margin (30% on total cost) _____

Total charge   £ _____

(b) Mrs R. Lightfoot. Raw materials: sheet aluminium £16.25; insulation £8.20; 2 chromium handles at £3.78 each. Factory labour costs: metal shop $4\frac{1}{2}$ hours at £3.80 per hour.

(c) Mr T. A. Alberga. Raw materials: timber £27.75; window frames (large) $3 \times £38.25$; window frames (small) $1 \times £16.30$. Factory labour costs: carpentry shop 14 hours at £3.25 per hour; joinery labour 6 hours at £2.25 per hour.

(d) Mrs R. Dickinson. Raw materials: steel framework £32.50; aluminium sheeting £26.85. Factory labour costs: metal shop 16 hours at £3.25 per hour.

(e) Mr E. Woods. Raw materials: timber £42.50; 2 doors £86.25 each. Factory labour costs: carpentry shop 6 hours at £3.25 per hour; painters 8 hours at £2.25 per hour; transport department 3 hours at £2.80 per hour.

12

Buying Prices, Selling Prices and Profit Margins

12.1 Mark-ups and selling prices

In manufacturing and service industries we are interested in costing to fix our selling prices. We find total costs and add a margin for profits. In ordinary retail trade the process is much simpler. All we need to do is to take the cost price of the goods we buy, add a profit **mark-up** and sell again. The profit mark-up must be large enough to cover all our overhead expenses and still leave enough profit as a reward to the retailer for his efforts. The mark-up is not all profit: rent, rates, labour costs, delivery charges, light, heat and many other expenses have to be covered by the mark-up. The biggest single cause of small shops going out of business is the failure of their proprietors to add on a large enough mark-up. Slow moving items need a bigger mark-up than fast selling items, and items which require wrapping, or delivery, or preparation before they can be sold, need a bigger mark-up too.

A good exercise for a student of business calculations is to go and stand in the middle of the most popular store in your home area and look around you at the bright lights, the lush carpets, the enormous stocks, the sales personnel, the security staff etc. Then think about one particular item that is on display and ask yourself how much must have been added to the price of that article to cover all the expenses connected with selling it. Clearly 5% is not enough, and even 20% would not be sufficient. Often 40% is the mark-up, while 100% is not unusual and 300% is not unheard of (though it may be profiteering).

Mark-up is usually done in percentage terms, using the simple formula:

Cost price + mark-up (%) = *selling price*

Consider the following examples.

Example: (a) A furniture shop buys coffee tables from a furniture manufacturer at £35 each. He adds a mark-up of 40%. What is his selling price?

$SP = £35 + (\frac{40}{100} \times 35)$ (cancelling by 10, 5 and 2)
$= £35 + £14$
$= £49$

Example: (b) A fashion boutique buys dresses at £8.50 each, adding a mark-up of 150%. What is their selling price?

$SP = £8.50 + (\frac{150}{100} \times £8.50)$
$= £8.50 + (1\frac{1}{2} \times £8.50)$
$= £8.50 + £8.50 + £4.25$
$= £21.25$

Cost price and selling price are often abbreviated to CP and SP, respectively.

12.2 Exercises: mark-ups

1 What will be the selling prices of the following items if a $33\frac{1}{3}\%$ mark-up is added to the cost price shown?

(a) 90p	(b) £1.50
(c) £2.40	(d) £25.20
(e) £38.70	(f) £55.50
(g) £78.00	(h) £94.92
(i) £128.55	(j) £166.50

2 In the calculations shown below, the cost price is given first and then the percentage mark-up. What will the selling prices be? (Answers correct to the nearest penny where necessary.)

(a) £1.50:30%	(b) £2.30:35%
(c) £3.80:40%	(d) £5.25:50%
(e) £5.60:45%	(f) £6.38:65%
(g) £7.25:60%	(h) £16.40:125%
(i) £18.50:150%	(j) £117.25:45%

12.3 Selling prices and retail branches

When we add a mark-up to cost price we arrive at a selling price. Today many retailers are run from Head Offices that operate a system by which the branches do not know the cost price of the goods they sell (that is a Head Office secret). Instead, the goods are sent to branches at selling price. The advantage is that the branch should then be able to account for the goods very easily. If we do a stock-taking operation at the shop and price the stock at selling price, we have only to find the difference between the two figures to find the amount the branch should have paid in. For example:

	£
Stock sent to branch (at selling price)	17 256
Less stock in hand (at selling price)	3 854
Money due to be paid in	£13 402

If we then find that the branch has only paid in £12 830 to its local bank, there is a shortage:

	£
Money due	13 402
Cash paid in	12 830
Shortage	572

Every shortage should be investigated. Is it due to shop-lifting, or theft from the tills by the staff, or theft of stock by the staff, or the giving away of stock by the staff? There are many possibilities.

Sometimes when you go shopping you will see someone checking the stock with a clip-board to which price lists are attached. This may be someone from Head Office doing the stock-taking, but it may also be a person from Head Office checking the prices that are being charged. If a manager adds a few pence to each item and charges more than the Head Office prices, he or she will cover-up any shortages and may even make a surplus. A dishonest manager may keep that extra sum, to cover any future shortages. This type of practice is criminal (apart from being an attempt to prevent Head Office knowing what is actually going on) and if it is discovered, often results in the dismissal of the person concerned.

12.4 Exercises: selling prices and retail branches

1 A branch shop has received £28 325.50 of goods from Head Office, sent to it at selling price. It has paid in £23 337.85 to the local bank for payment to Head Office accounts. How much stock should be on the shelves?

2 A supermarket receives £47 825.50 of goods from Head Office, sent at selling price. The manager has paid in £32 567.25. What is the value of the goods still on the shelves (at selling price)?

3 A supermarket manager is about to be confirmed as a full manager after a probationary period. The supermarket has received £273 285.85 of goods at selling prices during her management; she has paid in £238 876.55 and goods on the shelves are valued (at selling price) at £34 286.50. (a) Is there a shortage or a surplus, and how much is it? (b) Would you confirm her appointment or not? Say why!

4 A supermarket has received £42 509.50 of goods from Head Office in a week. When the week began goods on the shelves were worth £8250.25. The manager paid in £38 500.50 during the week for cash sales. How much stock should still be on the shelves now?

5 A supermarket has received £127 246.50 of goods from Head Office in a month. Stock at the start of the month was priced at £18 245.40. The manager paid in £131 472.80 during the month. What is the value of the stock still on the shelves?

12.5 Selling prices and profit margins

A margin is that part of the selling price which is profit, and therefore it is often called the *profit margin*. It might be thought that this margin is the same as the mark-up added on to the cost price; it is indeed, but in percentage terms it is a different percentage, which some students find confusing. Consider the following example:

Cost price + % mark-up = selling price
£100 + 20% mark-up = £100 + £20 = £120
Selling price − margin = cost price
£120 − £20 = £100

However, the £20 we deduct is not 20% (as it was in the mark-up) as we soon find if we deduct 20% from £120.

$$£120 - 20\% = £120 - (\tfrac{20}{100} \text{ of } £120)$$
$$= £120 - £24$$
$$= £\ 96$$

If we use the same percentage we do not arrive back at the correct low price. This is because the first 20% is based on the £100 cost price (20% of £100), whereas the second 20% is based on £120 (20% of £120).

We shall see later that there is a simple relationship between mark-up and margin, but first let us be clear that margins are always referred to when dealing with selling prices (whereas mark-ups refer to the profit element added on to cost price). Consider the following examples.

Example: (a) What was the cost price of goods sold at £160, of which 25% is the profit margin?

Cost price = selling price − profit margin
$$= £160 - (25\% \text{ of } £160)$$
$$= £160 - £40$$
$$= £120$$

Example: (b) What was the cost price of goods sold at £230, of which $33\tfrac{1}{3}\%$ is profit? (Answer correct to the nearest penny.)

$$CP = SP - \text{profit margin}$$
$$= £230 - (33\tfrac{1}{3}\% \text{ of } £230)$$
$$= £230 - (\tfrac{1}{3} \times £230)$$
$$= £230 - £76.67$$
$$= £153.33$$

Example: (c) What was the cost price of goods sold at £18.50 of which 40% is profit?

$$CP = SP - (\tfrac{40}{100} \times SP)$$
$$= £18.50 - (\tfrac{2}{5} \times £18.50)$$
$$= £18.50 - £7.40 \ (\tfrac{1}{5} = £3.70)$$
$$= £11.10$$

12.6 Exercises: selling prices and profit margins

1 Find the cost price of each of the articles whose selling prices are listed below. In each case the profit margin is $33\tfrac{1}{3}\%$.

(a) SP = £9   (b) SP = £36
(c) SP = £14.40   (d) SP = £26.40
(e) SP = £58.50   (f) SP = £73.80

2 Find the cost price of each of the articles whose selling prices are listed below. The profit margin has been stated in brackets alongside each.

(a) £5 (20%)   (b) £45 (25%)
(c) £30 (25%)   (d) £56 (50%)
(e) £43.50 ($33\tfrac{1}{3}\%$)   (f) £81.60 ($16\tfrac{2}{3}\%$)
(g) £200 ($12\tfrac{1}{2}\%$)   (h) £75 (30%)
(i) £160 (40%)   (j) £85 (60%)

12.7 The link between mark-up and margin

There must be a simple relationship between mark-up and margin. Take the simple example used before:

$$CP + \text{mark-up} = SP$$
$$£100 + 20\% \text{ of } £100 = £100 + £20 = £120$$

When we try to work this backwards, that is from the selling price to the cost price, the percentage is different. What percentage is needed to bring us back to the original cost price?

$$SP - \text{margin} = CP$$
$$£120 - ?\% = £100$$

Clearly the margin has to be £20. But what percentage is £20 of £120? The answer is $\tfrac{20}{120} \times 100$ (*not* $\tfrac{20}{100} \times 100$). Therefore:

$$\frac{20^1}{120} \times 100 \text{ (cancelling by 10 and 2)}$$
$$= \tfrac{1}{6} \times 100$$
$$= 16\tfrac{2}{3}\%$$

So 20% on the cost price becomes $16\tfrac{2}{3}\%$ off the selling price. There does not seem to be anything very remarkable in this relationship but if we turn the percentages into fractions we do get a remarkable relationship:

$$20\% \text{ on } CP = 16\tfrac{2}{3}\% \text{ off the } SP$$
$$\tfrac{1}{5} \text{ on } CP = \tfrac{1}{6} \text{ off the selling price}$$

Note that the denominator of the fractions off the selling price is one more than the denominator of the fraction on the cost price. This is because when we add $\frac{1}{5}$ to the CP we get $1\frac{1}{5}$ or $\frac{6}{5}$. To take that $\frac{1}{5}$ off again we have to deduct $\frac{1}{6}$, not $\frac{1}{5}$. There are now six fifths in the selling price, not five fifths. This works for all other mark-ups and margins:

$$\frac{1}{2} \text{ on the CP} = \frac{1}{3} \text{ off the SP}$$
$$\frac{1}{3} \text{ on the CP} = \frac{1}{4} \text{ off the SP}$$
$$\frac{1}{4} \text{ on the CP} = \frac{1}{5} \text{ off the SP}$$
$$\frac{1}{5} \text{ on the CP} = \frac{1}{6} \text{ off the SP}$$
$$\frac{1}{6} \text{ on the CP} = \frac{1}{7} \text{ off the SP}$$
$$\frac{1}{7} \text{ on the CP} = \frac{1}{8} \text{ off the SP}$$
$$\frac{1}{8} \text{ on the CP} = \frac{1}{9} \text{ off the SP}$$

The list continues for any mark-up you like, for example $\frac{1}{20}$ on the cost price $= \frac{1}{21}$ off the selling price. So:

$$£100 + 5\% = £100 + \tfrac{1}{20} = £100 + £5 = £105 \text{ SP}$$

To turn the selling price back to cost price:

$$£105 - (\tfrac{1}{21} \times £105)$$
$$= £105 - £5$$
$$= £100$$

This relationship often crops up in examination questions, and while the sums are easy to solve if you know the relationship, they lead to many candidates losing valuable marks because they have not understood this link between mark-ups and margins. Consider the following examples.

Example: (a) A retailer marks up an article by 50% on cost price and sells it for £15. What did the article cost originally? What was the margin on selling price?

$$\text{Mark-up} = 50\% = \tfrac{1}{2}$$
$$\tfrac{1}{2} \text{ on the cost price} = \tfrac{1}{3} \text{ off the selling price}$$
$$\tfrac{1}{3} \text{ as a percentage} = 33\tfrac{1}{3}\%$$
$$\text{therefore margin on SP} = 33\tfrac{1}{3}\%$$

$$\text{Original cost} = £15 - (\tfrac{1}{3} \times £15)$$
$$= £15 - £5$$
$$= £10 \text{ CP}$$

Check: If we work this forwards we should now find the selling price easily enough:
CP + mark-up = SP
£10 + 50% of £10 = £10 + £5
= £15, so our calculation is correct

Where the original mark-up is not as simple as in

the list of mark-ups and margins above ($\frac{1}{2}$ on CP = $\frac{1}{3}$ off SP etc.) we still follow the same rule really.

Example: (b) A retailer marks-up an article by 60% on cost price and sells it for £64. What was the margin on selling price? What did the article cost originally?

$$CP + 60\% = £64$$

If we regard the CP as 100% then:

$$100\% + 60\% = 160\%$$

Therefore the CP is $\frac{100}{160}$ of £64 and the margin is $\frac{60}{160}$

$$CP = \tfrac{100}{160} \times £64^4$$
$$= 10 \times 4 \text{ (cancelling by 10 and 16)}$$
$$= £40$$

Margin on selling price:

$$= \frac{\overset{3}{\cancel{60}}}{\underset{8}{\cancel{160}}} \times \cancel{100}^{25}$$
$$= \frac{75}{2} \text{ (cancelling by 10, 2 and 4)}$$
$$= 37\tfrac{1}{2}\%$$

12.8 Exercises: mark-ups and margins

1 Ten retailers mark up the cost of articles by the percentages shown below, so that the selling prices reach the figures shown. In each case find (a) the cost price of each article, and (b) the margin of profit per cent on the *selling price*.

	Mark-up on CP	*SP*		*Mark-up on CP*	*SP*
(a)	50%	£15	(b)	50%	£24
(c)	$33\tfrac{1}{3}\%$	£1.60	(d)	$33\tfrac{1}{3}\%$	£120
(e)	25%	£100	(f)	25%	£5.60
(g)	20%	£12	(h)	20%	£72
(i)	$12\tfrac{1}{2}\%$	£36	(j)	$12\tfrac{1}{2}\%$	£90

2 Six retailers mark up the cost price of the articles shown below by the percentages given, and thus achieve the selling prices shown. In each case find (a) the cost price of the article, and (b) the margin per cent of profit on the *selling price*. (Answer correct to one decimal place.)

	Mark-up on CP	SP		Mark-up on CP	SP
(a)	30%	£2.60	(b)	40%	£4.20
(c)	60%	£32	(d)	60%	£7.20
(e)	45%	£17.40	(f)	55%	£37.20

3 A jeweller sells a gold bracelet with charms for £544, having made a 36% profit on his cost price. What did the bracelet cost?

4 A video machine is sold for £420 after a retailer has marked it up by 68% on the cost price. What did it cost?

5 A dishwasher retails at £248.50 after being marked up by 75% on cost price. What did it cost?

13
Simple Interest

13.1 Saving and borrowing

Money is the reward paid to those who supply factors of production to work in industry, commerce and personal services. The factors of production are land, labour and capital. Land earns rent, labour earns wages and capital earns interest. Those who have money to spare save it, and this is called money capital. This money capital is usually saved in banks, building societies etc. and it earns interest, which is a payment of money for the use of money capital. Those who want to borrow money, either for buying a house, starting a business or just for every-day domestic use (for example, to buy a washing machine or a motor car), must pay interest on the loan.

When saving or borrowing, certain special words are used that we must learn:

(a) The **principal** is the sum of money saved, or borrowed. It is often called the 'capital sum'. It need not be very large, even a few pounds is capital, and many people accumulate quite large capital sums by saving regularly each week or month. The Government runs a special SAYE scheme: save as you earn. It earns a high rate of interest, to encourage small savers.

(b) The **rate of interest** is expressed as a percentage of the principal, and always refers to the use of money for a period of one year. So the rate of interest might be '8% per annum', or '$11\frac{1}{4}$% per annum'.

(c) The **time period** is also important. Various words are used to express this time, but they are all related to a year. Thus a daily rate is worked out as $\frac{1}{365}$ of a year, and a monthly rate would be $\frac{1}{12}$ of a year.

(d) The **investor** is the person who is saving money and is prepared to lend it to someone who needs it, in return for the payment of interest. Usually, ordinary people invest in a bank or building society and leave it to the organisation to lend the money to a borrower. Such institutions that specialise in borrowing and lending money are called **institutional investors**.

13.2 Simple interest and compound interest

Simple interest is interest that is paid yearly to the investor. Thus if I invest £500 in a firm, and the owner of the firm pays me 10% interest per annum I shall draw £50 interest each year and the principal of £500 will remain on loan for the following year (or for as long as I do not demand repayment).

Compound interest is a different system. I do not draw out the interest each year, but leave it in as an extra investment. Next year I shall get 10% interest on £550, which is £55. The table below shows what happens over a ten-year period.

Year	Principal (£)	Interest (£)	End of year total (£)
Year 1	500	50	550
Year 2	550	55	605
Year 3	605	60.5	665.5
Year 4	665.5	66.55	732.05
Year 5	732.05	73.20	805.25
Year 6	805.25	80.52	885.77
Year 7	885.77	88.58	974.35
Year 8	974.35	97.44	1071.79
Year 9	1071.79	107.18	1178.97
Year 10	1178.97	117.90	1296.87

Notice that the money quickly doubles in value at a 10% rate of interest. In eight years we have reached £1071.79, more than twice the amount originally invested.

Compound interest is dealt with later in this book (Chapter 31). Here we only deal with simple interest.

13.3 The simple interest formula

Simple interest is usually calculated by a formula. This is:

$$I = \frac{PRT}{100}$$

Here the letter I stands for 'interest', P stands for 'principal', R stands for 'rate' of interest, and as this is always expressed as a percentage, the 100 below the line in the formula is the denominator of this percentage. So 8% is written $\frac{8}{100}$ and 14% is written $\frac{14}{100}$. T stands for 'time in years'. (Some people use N instead for 'number of years' and use the formula $I = \frac{PRN}{100}$.)

Those who know their algebra will understand that when we use letters as symbols in a formula of this sort, letters written side by side are multiplied together. We save time by leaving out the multiplication signs. So:

$$I = \frac{PRT}{100} \text{ means } I = \frac{P \times R \times T}{100}$$

or $I = \dfrac{\text{Principal} \times \text{Rate} \times \text{Time in years}}{100}$

Consider the following examples.

Example: (a) Mrs Brown invests £1200 at 8% for 1 year. How much interest will she earn?

In every simple interest sum we begin by setting down the formula, and then substituting in the actual figures of the calculation in place of the symbols of the formula. As we change the symbols to the actual figures we must remember to put the multiplication signs in. Then we cancel if we can and continue in the usual way with any fraction sum, multiplying the numerators etc.

$$I = \frac{PRT}{100}$$

$$= \frac{£12\cancel{00} \times 8 \times 1}{1\cancel{00}} \quad \text{(cancelling by 100)}$$

$$= £12 \times 8$$

$$= £96$$

Example: (b) Mrs Awolowo invests £850 at 11% for 2 years. How much interest does she earn altogether?

$$I = \frac{PRT}{100}$$

$$= \frac{\overset{17}{£8\cancel{50}} \times 11 \times \overset{1}{\cancel{2}}}{\underset{1}{1\cancel{00}}} \quad \text{(cancelling by 10, 5 and 2)}$$

$$= £17 \times 11$$

$$= £187$$

Example: (c) R. Fischer invests £10 000 at $13\frac{1}{4}$% for $3\frac{1}{2}$ years. How much interest will he earn altogether?

$$I = \frac{PRT}{100}$$

$$= \frac{\overset{25}{£10\cancel{000}} \times 53 \times 7}{1\cancel{00} \times \cancel{4} \times 2} \quad \text{(cancelling by 100 and 4)}$$

$$= \frac{£25 \times 53 \times 7}{2}$$

$$= £4637.50$$

$$
\begin{array}{r}
25 \\
53 \\
\hline
75 \\
1250 \\
1325 \\
\times 7 \\
\hline
2\overline{)9275} \\
\hline
4637.50
\end{array}
$$

(*Note:* $13\frac{1}{4}$ has to be changed to $\frac{53}{4}$ and $3\frac{1}{2}$ has to be changed to $\frac{7}{2}$.)

Example: (d) Find the simple interest on £4800 invested at $9\frac{1}{4}$% per annum for 219 days. (A day is always taken as $\frac{1}{365}$ of a year, even in a leap year.)

$$I = \frac{PRT}{100}$$

$$= \frac{£4800 \times 9\frac{1}{4} \times 219 \text{ days}}{100}$$

$$= \frac{£4800 \times 37 \times 219}{100 \times 4 \times 365}$$

We cancel by 100, 4 and 73 $(5 \times 73 = 365; 3 \times 73 = 219)$.

The calculation continues:

$$= £12 \times 37 \times \tfrac{3}{5}$$

$$= \frac{£1332}{5}$$

$$= £266.40$$

	37
	$\times 12$
	444
	$\times 3$
	1332

13.4 Exercises: simple interest

1 Find the simple interest earned on each of the following investments over the period shown.

(a) £200 at 6 per cent per annum for 5 years
(b) £700 at 9 per cent per annum for 2 years
(c) £300 at 14 per cent per annum for 9 years
(d) £6000 at 12 per cent per annum for 3 years
(e) £400 at 13 per cent per annum for $7\frac{1}{2}$ years

2 Find the simple interest payable on the following loans over the period shown.

(a) £500 at 7 per cent per annum for $8\frac{1}{2}$ years
(b) £2100 at 11 per cent per annum for $6\frac{1}{4}$ years
(c) £3000 at $8\frac{1}{4}$ per cent per annum for $4\frac{1}{2}$ years
(d) £19 000 at $13\frac{1}{2}$ per cent per annum for $7\frac{1}{2}$ years
(e) £1250 at $12\frac{1}{2}$ per cent per annum for $2\frac{3}{4}$ years

3 Find the simple interest payable on each of the following loans. (If necessary, give the answers correct to the nearest penny.)

(a) £330 at 21 per cent per annum for $2\frac{1}{2}$ years
(b) £670 at 12 per cent per annum for $7\frac{1}{4}$ years
(c) £920 at 13 per cent per annum for $5\frac{3}{4}$ years
(d) £550 at $17\frac{1}{2}$ per cent per annum for $3\frac{1}{2}$ years
(e) £680 at $15\frac{1}{2}$ per cent per annum for $4\frac{1}{4}$ years

4 Find the simple interest on each of the following investments.

	Principal	Rate (%)	Time
(a)	£720	$8\frac{1}{4}$	$2\frac{1}{2}$ years
(b)	£380	$10\frac{1}{2}$	$3\frac{3}{4}$ years
(c)	£4800	$11\frac{1}{4}$	7 months
(d)	£7800	$7\frac{1}{2}$	146 days
(e)	£1460	$13\frac{1}{2}$	50 days

13.5 Transposing the formula

In the examples already given, the unknown item was always the interest payable. Sometimes we will need to alter the formula in order to be able to calculate some other unknown item, such as the principal, or the rate of interest, or the time. This requires us to carry out a simple process called the transposition of the formula, explained in detail below. Let us first look at the answers we will get when we transpose the formula:

The simple interest formula is $\quad I = \dfrac{PRT}{100}$

The formula to find the principal is $\quad P = \dfrac{100\,I}{RT}$

The formula to find the rate of interest is $\quad R = \dfrac{100\,I}{PT}$

The formula to find the time an investment is left in for is $\quad T = \dfrac{100\,I}{PR}$

We can see that these are all very similar, they have $100\,I$ on the top line and the other two terms underneath. We can now answer some simple problems using these formulae.

Example: (a) What principal was invested if £500 interest is earned in 4 years at 10% per annum?

Naturally we use the formula to find the principal.

$$P = \frac{100\,I}{RT}$$

$$= \frac{\overset{25}{\cancel{100}} \times £500}{\underset{1}{\cancel{10} \times \cancel{4}}} \quad \text{(cancelling by 10 and 4)}$$

$$= 25 \times £50$$

$$= £1250$$

Example: (b) What rate of interest was charged if £3000 borrowed to buy a car must be repaid with £1080 interest in three years?

Using the formula for the rate of interest we have:

$$R = \frac{100\,I}{PT}$$

$$= \frac{1\cancel{00} \times £108\cancel{0}}{£3\cancel{000} \times 3} \quad \text{(cancelling by 100 and by 10)}$$

$$= \frac{£108}{£9}$$

$$= \underline{\underline{12\%}}$$

(*Note:* In example (b) the £ signs cancel out as well as many of the figures and we finish up with a number 12, which is of course 12%, since we are finding the rate.)

Example: (c) How long was an investment of £6250 made for, if it earned £250 at 8%?

Using the formula for time we have:

$$T = \frac{100\,I}{PR}$$

$$= \frac{\overset{5}{\cancel{1\cancel{00}}} \times \overset{125}{\cancel{£250}}}{\cancel{£6250} \times \underset{\underset{2}{4}}{\cancel{8}}} \quad \text{(cancelling by 10, 2 and 2)}$$

$$= \frac{\overset{1}{\cancel{£625}}}{\underset{1}{\cancel{£625}} \times 2} \quad \text{(cancelling by 625)}$$

$$= \tfrac{1}{2} \text{ year}$$

$$= \underline{\underline{6 \text{ months}}}$$

(*Note:* Once again the £ signs cancel out to give an answer, $\tfrac{1}{2}$, which is a number only, and since we are finding the time for which the investment was made must be $\tfrac{1}{2}$ year, or six months.)

Before working some exercises in these matters, let us just explain the transposition of the formula used above.

Altering an equation

Our formula is a simple equation: that is, a mathematical statement with an equals sign in it:

$$I = \frac{PRT}{100}$$

The rule is that if you have an equation you can change it in any way you like, so long as you do the same thing to both sides, and it will still be true. Let us explain this by a very simple equation:

$$5 = 2 + 3$$

Let us now change this formula by doing the same thing to both sides, and we shall find it remains true.

Addition: let us add 1 to both sides

$5 + 1 = 2 + 3 + 1$. This is till true! $6 = 6$

Subtraction: let us subtract 3 from both sides

$5 - 3 = 2 + 3 - 3$. This is till true! $2 = 2$

Multiplication: let us multiply both sides by 4

$$5 \times 4 = (2 + 3) \times 4$$
$$20 = 20. \text{ It is still true.}$$

Division: let us divide both sides by 5

$$5 \div 5 = \frac{(2 + 3)}{5}$$
$$1 = 1. \text{ It is still true.}$$

Another thing that is true about equations is that you can turn them round completely and they are still true.

$$5 = 2 + 3$$
$$2 + 3 = 5$$

Nothing has changed, except that the two sides have been transposed (that is, moved to the opposite position).

Now let us try the same process with our formula to give us different formulae. We don't want a formula to tell us the interest, but one to tell us the principal, or the rate, or the number of years (the time). How shall we change

$$I = \frac{PRT}{100}$$

into P = ?

or R = ?

or T = ?

It is quite simple. Let us find a formula for $P = ?$

Start with the original formula

$$I = \frac{PRT}{100}$$

Transpose the formula

$$\frac{PRT}{100} = I$$

We want to leave P where it is and move R, T and 100 out of the way. How shall we get rid of each of these?

We obey the rules of equations. Multiply both sides by 100 to remove the hundred:

$$\frac{PRT}{100} \times 100 = 100\,I \quad \text{(cancelling by 100)}$$

$$PRT = 100\,I$$

How shall we remove R to get rid of it? Answer: divide both sides by R. The R will cancel out on the left-hand side.

$$\frac{PRT}{R} = \frac{100\,I}{R} \quad \text{(cancelling R)}$$

$$PT = \frac{100\,I}{R}$$

How shall we remove T from the left-hand side? Divide both sides by T.

$$\frac{PT}{T} = \frac{100\,I}{RT} \quad \begin{array}{l}\text{(cancel the Ts on}\\ \text{the left-hand side)}\end{array}$$

$$P = \frac{100\,I}{RT}$$

This is the formula we used in the examples already given to find the principal invested or borrowed.

If we use the method shown above we can similarly find the other formulae:

$$R = \frac{100\,I}{PT} \quad \text{and} \quad T = \frac{100\,I}{PR}$$

13.6 Exercises: more difficult simple interest calculations

1 What simple interest was earned altogether in the period shown? (Answer correct to the nearest penny.)

	Principal (£)	Rate (%)	Time (years)
(a)	2855	7	3
(b)	5700	$4\frac{1}{2}$	$8\frac{3}{4}$
(c)	1250	$6\frac{1}{2}$	$2\frac{1}{4}$
(d)	825	12	$\frac{1}{2}$
(e)	2700	$12\frac{1}{2}$	$4\frac{1}{4}$

2 Find the principal borrowed in each of the following loans.

	Interest earned	Rate per cent	Number of years
(a)	£365	8	5
(b)	£4500	15	6
(c)	£490	14	$3\frac{1}{2}$
(d)	£266	$9\frac{1}{2}$	7
(e)	£560	$12\frac{1}{2}$	2

3 Find the rate of interest charged on each of the following loans.

	Principal	Interest earned	Time in years
(a)	£200	£100	4
(b)	£900	£225	$2\frac{1}{2}$
(c)	£1500	£675	6
(d)	£2250	£630	$3\frac{1}{2}$
(e)	£3250	£1755	$4\frac{1}{2}$

4 For how long were the following sums of money invested at the rates of interest per annum shown in the table, if they earned interest as listed?

	Principal	Interest earned	Rate per cent
(a)	£1400	£280	8
(b)	£400	£325	$12\frac{1}{2}$
(c)	£840	£273	13
(d)	£2300	£920	$12\frac{1}{2}$
(e)	£9000	£2295	$8\frac{1}{2}$

14

Foreign Money and Exchange Rates

14.1 Foreign money

Every country has its own currency. The United Kingdom has its pound sterling, the Americans have their dollar (a currency copied by many other countries), the French use the franc, the Italians use the lira, the Russians use the rouble, and so on. All these currencies are subdivided into small coins so that even quite tiny payments can be made in the official currency. Usually the main coinage is divided into 100 parts (often called cents) or 1000 parts (called mils), after the Latin words for 100 and 1000 respectively. When the main currency unit is a very small unit itself there is no point in dividing it into smaller parts, and consequently there are no coins smaller than the unit itself. This is particularly the case with the lira and the yen. At the time of writing (1984) there are 326 yen to £1 and 2339 lire to £1. The most important currencies are listed in Table 14.1, with their exchange rates for sterling at the time of writing. These rates change every day and can be found in any major newspaper.

If you travel to any country, or trade with any country, you will need to obtain a supply of the currency of that country. You can do this at any bank, provided you give the bank notice of a few days before you travel or have to pay for the goods you are buying from abroad. Of course, the more regularly used currencies are usually available at most banks and can be obtained on demand. Also at ports and airports there will be special counters where currency can be exchanged, and in continental countries there are often officials on trains who travel up and down the corridors of the trains selling currency to those moving from one country to another.

Foreign money and exchange rates

Country	Currency unit	Rate of exchange per £1 (31 March 1984) (when changing sterling to the foreign currency)	Smaller coins
Australia	dollar	1.53 dollars	100 cents
Belgium	franc	76.9 francs	100 centimes
Canada	dollar	1.86 dollars	100 cents
France	franc	11.6 francs	100 centimes
West Germany	Deutschmark	3.76 Deutschmarks	100 pfennigs
Holland	guilder	4.24 guilders	100 cents
Italy	lira	2339 lire	—
Japan	yen	326 yen	—
Sweden	krona	11.2 kronor	100 oere
Switzerland	franc	3.12 francs	100 centimes
UK	pound	—	100 pence
USA	dollar	1.46 dollars	100 cents

Table 14.1

14.2 Rates of exchange

As explained above, rates of exchange change every day in the free enterprise countries of the world. In many communist countries the rate of exchange is fixed at an official rate and rarely varies, but there are certain disadvantages connected with exchange rates that are fixed and people in communist countries do not often travel outside their own countries partly because of foreign exchange problems.

You will see the foreign exchange rates displayed on notice-boards at banks, ports and airports. There are many subtle points to learn about exchange rates, but for the present we need only consider how much foreign currency we would receive for a given amount of United Kingdom currency. Consider the following examples.

Example: (a) A family bound for a Swiss skiing holiday decides to take £300 with them for pocket money. The rate of exchange is 3.12 francs = £1. How many francs will they receive for their pounds?

$$£1 = 3.12 \text{ francs}$$
$$£300 = 300 \times 3.12f$$
$$= 3 \times 312 \text{ (multiplying by 100)}$$
$$= 936 \text{ francs}$$

We simply multiply the exchange rate for £1 by the number of pounds we wish to exchange.

Example: (b) On their return, the family has 200 Swiss francs left. The exchange rate is now 3.25 francs = £1. How much will they receive for the 200 Swiss francs when they convert them back to £ sterling?

This time they will receive £1 for every 3.25 francs. So the question is: how many times does 3.25 go into 200? This is, of course, a division sum:

$$200 \div 3.25$$
$$= 20\,000 \div 325 \quad \text{(make the divisor a whole number, etc.)}$$

$$= £61.53$$

```
        61.538
325)20000
     1950
      500
      325
     1750
     1625
     1250
      975
     2750
```

(*Note*: Although to the nearest penny the answer would be £61.54, it is unlikely the bank would pay the extra penny. We must expect little losses when we exchange currency. The fact is, the family did not bring home enough to deserve £61.54.)

Example: (c) A furniture manufacturer is buying timber from Nigeria. The price is 680 Naira per tonne, and he has ordered 300 tonnes. The rate of exchange is £1 = 1.8 Naira. How much sterling must he pay to obtain the necessary Nigerian currency?

$$\text{Total price of timber} = 300 \times N680$$
$$= 3 \times N68\,000$$
$$= N204\,000$$

Sterling required is £1 for every 1.8 Naira.

Therefore sterling needed

$$= \frac{204\,000}{1.8} \text{ pounds}$$
$$= \frac{£2\,040\,000}{18}$$
$$= £113\,333.33$$

```
         113333
18)2040000
   18
    24
    18
    60
    54
     6 etc.
```

14.3 Exercises: simple exchange transactions

Where necessary, calculations in these exercises should be correct to the nearest penny.

1 Change the following amounts of pounds sterling into the foreign currencies shown at the rates of exchange given.

(a) £200 to Deutschmarks at £1 = 3.83 DM
(b) £200 to Naira at £1 = 1.65 Naira
(c) £200 to United States dollars at £1 = US$1.48
(d) £1500 to Swiss francs at £1 = 3.36 Swiss francs
(e) £2000 to Australian dollars at £1 = A$1.56
(f) £1500 to Bahrain dinars at £1 = 0.45 dinars
(g) £7000 to French francs at £1 = 11.28 francs
(h) £5000 to Swiss francs at £1 = 3.48 Swiss francs
(i) £9000 to Mexican pesos at £1 = 75 pesos
(j) £8000 to Finnish markka at £1 = 7.89 markka

2 Change the following amounts of foreign currency to sterling at the exchange rates shown.

(a) 4000 USA dollars at $1.63 = £1
(b) 6500 Japanese yen at 348 yen = £1
(c) 3500 Norwegian kroner at 10.7 kroner = £1
(d) 86000 Italian lire at 2427 lire = £1
(e) 725 Belgian francs at 78.3 francs = £1
(f) 386 Deutschmarks at 4.23 DM = £1
(g) 500 Australian dollars at A$1.47 = £1
(h) 24000 Brazilian cruzeiros at 286 cruzeiros = £1
(i) 76000 Naira at N 1.71 = £1
(j) 845 Swedish kronor at 11.15 = £1

3 Change the following amounts of sterling to the foreign currency shown at the rates of exchange given.

(a) £4900 to US dollars at £1 = $1.49
(b) £9680 to Japanese yen at £1 = 349 yen
(c) £7350 to Norwegian kroner at £1 = 11.15 kroner
(d) £6900 to Italian lire at £1 = 2726 lire
(e) £11 800 to Belgian francs at £1 = 81.5 francs

4 Change 65 880 Dutch guilders to pounds when £1 = 5.49 guilders

5 Change 1102000 Portuguese escudos to pounds when £1 = 145 escudos
6 Change 19 530 Austrian schillings to pounds when £1 = 42 sch.
7 A German importer buys 20 machines from the United Kingdom at £585 each. What sum in Deutschmarks will he need to exchange to sterling to make payment at DM 3.76 = £1?
8 A supermarket buys Swiss dairy cheeses at an exchange rate of Sfr 3.06 = £1. The order is for 380 cheeses at 24 francs per cheese. How much sterling must the supermarket provide to finance the purchase?

14.4 'Spot' rates and 'forward' rates

The exchange rates used in the examples of the first sections of this chapter (14.1 to 14.3) were all 'spot' rates, that is, the rates payable to anyone who has foreign currency to exchange now—'on the spot', as we say—or who wants foreign currency immediately in exchange for sterling. Many businesses who deal with overseas countries do not receive payment at once, and are always worried about the exchange rates that will prevail in the future. These are called 'forward' rates.

Example: A. Steelmaker makes a contract to sell steel to an American manufacturer for 32 000 dollars, payment to be three months later. What will happen to the present value of the dollar (say $1.60 = £1) in the three months ahead? Let us see the effect of a changing exchange rate.

Present value of $32 000
$$= \frac{£32\,000}{1.60} = \frac{£320\,000}{16} = \underline{\underline{£20\,000}}$$

Suppose the dollar begins to harden (get more valuable) and £1 = $1.59, then $1.58, $1.57 etc. (*Note*: As the dollar gets more valuable we get *less* dollars to our £1.)

Then suppose the price of the dollar hardens in the three months until £1 = $1.50.

Forward value of $3200
$$= \frac{£32\,000}{1.50} = \frac{£320\,000}{15} = \underline{\underline{£21\,333.33}}$$

By being forced to wait for his money, A. Steelmaker will gain if the dollar hardens in the meantime; the actual increase is £1333.33.

Now what happens if the dollar weakens (gets less valuable), and £1 = $1.61, or £1 = $1.62 etc? (*Note*: As the dollar weakens we get *more* dollars for our pound.) Suppose after three months it finishes up at £1 = $1.70 on the day that A. Steelmaker is paid his 32 000 dollars.

$$\$32\,000 = \frac{£32\,000}{1.70} = \frac{£320\,000}{17} = \underline{\underline{£18\,823.53}}$$

Clearly, A. Steelmaker has suffered a *loss on exchange* of £1176.47. This is quite a serious loss.

Speculators and foreign exchange

We have seen that the owners and managers of ordinary businesses may gain money sometimes, or lose money sometimes, by changes in the exchange rates. This is one of the risks of business, but it is not one of the risks ordinary people wish to run. Fortunately, there is a type of wealthy business person who is prepared to carry such risks. We use the name **speculator** for these people. The word means 'to form an opinion about future possibilities'. We all speculate as to whether it will rain on a particular day when we are fixing the date of some special occasion, like a wedding, a sporting attraction, a garden fête etc. Foreign exchange speculators speculate on what will happen to the value of foreign currencies. They then make bargains to buy or sell foreign currency at firm prices in the future, which will be honoured whatever happens. These prices are fixed in the money market, usually by telephone, and the bargains struck are recorded. They are quoted next day in the newspapers, like this:

Three months forward
USA   0.83–0.78c premium
Italy   18–23 lire discount

The short line is not a minus sign, it is a hyphen. It means 'to'. The word 'premium' means the price of the dollar is expected to be above the present price, the word 'discount' means the Italian lira is expected to be worth less than the present price.

So the first line really says: yesterday foreign exchange dealers struck bargains for dollars to be delivered in three months time ranging from 0.83 cents up on present prices to 0.78 cents up on present prices. The average bargain struck was therefore at a premium of about 0.805 cents for three months forward dollars.

The second line says that the bargains were struck at from 18 lire discount to 23 lire discount, since the speculators expect the lira to fall in price in the next few months.

So, if A. Steelmaker does not wish to run any risks on his contract, he could ask his bank to arrange a forward contract on the foreign exchange market. Suppose they made the bargain at a premium of 0.81 cents. This means instead of the spot rate:

£1 = $1.60   (he will give up 81 hundredths of a cent less for each £1)

and he will get £1 = $1.5919

This is a firm bargain, which both sides must honour in three months time. When A. Steelmaker receives his 32 000 dollars he must surrender them in exchange for:

$$\$32\,000 = \frac{£32\,000}{1.5919} = \frac{£320\,000\,000}{15919} = \underline{\underline{£20\,101.76}}$$

A. Steelmaker has made a small profit on exchange. What has happened to the speculator? This depends on how the dollar really did change. If it went to £1 = $1.50, the speculator made a good profit, getting £21 333.33. If it went to £1 = $1.70 he or she made a serious loss, only getting £18 823.53 for the dollars, which had just cost them £20 101.76 paid to A. Steelmaker. In one recent case, a speculator on the silver market lost over $200 million. Now consider the following examples.

Example: (a) Dollars are quoted as follows:

Spot   Three months
1.5590   (0.85c–0.92c premium)

A. Trader expects to receive $92 500 in three months time. His bank makes a bargain on the foreign exchange market for him at 0.90 cents premium. How much will he get for the dollars in three months time? (Answer correct to the nearest £1.)

Forward price is $1.5590 − 0.0090 = $1.55 to the £1

(*Note*: As the price is at a premium, the dollar is expected to get more valuable, so we will exchange less dollars for £1. We have to subtract the 0.90 cents from the present exchange rate.)

When the dollars become available, A. Trader receives:

$$\$92\,500 = \frac{£92\,500}{1.55}$$

$$= \frac{£9\,250\,000}{155}$$

$$= £59\,677$$

```
         59677.4
155)9250000
    775
    1500
    1395
     1050
      930
     1200
     1085
      1150
      1085
       650
       620
```

Example: (b) Pesetas are quoted as follows:

Spot	Three months
179 pesetas	(3.5–4.5 discount)

An importer of Spanish wine requires to pay 20 000 000 pesetas in 3 months' time. Her bank makes a forward contract for her at 4 pesetas discount. How much will she have to pay for the pesetas when her payment becomes due? (Answer correct to the nearest £1.)

Spot price:

179 pesetas = £1

forward price:

179 + 4 pesetas = 183 pesetas to the £1

(Since the price is falling, she will get more pesetas for each pound, so we have to add on the 4 pesetas.)

$$\text{Sum required} = \frac{20\,000\,000}{183} \text{ pounds}$$

= £109 290

```
         109289.6
183)20000000
    183
    1700
    1647
     530
     366
     1640
     1464
      1760
      1647
      1130
      1098
```

14.5 Exercises on spot and forward rates

1 Dollars are quoted as follows: spot £1 = $1.6410; forward 3 months 0.90 cents premium. What will each of the following traders receive for the sums shown, which are due in 3 months time, when converted to sterling?

(a) $3264
(b) $16 320
(c) $48 960
(d) $80 000
(e) $1 000 000

2 Lire are quoted as follows: spot £1 = 2240 lire; forward 3 months 24 lire discount. What will each of the following traders receive for the sums shown, which are due to be earned from Italian importers in three months time, if they make forward contracts for conversion to sterling?

(a) 1 132 000 lire
(b) 9 056 000 lire
(c) 679 200 lire
(d) 20 000 000 lire
(e) 45 000 000 lire

3 A. Trader agrees to sell 20 000 Norwegian kroner at K11.15 = £1. He is due to receive the money in 3 months time and K11.15 is the forward rate, a premium of 80 oere (cents) on the spot price. (a) How much will he get for his 20 000 kroner? (b) On the due date the price of

the kroner had actually hardened to K10.68 = £1. Did the speculator make a profit or a loss? How much did he gain or lose?

4 A trader who is due to pay 477 500 French francs in 2 months time is quoted a forward price of a premium of 80 centimes on the present spot price of Ff10.35 = £1. She makes this forward exchange bargain. (a) How much will she have to pay in due course to obtain the 477 500 French francs? (b) Suppose the franc has not strengthened, but become 25 centimes weaker than the original spot price. Has the speculator made a profit or a loss? How much profit (or loss)?

5 A trader agrees to sell 200 000 Portuguese escudos which are coming to him in three months' time. The current spot price is 122 escudos = £1, and the forward rate is a discount of 3 escudos. (a) How much sterling will he get when the Portuguese funds become available? (b) In fact the escudo hardened in the three-month period to 120 escudos = £1. Did the speculator make a profit or a loss, and how much was it?

15

Overhead Expenses 1: Gas and Electricity Charges

15.1 Overhead expenses

In business there are many expenses to be borne that arise from the very act of starting a business. Thus we must pay rent and rates for the use of property (although sometimes we buy the property outright to avoid paying rent). We must pay for gas, electricity, water, telephone services and so on. We call these expenses, 'overhead expenses'. Other overheads include advertising, insurance, cleaning, security costs and many others. All these expenses have to be recovered from the profit we make on goods we sell, or the services we render to our customers. In Chapters 15 to 19 we shall look at some of the calculations which are necessary in order to ensure that we only pay the correct amount for these overhead expenses.

The term 'overhead' is used to distinguish these expenses from those other expenses that are concerned with a particular product and get worked into the product. If you buy a motor car it has so much metal, windows, components, upholstery etc., which have been made from various raw materials (steel, copper, leather, glass etc.). These are not overhead expenses. We cannot actually see how much rent, rates, lighting, hot water, advertising etc. went into that car, but these expenses were incurred in manufacturing the car just the same. These costs had to be borne just to get a roof over the workers' heads and keep them warm and dry while they worked. Hence the word 'overheads'.

When we are due to pay these expenses, the authority concerned (the Local Council, the Gas, Electricity or Water Board etc.) will send us a bill. Just because someone sends us a bill does not mean we have to pay it unthinkingly, for every account sent to us should be checked to see if it is in accordance with the agreed terms on which the

goods or services were supplied. Some criminals specialise in sending out 'phoney' bills, knowing that some firms pay bills that are sent to them without checking whether they are genuine or not. All such 'phoney' bills should be reported to the Police, who will follow up the fraud and find who is responsible. There is a special Fraud Squad to investigate such matters.

15.2 Electricity charges

In the United Kingdom electricity is supplied by nationalised Area Boards who supply power to every person who requires it, provided the person is within reach of the electricity authority's supply cables. There are still some people in remote areas who do not have electric power.

Charges are based partly on a standing charge (levied to meet the Board's capital costs of building power stations, pylons and distribution networks), and partly on the units of electricity used. A unit is a *kilowatt hour*, the cost of burning an appliance which uses one kilowatt per hour. Many small electric fires are 1 kilowatt fires; bigger electric fires are usually 3 kilowatt fires, and burn 3 units in one hour.

The charge for a unit depends on the geographical situation of the customer and also on how much electricity the customer uses. Customers in remote areas pay more. Large users of electricity get cheaper rates per unit, as do those who use electricity during off-peak hours. A bakery, making bread all night when no one else needs electricity, may get their power very cheaply. Storage heaters, which are switched on all night to store heat but are switched off in the daytime, similarly get cheap rate electricity.

Some people purchase electrical appliances on

Figure 15.1 An electricity bill

METER READING		UNITS USED	PENCE PER UNIT	AMOUNT £	STANDING CHARGE £	V A T	
THIS TIME	LAST TIME						
23721	22405	1316	4.25	55.93	6.37	O	62. 30
48642	45988	2654	1.85	49.10		O	49. 10
INST 7 of 12 COOKER						A	37. 71

YOUR CUSTOMER NUMBER IS	YOU CAN PHONE US ON	PERIOD ENDING		AMOUNT DUE NOW
17 2046 3129 54	01 000 0000	31 MARCH 19....		£ 149. 11

hire purchase, and the quarterly charges are added to the electricity bill. Such bills are printed out by computers these days, and are designed so everyone can easily see how much he or she is to pay and exactly what charges have been made. A typical bill is shown in Figure 15.1 and explained in the notes (a) to (e) below it. As these notes are self-explanatory, no further examples need be given.

(a) To find the units used, deduct the 'LAST TIME' reading from the 'THIS TIME' reading.

(b) To get the amount of the charge, multiply the charge in pence per unit by the units used. The standing charge is added to this to get the total.

(c) The second set of meter readings is for 'off-peak' electricity at a much cheaper rate.

(d) The last charge refers to an instalment for the purchase of a cooker.

(e) Note that electricity is zero-rated for VAT. The code A in the VAT column on the hire purchase line stands for 'advised', meaning that the customer was charged this VAT charge earlier, when the cooker was purchased.

15.3 Exercises: electricity charges

1 Work out the electricity charges for the five householders (a) to (e), below, who used the quantity of electricity shown at 4.85p per unit and paid other charges as shown.

	Units used	Standing charge	Other charges
(a)	2841	£6.95	£37.20 HP
(b)	3268	£8.50	—
(c)	2954	£6.95	—
(d)	1634	£6.95	£11.44 HP
(e)	3874	£10.56	—

2 Work out the electricity charges for the following businesses which used both standard rate (4.65p per unit) and off-peak electricity (2.25p per unit). Other charges are as listed.

	Standard units	Off-peak units	Standing charge	Other charges
(a)	1 789	4 825	£29.55	£268.80 HP
(b)	2 321	4 368	£36.45	£76.50 installations
(c)	3 468	17 254	£127.25	£14.55 service
(d)	13 742	2 864	£45.80	£325.60 HP
(e)	8 564	4 735	£38.65	£32.50 service

3 What is the charge for electricity made to the following 'heavy user' customers who pay the standard rate (4.85p per unit) for a quota of electricity but if they use more than this quota are only charged at the 'off-peak' rate of 2.15p per unit?

	Units used	Quota agreed	Standing charge	Other charges
(a)	33 520	10 000	£100	£224 service
(b)	48 257	15 000	£100	£1860 installation
(c)	68 320	15 000	£100	£385.50 service
(d)	72 551	25 000	£150	£425.95 leasing
(e)	98 328	25 000	£150	£850.00 leasing

15.4 Gas charges

Gas charges are based upon a unit of gas called a *therm*. This is a Greek word meaning 'heat'. (We are all familiar with a thermometer, which measures the temperature of our bodies, and it has the same word-root.) The gas is metered in hundreds of cubic feet, but the number of therms used takes account of the calorific value of the gas (a technical measure devised by the gas industry, which ordinary householders cannot value). It is shown on our bills as the value of 1 cubic foot in therms.

As with electricity bills, there is a standing charge to cover the costs of the distribution network and the safety problems associated with it, for gas is a dangerous substance and skilled maintenance of the network is essential. VAT is not charged on gas. Hire purchase facilities for apparatus and installation expenses are common features of gas bills, especially as some people might be tempted to do installations themselves if easy payment schemes were not available. This could be very hazardous for the general public as well as the householder concerned.

Once again, heavy gas users are usually charged cheaper per-unit rates which are the subject of individual bargaining between the industrial user and the gas industry representatives. A typical domestic bill is shown in Figure 15.2, below.

(a) To find the volume of gas supplied in the current period, take the 'PREVIOUS' reading from the 'PRESENT' reading.
(b) This is multiplied by the calorific value to convert the gas to therms.
(c) This answer is multiplied by the price per therm to give the amount payable.
(d) To this amount (£78.77 in the example) must be added the standing charge and any hire purchase instalments due.

Consider the following examples.

Example: (a) A householder has used 274 therms at 35.5p per therm. The standing charge is £7.36 and an instalment of hire purchase is due, £34.25. What is the quarterly charge payable?

Figure 15.2   A gas bill

DATE	METER READING		GAS SUPPLIED		PRICE PER THERM (PENCE)	AMOUNT £	VAT CODE	VAT CHARGES	HIRE PURCHASE
	PRESENT	PREVIOUS	CUBIC FEET (HUNDREDS)	THERMS					CASH SETTLEMENT VALUE
19....	1565	1342	223	227.658	34.600	78.77		0.00	
1 April	STANDING CHARGE					9.90		0.00	
	TOTAL VAT					0.00		0.00	
	HIRE PURCHASE	6 of 8				24.26			
									45.20 (AFTER PAYMENT OF THIS ACCOUNT)

CALORIFIC VALUE	£112. 93	AMOUNT NOW DUE
1.020888 TH/ft^3		

```
                    274
                   35.5
                 ──────
                   1370
                  13700
                  82200
                 ──────
                 9727.0 pence
                 ══════

      9727 pence =   £  97.27
      Standing charge     7.36
      Hire purchase      34.25
                       ──────
      Total charge   £ 138.88
                       ══════
```

Example: (b) An industrial user pays 35.5p per therm for the first thousand therms used and 25.5p for each therm above the quota of 1000. There is no standing charge, but an 'industrial user' servicing charge of £250 per quarter is payable. What will the quarterly charge of XYZ Crispmakers be if the total number of therms used is 13 850?

Charge for first 1000 therms at £0.355 = £355

```
Charge for 12850 therms at £0.255       12850
                                        0.255
                                      ────────
                                        64250
                                       642500
                                      2570000
                                      ────────
                                      3276.750
```

```
Therefore total charge:
  First 1000 therms        = £355.00
  Balance of supply        = £3276.75
  Quarterly service charge = £250
                           ─────────
                  Total     £3881.75
                           ═════════
```

15.5 Exercises: gas charges

1 Calculate the total gas bills for the following domestic consumers.

	Therms used	Charge per therm (pence)	Standing charge (£)	Hire purchase
(a)	227	34.5	6.75	£24.25
(b)	381	34.5	7.50	—
(c)	285	34.5	6.75	£13.85
(d)	426	34.5	8.50	£36.35
(e)	193	34.5	5.00	£12.70

2 Calculate the total gas bills for the following small business users.

	Therms used	Charge per therm (pence)	Service charge (£)	Hire purchase
(a)	486	32.5	55	—
(b)	1325	32.5	55	—
(c)	1728	31.5	65	£28.50
(d)	785	32.5	55	—
(e)	2021	31.5	65	£56.75

3 The following major gas users, (a) to (e), have agreed special contracts with the gas industry which permit them to pay a standard charge per therm for a small quota of gas, followed by a cheaper rate for supplies in excess of the quota. The standard charge is 34.8p per therm. The cheap rate is 25p per therm. A quarterly service charge as shown is also payable. Calculate the total bill for these users.

	Quota	Therms used	Service charge
(a)	5000	15 821	£150
(b)	5000	16 008	£150
(c)	10 000	19 524	£175
(d)	10 000	21 864	£250
(e)	15 000	37 256	£300

15.6 From therms to thermometers

As we have just referred to therms as a unit of heat, it seems appropriate at this point to mention thermometers, which frequently feature in simple arithmetic examinations.

Fahrenheit and Celsius thermometers

Traditionally there have always been two ways of measuring temperature: Fahrenheit and Centigrade. The latter name posed a problem, as some countries used the term for another matter altogether, so under the SI system of units the word Celsius was adopted instead. The Celsius scale is used in all scientific work; the Fahrenheit scale is widely used in the United Kingdom for temperatures concerned with the weather. Meteorologists usually give both scales, for example in weather forecasts.

The scales are compared in Figure 15.3, and explained in the notes (a) to (d) below it.

Figure 15.3 The Fahrenheit and Celsius scales

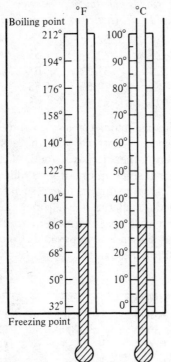

(a) The Fahrenheit scale goes from freezing point at 32° to boiling point at 212°.
(b) The Celsius scale goes from 0° at freezing point to 100° at boiling point.
(c) The scales are therefore in the ratio 180:100. There are one hundred and eighty degrees between freezing and boiling on the Fahrenheit scale (32° to 212°) and one hundred degrees on the Celsius scale (0° to 100°).
(d) 180:100 = 9:5 (cancelling down to the lowest terms).

Converting Fahrenheit to Celsius, and Celsius to Fahrenheit

To change a Fahrenheit measurement to Celsius we go through a simple procedure, which takes account of two things: (a) the higher starting point of 32° of the Fahrenheit scale, and (b) the ratio of 9:5 mentioned in the notes to Figure 15.3,

i.e. for every nine Fahrenheit degrees there are only five Celsius degrees.

To convert *Fahrenheit to Celsius*, the rule is:

first deduct 32°, divide by 9, then multiply by 5

Let us take an example.

Example: (a) Convert 140°F to Celsius.
$$140 - 32 = 108 \text{ (deduct } 32°)$$
$$108 \div 9 = 12 \text{ (divide by 9)}$$
$$12 \times 5 = \underline{\underline{60}} \text{ (multiply by 5)}$$

So, 140°F = 60°C.

To convert *Celsius to Fahrenheit*, we reverse the rule explained above:

first divide by 5, multiply by 9, then add 32°

Let us take an example.

Example: (b) Convert 10°C to Fahrenheit.
$$10 \div 5 = 2 \text{ (divide by 5)}$$
$$2 \times 9 = 18 \text{ (multiply by 9)}$$
$$18 + 32 = \underline{\underline{50}} \text{ (add on 32°, because Fahrenheit starts at 32°)}$$

So, 10°C = 50°F.

15.7 Exercises: converting Fahrenheit to Celsius and vice versa

1 Convert the following Fahrenheit temperatures to Celsius. (Answers correct to one decimal place where necessary.)

(a) 59°F	(b) 77°F
(c) 95°F	(d) 84°F
(e) 105°F	(f) 126°F
(g) 109°F	(h) 121°F
(i) 138°F	(j) 174°F

2 Convert the following Celsius temperatures to Fahrenheit. (Answers correct to one decimal place where necessary.)

(a) 20°C	(b) 25°C
(c) 30°C	(d) 17°C
(e) 24°C	(f) 27°C
(g) 44°C	(h) 48°C
(i) 52°C	(j) 82°C

16

Overhead Expenses 2: Rates

16.1 Rates and rateable values

Rates are a form of tax, paid by people who live in a certain locality, and are a means of raising money for local services such as education, police and fire services, refuse collection etc. Rates are based upon landed property. Those who own property or rent property have to pay rates. The system is based upon a **rateable value (RV)** which is applied to every property by an official called the **valuation officer**. The rateable value of a small house might be £120 a year, a larger house might have a rateable value of £300 a year, a cinema might be rated at £3800 a year and a department store at £10 000. This does not mean that the rates on these properties are £120, £300 etc. The rateable value is only a basis for comparing the properties.

When all the rateable values of the properties in a town or district are added together we get the **aggregate rateable value** of the town or district. It might, for example, come to £24 million. We now have a simple basis for working out how much money to charge the householders. This simple basis is the **penny rate**. If we charge a 'penny in the pound' rate, it means that the property owners mentioned above must pay 120p, 300p, 3800p and 10000p respectively. The whole town or district will pay 24 000 000p, that is, £240 000. This is said to be the 'yield of a penny rate'. Let us pause at this point and look at some simple calculations.

Example: (a) A shopkeeper's property has a rateable value of £480. How much will the shopkeeper pay for a penny rate?

The answer is, of course, 480p = £4.80.

Example: (b) The rates are actually fixed by the town council at 78.5p in the £1. How much must the shopkeeper pay now?

78.5p in the £

RV of £480 means that the shopkeeper must pay:

480 × 78.5 pence

$$= £\frac{\overset{24}{\cancel{480}} \times \overset{15.7}{\cancel{78.5}}}{\underset{1}{\cancel{100}}} \quad \text{(cancelling by 10, 5 and 2)}$$

$$= £24 \times 15.7$$

$$= £376.80$$

$$
\begin{array}{r}
15.7 \\
24 \\
\hline
628 \\
3140 \\
\hline
376.8
\end{array}
$$

Example: (c) A town's aggregate rateable value is £3 250 760. What will be the yield of a penny rate from the whole town?

£3 250 760 at 1p in the £

= 3 250 760 pence

= £32 507.60   (dividing by 100)

16.2 Exercises: simple rate calculations

1 What will each householder have to pay for a penny rate for their properties if the rateable values are as shown below?

(a) £120   (b) £165
(c) £240   (d) £265
(e) £380   (f) £455
(g) £760   (h) £850
(i) £984   (j) £2325

2 A council fixes the rates at 87p in the £1. What will each of the householders below have to pay if the rateable values of their properties are as shown below?

(a) £140   (b) £185
(c) £220   (d) £245
(e) £350   (f) £388
(g) £726   (h) £845
(i) £1000   (j) £1250

3 What will a rate of 76p in the £1 cost the owners of the following properties?

(a) a flat rated at £320
(b) a house rated at £560
(c) an office rated at £175
(d) an office rated at £840
(e) a factory rated at £1360
(f) a factory rated at £24 750
(g) a hotel rated at £9400
(h) a hotel rated at £27 500
(i) a supermarket rated at £4840
(j) a department store rated at £36 000

4 The aggregate rateable values of ten districts are given below. How much will their respective councils be able to collect in rates for each penny rate levied?

(a) £260 000   (b) £385 240
(c) £760 000   (d) £685 600
(e) £2 427 350   (f) £3 500 850
(g) £4 720 850   (h) £9 726 340
(i) £24 386 725   (j) £33 728 448

16.3 Fixing the rates

The services provided by local government are not paid for entirely by local people. Some of the money is provided by the central Government, through a mechanism called the 'rate support grant'. On certain matters this may be as much as 100 per cent of the expense incurred, on others it may be quite low. For example, main highways which happen to pass through a district are of concern to the whole nation, and while their repair may be carried out by local authorities, payment will largely be made by the central Government. This is not true of minor roads, which are of greater importance to local people, who consequently bear a larger share of the expenses of repair.

The process of fixing the rates starts with a process called **budgeting**. Each department of local government prepares a budget, or forecast of expenditure to be incurred in the coming year. This may include both **capital budgets** and **revenue budgets**. Capital budgets are for the purchase or creation of long lasting assets, such as vehicles, schools, fire stations etc. Revenue budgets are budgets concerned with day-to-day running of the services required, repairs, renewals, wages, lighting and heat etc.

Budgets are then scrutinised to decide on priorities once the total figure for all the budgets has been arrived at. Like every householder, councils cannot order everything they think people need for a full life. A balanced programme of services must be devised and certain items will be struck out of the budgets year after year. Finally, the amount the central Government is prepared to pay will be deducted from the total, to give the amount the council must afford. Some of this may be financed by borrowing, particularly the capital items that will last many years and may earn revenue to repay the sum borrowed. Thus a swimming pool might earn enough revenue from admission charges to repay the capital borrowed to build it.

The final result is a sum of money that has to be found by the rates. As every council knows the yield of a penny rate, we can fix the rates payable by local people using the following formula:

$$\text{Rate payable in pence} = \frac{\text{total sum required}}{\text{yield of a penny rate}}$$

Consider the following examples.

Example: (a) A council, whose area produces £217 000 for each penny rate levied, has to finance total expenditures of £6 510 000. What rate must be levied?

$$\text{Rate in pence} = \frac{\text{total required}}{\text{yield of 1p rate}}$$

$$= \frac{£6\,510\,\cancel{000}}{£217\,\cancel{000}} \quad \text{(cancelling by 1000)}$$

$$= \frac{6510}{217} \qquad \begin{array}{r} 30 \\ 217\overline{)6510} \\ \underline{651} \\ \dots 0 \end{array}$$

$$= 30\text{p}$$

(*Note:* The £ signs cancel out in the calculation leaving us with a number, 30. This is the pence rate required.)

Example: (b) A council, whose aggregate rateable value of property in the area is £27 500 000, has to finance expenditure of £3 875 500. What rate will be required, to the nearest tenth of a penny?

Here we have to calculate the yield of a penny rate first. This is, of course, 1p in every £1 of the aggregate RV = £275 000. Now:

$$\text{Rate in pence} = \frac{£3\,875\,5\cancel{00}}{£275\,0\cancel{00}} \quad \begin{array}{l}\text{(cancelling by}\\ \text{100 and by 5)}\end{array}$$

$$= \frac{7751}{550}$$

$$= \frac{775.1}{55} \qquad \begin{array}{r} 14.09 \\ 55\overline{)775.1} \\ \underline{55} \\ 225 \\ \underline{220} \\ 510 \\ \underline{495} \\ 15 \end{array}$$

$$= 14.1\text{p in the £1}$$

Example: (c) A council is constantly troubled by flood damage to a lower part of the town. The recommended solutions are as follows: raise the river banks in the lower part of the town at a cost of £2.4 million and, at the same time, purchase a claypit higher up the catchment area to use as a flood-relief area in periods of high flow, at a cost of £1.2 million. Fifty per cent of flood-relief work is payable by the central Government. A penny rate raises £720 000. What rate will be needed to finance this project?

Cost of project = £2.4 million + £1.2 million

$$= £3.6 \text{ million}$$

Cost to local
ratepayers = half £3.6 million

$$= £1.8 \text{ million}$$

$$\text{Rate required} = \frac{£1\,800\,000}{£720\,000}$$

$$= \frac{180}{72}$$

$$= \frac{15}{6} \quad \text{(cancelling by 12)}$$

$$= \frac{5}{2}$$

$$= 2\tfrac{1}{2}\text{p or } 2.5\text{p}$$

Example: (d) What rate will a council need to raise to finance total expenditure of £24 250 725 if a penny rate yields £204 000? (Answer correct to the nearest penny.)

$$\text{Rate required} = \frac{\text{total to be raised}}{\text{yield per penny rate}}$$

$$= \frac{£24\,250\,725}{£204\,000}$$

$$= \frac{24\,250.725}{204} \qquad \begin{array}{r} 118.8 \\ 204\overline{)24250.725} \\ \underline{204} \\ 385 \\ \underline{204} \\ 1810 \\ \underline{1632} \\ 1787 \end{array}$$

$$= 119\text{p}$$

(*Note:* In this example the ratepayers will have to pay more than £1 in the £1: the rate will be £1.19 in the £1. This is quite common and presents no difficulty, except to the ratepayer trying to find the money.)

16.4 Exercises: more difficult rate calculations

1 What sum must each of the ratepayers below find if the rates are fixed at the figure shown?

	Rateable value (£)	Rate fixed		Rateable value (£)	Rate fixed
(a)	360	78p	(b)	450	39p
(c)	420	£1.04	(d)	650	£1.15
(e)	540	£1.17	(f)	920	£1.25
(g)	680	£1.21	(h)	1250	£1.37
(i)	750	£1.30	(j)	2440	£1.44

2 A town proposes to provide the following facilities at the costs shown below. A penny rate yields £425 000. What rate will be needed for each facility? (Answer correct to the nearest tenth of a penny.)

Facility	Estimated cost
(a) Secondary school	£3.25 million
(b) Swimming pool	£1.68 million
(c) Children's playground	£108 000
(d) Clinic	£687 500
(e) Workshop for physically handicapped	£2.25 million

3 The five district councils shown below have to finance total expenditures as listed. The yield of a penny rate in each area is shown. What will be the rate in each case? (Answer correct to the nearest tenth of a penny.)

	Total expenditure	Yield of a penny rate
(a)	£2 276 525	£48 500
(b)	£3 824 725	£55 000
(c)	£14 982 650	£135 000
(d)	£27 235 425	£330 500
(e)	£35 327 420	£285 000

4 A road development project is costed at £17 million, of which central Government is prepared to pay 65%. A county council is required to finance the balance of the project. What rate must the council levy to raise the necessary money, if the penny rate yields £480 000? (Answer correct to one decimal place of a penny.)

5 In a certain town, a penny rate yields £18 754. The council levies a rate of 47p in the £1. Calculate (a) how much money it will receive, and (b) how much extra rate (to the nearest tenth of a penny) it would need to raise in order to finance a new business studies department at a college of further education, costed at £175 000.

6 A residential complex for mentally handicapped patients is costed at £758 000. It is also estimated that £78 000 a year will be needed to run the complex once it is built. Of the capital cost, 40% can be claimed from Government funds. A penny rate in the area raises £176 000. What rate must be levied (a) to finance the rest of the capital cost, and (b) to finance the running costs? (In each case give your answer correct to one-tenth of a penny.)

7 A city has an aggregate rateable value of £37 850 000. Its total budget for the coming year is £24 750 600, of which the Government will provide 54% as the rate support grant. You are asked to calculate (correct to the nearest penny):

(a) the yield of a penny rate in the city
(b) the amount of money the city requires for its activities in the coming year
(c) the rate it must levy to finance its budgeted expenditure

8 A county council has to budget for a total expenditure after claiming all available Government aid of £17 126 528. To allow for a special contingency reserve, the council always rounds its rating calculations to the next penny *above* the calculated figure (that is, not to the nearest penny) and then adds on a further 2 pence for contingencies. What rate will it levy, if a penny rate brings in £425 000?

17

Overhead Expenses 3: Transport Costs

17.1 Motor vehicle costs

Although motor vehicle costs are an important element in every business, they are also of general interest. We all hope to drive a motor vehicle for domestic purposes at some time (and the way things are in the modern world, it is better to learn to drive sooner than later). Let us therefore consider the costs of running a family motor-car at the present time (1984). These divide into two parts: capital costs and running costs.

Capital costs are the costs of buying the vehicle itself. We can enter the car market at all sorts of prices: a new family car can cost anything from about £3000 to £30000, while second-hand cars are available for a few hundred pounds. This cost can be met by savings (if we save sufficient funds to buy a vehicle outright), or by savings and finance on hire purchase, or by a personal loan scheme. Hire purchase is dealt with later (Chapter 20), so we will not pursue capital costs any further at this point.

Running costs are the costs of actually running the vehicle. They include the following: petrol, oil, tyres, vehicle taxes, insurance, repairs, and de-preciation (discussed in Chapter 23). Listed and explained briefly, some imaginary costs might be as shown in Table 17.1. They are given as annual costs, because many of them (for example, servicing and repairs) do not occur every week, and have to be averaged over the year.

While the householder is chiefly interested in the weekly costs of running a car (to make decisions about whether he or she can afford personal transport), the business user is often more concerned with the cost of running a vehicle per unit of distance, i.e. **cost per kilometre**. This is one of the most useful ways of comparing one vehicle with another. We need to make such comparisons when deciding what vehicle to purchase, but they are also useful to compare one driver's performance with another. For example, if one lorry costs on average 13.25p per kilometre, and another similar vehicle costs 14.55p per kilometre, there must be some explanation for the difference. A dishonest driver may arrange to charge his own personal supplies of fuel to the firm's account, for example. Statistical controls of this sort can often detect dishonesty.

Running cost	Explanation	£
Petrol (gasoline)	Varies with mileage (or kilometres) covered	520.00
Oil	Varies with mileage and with age of car	10.00
Tyres	Last about 2 years (less on very small cars)	40.00
Taxation	Varies at Government whim	90.00
Insurance	Varies with cover required, age of vehicle, record of driver	90.00
Repairs	Say, service twice a year	120.00
Depreciation	Cars wear out quickly	500.00
		£1370.00

$$\text{Costs per week} = \frac{£1370.00}{52} = \underline{£26.35}$$

Table 17.1

To find the cost per kilometre we use the formula:

$$\text{Cost per kilometre} = \frac{\text{total cost in period}}{\text{kilometres run in period}}$$

Consider the following example.

Example: A motorist keeps a record of costs as follows for the 13-week quarterly period Jan.–March: petrol £176.45, oil £4.25, tyres £14.68, repairs £23.46, taxation £22.50, insurance £26.50, depreciation £135.50. Find (a) the cost per week (correct to the nearest penny), and (b) the cost per kilometre run (correct to the nearest tenth of a penny). The vehicle covered 5500 kilometres in the period.

$$\begin{array}{r}
£ \\
\text{(a) Total costs} = 176.45 \\
4.25 \\
14.68 \\
23.46 \\
22.50 \\
26.50 \\
135.50 \\
\hline
403.34 \\
\hline
\end{array}$$

$$\begin{array}{r}
31.026 \\
\text{Weekly cost} = 13\overline{)403.34} \\
39 \\
\hline
13 \\
13 \\
\hline
..34 \\
26 \\
\hline
80 \\
= £31.03
\end{array}$$

(b) Cost per kilometre run $= \dfrac{£403.34}{5500}$

$$= \frac{40334}{5500} \text{ pence}$$

$$\begin{array}{r}
7.33 \\
= 55\overline{)403.34} \\
385 \\
\hline
183 \\
165 \\
\hline
184 \\
\hline
= 7.3\text{p per km}
\end{array}$$

17.2 Exercises: motor vehicle costs

1 The motorists listed below incur the costs shown for motoring during the year. What is the *weekly* cost to each? (Answer correct to the nearest penny.)

Motorist	Petrol and oil (£)	Tax and insurance (£)	Servicing and repairs (£)	Depreciation (£)
(a)	385	150	48.20	500
(b)	535	180	156.85	650
(c)	725	165	194.50	720
(d)	840	195	126.25	850
(e)	926	215	208.80	1125

2 The motorists referred to in question 1 covered the following distances in the year: (a) 10 000 km, (b) 13 500 km, (c) 15 000 km, (d) 21 000 km, (e) 22 000 km. Find the cost in pence per kilometre in each case. (Answers correct to the nearest tenth of a penny.)

3 At the start of the business year, a businessman bought a car for £7920. The tax for the year was £90 and the insurance premium was £212. Petrol costs 40p per litre and the car (which averaged 15 kilometres per litre) was driven a total of 30 000 kilometres during the year. It used 1 litre of oil (costing £1.50) every 2000 kilometres. At the end of the year the car was sold for 25 per cent less than it cost. The balance was treated as depreciation. Calculate (a) the cost of the year's motoring, and (b) the average cost per kilometre (correct to the nearest 0.1p).

4 At the start of the business year, a businessman bought a van for £3840. The tax for the year was £90 and the insurance premium was £162. Petrol cost 40p per litre and the van (which averaged 16 kilometres per litre) was driven a total of 24 000 kilometres during the year. It used 1 litre of oil (costing £1.50) every 2000 kilometres.. At the end of the year the van was sold for $33\frac{1}{3}\%$ less than it cost. The balance was treated as depreciation. Calculate (a) the total cost of the van for the year, and (b) the average cost per kilometre (correct to the nearest 0.1p).

5 A firm operates four lorries, of a similar type, whose costs and distances covered are shown below.

Lorry	Annual costs	Kilometres travelled
(a)	£14 016	64 000
(b)	£15 372	72 000
(c)	£13 832	56 000
(d)	£21 624	68 000

All the vehicles have been operated in a similar way but lorry (d) was in a collision during the year and its costs included £6800 for repairs, which are to be deducted for the purposes of any control calculations. It is suspected that one of the vehicles is being operated fraudulently and it is decided to calculate the costs per kilometre travelled for each vehicle. Which vehicle do you suspect of being improperly operated?

6 A firm has five delivery vans, all the same model, whose costs and distances covered are shown below. During the course of a routine check the costs per vehicle kilometre are calculated. What would you report to senior management after doing the calculations? Note that the costs of vehicle (b) include £1250 for repairs which are the subject of an insurance claim, and may be disregarded when doing the calculation.

Vehicle	Annual costs	Kilometres travelled
(a)	£8 400	24 000
(b)	£10 366	26 500
(c)	£8 664	22 800
(d)	£6 908	20 200
(e)	£10 060	28 500

18

Overhead Expenses 4: Telephone, Telex and other Overhead Charges

18.1 Telephone charges

Today the telephone bill is one of the largest overhead expenses for many firms. The sophistication of a modern telephone service is such that it is very convenient and cheap to install a good system. Antiquated systems have hidden costs, such as getting up to go and see whether you can find Mr Jones who is not at his desk. With a modern system Mr Jones would simply instruct his telephone to 'follow me anywhere'; in other words, he would divert incoming calls to the room or work area he is about to visit and his own desk-telephone would not even ring.

Today the vast majority of routine matters are settled by telephone. It costs about £4 to type and post a letter in many offices, when all the overhead expenses are included. With a ten-second telephone call you can deal with the matter at once for about 5p.

The elements in a telephone bill are as follows:

(a) A quarterly rental, which varies with the number of extensions etc.
(b) A charge for the units used. These are controlled by a clock mechanism that can determine the time the call was made. More units click up at busy times of the day. There are peak periods, standard rate periods and cheap rate periods.
(c) Operator charges for operator-controlled calls.
(d) Transfer charges for calls transferred from public call boxes etc., which the subscriber has agreed to pay for.
(e) VAT charged on all these services.

Figure 18.1 shows a typical telephone account.

Figure 18.1   A telephone account

Rental and standing charges	1 Feb - 30 Apr			17.65
Units used	Date	Meter reading	Used	
	2 Feb	008318		
	7 Nov	004523	3795	
	Cost at 4.40p			166.98
	Operator-controlled calls			
	19 Nov	ALARM		0.44
	22 Dec	ALARM		0.44
	2 Jan	Transfer call - Luton Airport		1.53
	Total			187.04
	VAT at 15%			28.06
			£	215.10

(*Note:* An alarm call is an early morning call to wake the subscriber in time to catch a plane etc. It may be made at other times of the day, when it is called a fixed-time call.)

Abuse of the telephone system

Abuse of the telephone system is widespread. Many members of staff feel that the making of private and free telephone calls from the workplace is a 'perk' to which they are entitled. Nothing could be further from the truth. When we offer employment to someone we do not undertake to pay for their telephone calls to every relative around the world. Many large firms ask for detailed reports on telephone calls, possible under the latest computerised systems, which can identify every extension user and every call made. This may seem unfair, but consider that a ten-minute telephone call made at peak times costs £2.64 and you can see how fast the charges could build up if a number of employees made 'free' calls. Misuse of telephones is theft, and in some cases prison sentences have been imposed for it. One au pair used her employer's telephone to make £1000 worth of phone calls to her sweetheart in Italy in two weeks.

18.2 Exercises: telephone charges

1 Telephone charges to the five subscribers below are based on the details given. Calculate the total charge if the charge per unit is 5p and VAT is added at 15%.

	Quarterly rental (£)	Units used	Operator-controlled calls
(a)	13.95	878	1.44
(b)	17.85	1 024	2.36
(c)	26.35	3 752	3.75
(d)	42.75	4 295	13.25
(e)	51.30	18 717	184.16

2 Telephone charges to the five subscribers shown below are based on the details listed. Calculate the total charge, when VAT at 15% has been added, if the charge per unit is 4.4p.

	Rental (£)	Meter reading at start	Meter reading at end	Operator-controlled calls (£)
(a)	8.95	017 425	019 425	1.65
(b)	13.25	008 684	013 254	—
(c)	17.25	062 954	069 785	2.38
(d)	95.50	073 271	085 621	8.38
(e)	380.25	053 784	067 218	12.95

18.3 Telex charges

A telex machine is a typewriter which transmits and receives messages over the telephone network. It enables messages to be sent and received instantaneously around the world. There are two difficulties with telex messages.

The first difficulty arises when we dial the code of a subscriber, because we need to know that the subscriber's machine has received the code and is ready to deal with us. It might, for example, be taking a message from someone else. To solve this difficulty, the machine that is contacted sends an answer-back code at once. For example, an organisation called Bureau Veritas, which verifies the classification of ships and aircraft, says on its letterhead: Telex 886201 BVLOND G. Anyone wishing to send them a telex message types 886201 to be connected to the Bureau Veritas machine. That machine immediately sends its answer-back code BVLOND G, which stands for Bureau Veritas, London. All answer-back codes end in G, which one wag suggested stands for GOT-ME. When we receive the answer-back code we know we have 'got' the firm we wanted.

The second difficulty is that the time differences between various countries mean that a telex sent in the middle of the working day from the United Kingdom arrives in Australia, for example, in the middle of the night. It often follows, therefore, that a telex operator's first job of the day is to distribute to the various departments the telex messages that have come in overnight. These may then be the subject of responses in the following day; which again will be distributed in the country of arrival as soon as the working day starts.

Telex charges are similar to telephone charges in many ways. The initial installation leads to an **installation charge** followed by a quarterly rental charge for the continued use of the machine or machines installed. The actual messages are charged for in units, which are based on the duration of the messages; called **call charges**, they vary with the distance the messages travel. Charges do vary, but at the time of writing (1984) the charges are:

2.75p per minute under 56 km
8.25p per minute over 56 km
22p per minute to Europe
33p per minute to the Middle East and
North Africa
45p per minute to North America
75p per minute to South America,
Australia etc.

This is really very cheap for instantaneous delivery of messages in written form to the other side of the world.

Certain calls have to be connected by the operator, and the charge is then based on a basic three minute message. Other charges accumulate in units which are charged at 2.75p per unit, the higher charges being achieved by reducing the time per unit to each charge area.

A typical quarterly account might therefore read as follows:

		£
Quarterly rental		185.00
Units used: 8250 at 2.75p		226.88
Operator-connected calls		15.25
		427.13
VAT at 15%		64.07
Total to pay		£491.20

18.4 Exercises: Telex Charges

1 The offices listed below pay telex charges based on the records shown. What will be the quarterly charge for each when VAT at 15% has been added? The charge per unit is 2.75p.

Firm	Quarterly rental (£)	Units used	Operator calls (£)	Installation charges (£)
(a)	85.90	3 852	4.52	—
(b)	121.50	7 269	13.75	142.50
(c)	185.90	9 581	12.25	—
(d)	165.20	12 386	29.50	—
(e)	140.35	13 725	32.65	176.85

2 The following factories use telex machines to notify wholesalers and other customers of the reference numbers of all spare parts supplied and completed machines sent to them. They have to meet charges as listed below, based on 2.75p per unit, and timed calls which are operator controlled. What is the total charge in each case, after adding VAT at 15%?

Factory	Quarterly rental (£)	Units used	Operator calls (£)	Other charges (£)
(a)	88.90	4 965	15.25	12.75 servicing
(b)	125.40	7 214	37.45	204.25 installation
(c)	163.50	8 975	56.90	—
(d)	175.80	11 256	73.50	—
(e)	240.25	17 358	140.50	37.46 servicing

18.5 Facsimile copying

Many documents are now sent abroad by facsimile copying. This is possible by the use of a machine called a transceiver, that is to say, a transmitter and a receiver. An electric eye detects points of light as the document is passed under it, and relays them over the telephone network. The charge is exactly the same as a four-minute telephone call, as the machine takes four minutes to scan a document. The machines can be bought outright (they cost between £1400 and £3000), or purchased on hire purchase terms. (Hire purchase calculations are dealt with in Chapter 20.) No exercises are set on this section, as facsimile-copying charges would be included on the telephone bill.

18.6 Arabic numbers and Roman numbers

An old, schoolchild joke asks: 'What did the Arabs invent that was useful in mathematics?' Answer: 'Nothing.' We don't know for sure that the Arabs did invent the zero, 0 (they may just have rediscovered it from ancient manuscripts), but they are usually given the credit for it. The idea of a zero to indicate place value, so that 1 could become 10, 100, 1000 etc., was a real stroke of genius.

Previous to the system of Arabic numerals as we know them today, the Roman system was in use. This is based on 5 (V) and 10 (X). So, we have:

I II III IV V	(4 is IV: 1 before 5)
VI VII VIII IX X	(6 is VI: 1 after 5; and 9 is IX: 1 before 10)

We continue:

XI XII XIII XIV XV (14 is XIV: 4 after 10)
XVI XVII XVIII XIX
XX

XX XXX XL L (L is 50)
LX LXX LXXX
XC C (C is 100; XC is 90)

Now we will show the hundreds:

C CC CCC CD D (D is 500; CD is 400)

DC DCC DCCC
CM M   (M is 1000; CM is 900)

See if you can convert LXXIV and MCMLXXXIV to Arabic numerals.

LXXIV is L (i.e. 50) + XX (i.e. 20) + IV (i.e. 4) = 74

MCMLXXXIV is M (i.e. 1000) + CM (i.e. 900) + L (i.e. 50) + XXX (i.e. 30) + IV (i.e. 4) = 1984

You can see why Arabic numbers are such an improvement.

Consider $25 \times 3 = 75$ in Roman numbers:

XXV times III   XXV
                 times III
                 ___
                 ???

The Romans could not do multiplication sums!

The chief uses for Roman numbers today are for dates on tombstones and for chapter numbers in books (but not this book).

Overhead Expenses 5:
Wages, Salaries and Commission

19.1 Wages and salaries

Wages and salaries are really the same thing, but the word 'salary' is used for the monetary reward paid to people who do work that is not manual or mechanical in nature. At one time you could rely on the fact that salaried staff were paid more than manual workers. This is not necessarily true to-day, but the use of the word 'salary' for higher-paid staff is very ancient, the word actually comes from the Latin word *salarium*, meaning 'salt money', a higher rate of pay in Ancient Rome to soldiers serving in North Africa who had to buy salt to replace the minerals lost through sweating when on desert campaigns.

A common distinction between wage workers and salaried staff is that wage workers often have to clock in and record the times of arrival and departure. If they work over the normal working day they usually receive overtime. Salaried staff usually are paid monthly and work whatever hours are necessary to complete their work, setting the unpaid overtime against the greater job security they enjoy. Even this distinction is breaking down today, and many modern firms work systems of flexible hours, often called 'flexitime' (this word is actually a trade-mark of the Hengster Flextime Co. Ltd.).

If you take a job with flexitime, you will be required to press a button on a main panel as you enter the building. This lights up a board in the main reception area so that the telephonist knows you are in the building and calls may be put through to you. It also starts a record of your working hours. This might seem a rigorous management control procedure, but that is not the only idea. It gives you certain ranges of freedom and leaves you free to choose your hours of work. If you want a long lunchtime to go shopping, you

take it and make up the lost time later. You don't, like a schoolchild, have to ask permission to be absent. You behave sensibly, and put in your fair working hours within the flexible-hours system.

19.2 Types of reward

We can be paid in one of the following ways:

(a) **Hourly rates**: a fixed rate per hour, say £2.30 for each hour worked. The question of the rate per hour is, of course, of vital interest under this system, and trade union negotiation of rates of pay is quite common. Work is usually paid to the nearest complete quarter-hour, and late arrival may be punished by the loss of a quarter-hour's pay. More than 3 minutes late usually means a loss of pay for 15 minutes.

(b) **Overtime rates**: any work over the time of a set working day (usually 8 hours, or $7\frac{1}{2}$ hours not counting the lunch break) is paid at overtime rates. These are usually time-and-a-quarter, or time-and-a-half, or double-time at weekends. They vary from firm to firm.

(c) **Weekly pay**: a set weekly wage, paid whatever the hours worked, and is usually paid to clerical staff and other low-paid office staff who will eventually become salaried staff paid on a monthly basis. Some firms pay fortnightly, to save endless weekly calculations, and the employee receives two weeks' wages at a time.

(d) **Monthly pay**: the pay for salaried staff.

(e) **Bonus rates**: these are rates paid to manual workers as an incentive to hard work, or to complete a particularly urgent job. There are a number of quite complicated bonus schemes, but they are too difficult for a book of this type.

(f) Commission: salesmen are often rewarded on a commission basis. They draw a small basic wage and are paid extra money called 'commission' for each piece of work done. Thus commission may be earned on each sale made, according to the value of the sale.

19.3 Deductions from wages and salaries

The trouble with wages and salaries is that the Government requires certain deductions to be made from them before they are paid over to the employee. It is these deductions, which are often earnings-related (those who earn more, pay more), which lead to difficulties when paying wages and salaries. They may be listed as follows:

(a) *Compulsory deductions*, which are required by law, and are:
  (i) National Insurance charges
  (ii) PAYE (Pay As You Earn) tax
  (iii) Pension contributions (if the company has a scheme that is a condition of employment)
(b) *Voluntary deductions*, which are made if the employee wishes, and include:
  (iv) Trade Union contributions
  (v) Charitable contributions
  (vi) SAYE (Save As You Earn) contributions, which are made in one of the National Savings schemes

The wage or salary payable before deductions are made is called the gross pay. We calculate the gross pay before we consider the deductions from it.

19.4 Simple wage calculations

The basis for simple wage calculations is the calculation of gross pay. Obviously where pay is weekly pay or monthly pay, the gross pay is the agreed weekly wage or monthly salary. Where the rate is on an hourly rate we have to have some record of the hours worked. These are usually obtained from clock-cards, which are kept in

racks near the entrance to the factory. An employee arriving for work takes his or her card from the rack, inserts it in the clock mechanism, pulls a lever which records the time on the card, and places it in the 'in' rack. On leaving work the process is reversed. The card is taken from the 'in' rack, punched to record the time of departure, and placed in the 'out' rack.

Figure 19.1 shows a typical clock-card and the notes below explain a few special points.

(a) The foundry works seven days a week, but workers are given two days off (a weekend) in rotation around the week. For the week shown, M. Freemantle has his weekend on Thursday and Friday.
(b) Actually he works on Thursday—earning double time, $8\frac{1}{4}$ hours and $8\frac{1}{4}$ hours overtime.
(c) On the other days, when overtime earns time-and-a-half, the full hours worked are paid at the standard rate and each extra hour above $7\frac{1}{2}$ hours earns an extra half-hour overtime. So, $\frac{3}{4}$ hour on Monday earns $\frac{3}{8}$ hour overtime.
(d) The total overtime is added to the total hours worked to give the 'hours to pay'.
(e) Gross pay is therefore $69 \times £2.85 =$ (for calculation see below)

Example of gross pay calculation:

M. Freemantle

Hours worked	$55\frac{3}{4}$	
Overtime	$13\frac{1}{4}$	
Hours to pay	$\underline{69}$	2.85
Gross pay	$= 69 \times £2.85$	$\underline{69}$
	$= £196.65$	25.65
		171.00
		$\underline{£196.65}$

19.5 Exercises: simple wage calculations

1 In each of the cases shown below, fill in the 'extra hours payable' column and then calculate the gross pay of the individual, before deductions. The standard week is 39 hours and all overtime is at time and-a-half. (Calculate to the nearest penny where necessary.)

Figure 19.1   A weekly clock-card

Name	M. Fremantle	Official weekend	Thurs - Fri
Dept.	Foundry	Normal stint	7½ hours
Clock No.	286		
Week No.	37	Commencing 14th December	

Day		Time In	Time Out	*Less* Breaks	Hours Worked	Overtime payable
Monday	am	6.00		¾	8¼	$\frac{3}{8}$
	pm		3.00			
Tuesday	am	6.00		¾	8½	½
	pm		3.15			
Wednesday	am	6.00		¾	8¼	$\frac{3}{8}$
	pm		3.00			
Thursday	am	6.00		¾	8¼	8¼
	pm		3.00			
Friday	am					
	pm					
Saturday	am	6.00		¾	11¼	$1\frac{7}{8}$
	pm		6.00			
Sunday	am	6.00		¾	11¼	$1\frac{7}{8}$
	pm		6.00			
Standard rate £ 2.85 *Overtime* Weekdays 1½ Weekends 2		Total + Overtime			55¾ 13¼	13¼
		Hours to pay			69	

Name	Hours worked	Extra hours payable	Standard rate (£)		Name	Hours worked	Extra hours payable	Standard rate (£)
(a) Mr A	39		1.90		(a) Mr F	45		1.95
(b) Mrs B	44		2.70		(b) Mrs G	49		2.85
(c) Miss C	43½		2.65		(c) Miss H	48		2.45
(d) Mr D	55		2.85		(d) Mr I	54		3.50
(e) Mr E	62		3.00		(e) Mrs J	56		3.15

2 In each of the cases below, the overtime worked above the standard week of 42 hours is weekend working and is payable at double-time. Fill in the 'extra hours payable' column, and then find the gross pay in each case.

19.6 Commission on sales

Many salaries involve some element of commission, in other words, a reward for selling. Commission is a convenient method of payment for employers, as they only have to pay when a salesman makes a sale. If the commission is set at such a rate that the salesman can achieve a good salary with reasonably hard work, and a very good salary with very hard work, there will be a real incentive to the salesman, which in turn will greatly benefit the employer. On the other hand, a salesman who has a difficult territory to cover may find the rewards difficult to earn, especially at first, before he has built up a chain of customers in the area. A basic salary may be necessary to encourage such a salesman. We therefore have the following variations:

(a) *A basic salary + a straight commission* on each sale.
(b) *A basic salary + commission above a certain quota of sales.* There is a quota of sales which do not earn commission. Once this quota has been passed all extra sales earn commission.
(c) *A graduated commission*: very high on the first few sales in the period to give the salesman a basic reward, rather lower on higher sales above a certain figure, and lower still on very large volumes of sales.

Many variations on these basic schemes are possible to meet particular needs in particular sales areas. Note that the word 'sales' does not necessarily mean sales of goods, such as video machines, washing machines etc. It may also mean sales involving labour and installation such as double glazing, central heating etc., or sales of pension schemes, financial help etc.

The following examples illustrate the various calculations:

Example: (a) *A basic salary + a straight commission.* A salesman is paid a basic salary of £140 a month plus a commission of 20% on all sales. His sales in the month total £1800. What was his gross pay?

Gross pay = salary + commission

$$= £140 + \frac{20}{1\cancel{00}} \times £18\cancel{00}$$

$$\text{(cancelling by 100)}$$

$$= £140 + £360$$
$$= \underline{\underline{£500}}$$

Example: (b) *A basic salary + commission above a certain quota of sales.* A commercial traveller is paid a basic salary of £360 per month plus a commission of 10% on all sales over £12000. In July she sells £18500 of goods. What was her salary for the month?

As the quota of sales required is £12000, she exceeds the quota by:

$$\begin{array}{r} £ \\ 18\,500 \\ -\,12\,000 \\ \hline £6\,500 \end{array}$$

Salary = wages + commission

$$= £360 + \frac{10}{1\cancel{00}} \times £65\cancel{00} \quad \text{(cancelling by 100)}$$

$$= £360 + £650$$
$$= \underline{\underline{£1010}}$$

Example: (c) *A graduated commission.* A salesman earns a basic salary of £40 per week, above which he earns 5% commission on the first £500 of sales, $7\frac{1}{2}\%$ on the next £2000 and 10% on all sales above this figure. In the first week he sells goods worth £5280. What is his gross pay for the week?

Gross pay = salary + commission

	£	
Salary =	40	
Commission at 5%		
on first £500 =	25	(500 ÷ 20 = £25)
Commission at $7\frac{1}{2}\%$		
on next £2000 =	150	($7\frac{1}{2}\%$ = £75 on
		every £1000)
Commission at 10%		5280
on balance of £2780 =	278	− 2500
	£493	2780

19.7 Exercises: commission on sales

1 What will be the commission on the following sales, at the rates shown in each case? (Answer correct to the nearest penny where necessary.)

(a) 20% on £3080   (b) 20% on £9495
(c) $33\frac{1}{3}\%$ on £5952   (d) $33\frac{1}{3}\%$ on £6783

(e) 10% on £4265   (f) 5% on £2974
(g) 5% on £6780   (h) 10% on £1342
(i) $2\frac{1}{2}$% on £4371   (j) $2\frac{1}{2}$% on £5283

2 What will the following salesmen earn per month if their basic salary (which reflects the difficulty of their sales area) is as shown, and commission on sales is fixed at 5 per cent?

Name	Basic salary (£)	Sales achieved (£)
(a) Mr A	100	12 200
(b) Mrs B	100	14 700
(c) Mr C	150	9 600
(d) Mr D	150	8 850
(e) Miss E	250	5 425

3 A firm rewards salesmen with a basic salary which reflects the difficulty of the sales area, and for which they must achieve a certain quota of sales. Above this quota all sales earn 10% commission. What will each of the following earn?

Name	Basic salary (£)	Quota to be achieved (£)	Actual sales (£)
(a) Mrs F	360	5000	9540
(b) Mr G	240	3000	7250
(c) Miss H	280	3000	6880
(d) Miss I	300	2500	4950
(e) Miss J	320	2400	5525

4 Five salesmen from different firms are comparing notes about gross pay per week. Their basic salaries, quotas, rates of commission and actual sales in the previous week had been as follows. (Miss P earns commission on all sales.)

Name	Basic salary (£)	Quota to be achieved (£)	Actual sales (£)	Commission rate on extra sales (£)
(a) Mr M	75.50	500	1780	10
(b) Miss N	63.70	750	2120	8
(c) Mr O	59.60	1000	4850	5
(d) Miss P	72.50	no quota set	4328	5
(e) Mr Q	60.75	1500	7860	$2\frac{1}{2}$

What does each salesman earn? Who earns the highest pay and who earns the lowest?

5 A firm does not pay its salesmen a basic salary but the commission is graduated to ensure that most earn a reasonable living. The first £2000 of sales each month earn 10% commission, the next £8000 earn 5% commission, the rest earn 3% commission. What will each of the following earn?

Name	Sales (£)
(a) Mr V	13 250
(b) Mrs W	17 380
(c) Miss X	19 460
(d) Miss Y	14 890
(e) Mr Z	11 750

19.8 Calculating take-home pay

Whether pay is hourly pay, weekly pay, monthly pay or commission, the gross pay has to be reduced by the various deductions referred to in Section 19.3 above. If wages are paid in cash, the wage packet must be made up in a special envelope with a wages slip giving details of the calculations. The first part of this calculation will be the addition of various types of income, as there may be salary, overtime pay, commission etc. From this there may be a deduction for pension contributions, as money saved for future pensions is tax free and consequently is deducted before the important tax computations are done. This first part of the calculation may give us the top part of a slip as shown in Figure 19.2.

Figure 19.2 Finding taxable pay (the first part of a payslip)

Payslip	Week Month 3 June: 6: July: 5
Name A. Barclay	Tax Code 261
Department Machine shop	
Earnings	£
Salary	420. 00
Overtime	127. 40
Commission	—
SSP	—
Other 1	—
Other 2	—
Gross pay	547. 40
Less superannuation	27. 37
Pay for tax purposes	520. 03

(a) SSP stands for statutory sick pay. If an employee is sick during the pay period, a sum of money called statutory sick pay will be included in the pay packet.

(b) Superannuation is the term used for pension savings.

(c) The pay for tax purposes is used in the tax calculation as explained in Figure 19.3 below.

Tax tables

In order to know what tax to deduct in any given weekly or monthly period, it is necessary to use tax tables supplied by the Inland Revenue. Two tables, called Table A and Table B, show how to make the calculation.

Table A (see Figure 19.3) shows the tax-free pay, at every time in the year, for every week (or month) in the year. For the example used in Figure 19.2 we need the monthy table, reproduced as Figure 19.3. It shows all the tax codes which can be allocated to various employees by the tax office. These codes take into account various reliefs such as personal allowances, age allowance, dependent relatives allowance, blind person's allowance etc. The higher your code, the more tax-free pay you are entitled to. A. Barclay, in Figure 19.2, has a Tax Code 261, and we are in Month 3 at the start of the year. If you look at Table A (Figure 19.3) and read notes (a)–(e) below, you will see how we calculate the tax deductable in Month 3 from A. Barclay's pay packet (Figure 19.2). These notes lead you into the other illustrations to follow the whole tax calculation.

(a) A. Barclay's code number is shown on his payslip as 261.

(b) His pay for tax purposes for this month (see payslip, Figure 19.2) is £520.03.

(c) When we add this to the pay for tax purposes received in Months 1 and 2 we find the gross pay to date for tax purposes is £1695.50 (see Figure 19.4).

(d) Looking at Table A we see that with Code 261 the tax-free pay is £654.75. So A. Barclay does not have to pay any tax on the first £654.75 of his income. Taking this from the 'gross pay to date for tax purposes' we find he *does* have to pay tax on £1040.75.

(e) We now need to turn to Table B (Figure 19.4), and read notes (i)–(iii) below.

(i) Table B simply consists of a list of taxable

earnings, and set against these earnings the tax due on them.

(ii) As A. Barclay's 'Taxable Pay to Date' is £1040.75, we look for this figure in the table. If the exact figure is not available we look at the next lowest figure, which is £1040. This tells us that the tax due to date is £312.00.

(iii) The beauty of the PAYE system is that it can at once put right any errors made in previous months, in the following way:

(i) The tax due to date is £312.

(ii) Suppose that up to last month A. Barclay had paid £365. This could easily happen if his code number changed in the month, because, for example, he had married and now had a married man's allowance to claim. In such a case, A. Barclay would be entitled to a refund of £53, which would be given to him at once. (iii) In this case (see Figure 19.5) no such refund was due. By looking at last month's records we can see how much tax Barclay had paid, and we find it was £288.50. He is therefore due to pay £23.50 this month, and this appears on the line for tax deductions on the payslip (£312 due less £288.50 = £23.50 to pay). (See Figure 19.5 and notes (a)–(e) below.)

(a) The tax deduction is £23.50.

(b) The National Insurance contributions (NIC) are found in another table supplied by the Department of Health and Social Security (see Figure 19.6). The table is based on gross pay, and is in two parts: a figure for the employee's contribution which is deducted from the employee's pay, and an employer's contribution payable by the employer. In this case the figures for £547 gross pay mean a deduction of £49.32.

(c) A. Barclay also pays a trade union contribution of £1.50 and a charitable contribution of 20p to Dr Barnardo's Homes. Although this does not seem a very large contribution, such a sum given by all employees is very helpful to the charity concerned. You may be asked to make such a voluntary contribution at your own place of employment.

(d) When all these deductions are added together, and deducted from 'pay for tax purposes' (see first part of the payslip, Figure 19.2), we get a net pay of £445.51.

Figure 19.3 Tax-free pay with various code numbers

TABLE A—FREE PAY

MONTH 3
June 6 to July 5

Code	Total free pay to date (3)	Code	Total free pay to date (3)	Code	Total free pay to date (3)	Code	Total free pay to date (3)	Code	Total free pay to date (3)	Code	Total free pay to date (3)	Code	Total free pay to date (3)	Code	Total free pay to date (3)
0	NIL	61	154·77	121	304·77	181	454·77	241	604·77	301	754·77	361	904·77	421	1054·77
1	4·77	62	157·26	122	307·26	182	457·26	242	607·26	302	757·26	362	907·26	422	1057·26
2	7·26	63	159·75	123	309·75	183	459·75	243	609·75	303	759·75	363	909·75	423	1059·75
3	9·75	64	162·27	124	312·27	184	462·27	244	612·27	304	762·27	364	912·27	424	1062·27
4	12·27	65	164·76	125	314·76	185	464·76	245	614·76	305	764·76	365	914·76	425	1064·76
5	14·76	66	167·25	126	317·25	186	467·25	246	617·25	306	767·25	366	917·25	426	1067·25
6	17·25	67	169·77	127	319·77	187	469·77	247	619·77	307	769·77	367	919·77	427	1069·77
7	19·77	68	172·26	128	322·26	188	472·26	248	622·26	308	772·26	368	922·26	428	1072·26
8	22·26	69	174·75	129	324·75	189	474·75	249	624·75	309	774·75	369	924·75	429	1074·75
9	24·75	70	177·27	130	327·27	190	477·27	250	627·27	310	777·27	370	927·27	430	1077·27
10	27·27	71	179·76	131	329·76	191	479·76	251	629·76	311	779·76	371	929·76	431	1079·76
11	29·76	72	182·25	132	332·25	192	482·25	252	632·25	312	782·25	372	932·25	432	1082·25
12	32·25	73	184·77	133	334·77	193	484·77	253	634·77	313	784·77	373	934·77	433	1084·77
13	34·77	74	187·26	134	337·26	194	487·26	254	637·26	314	787·26	374	937·26	434	1087·26
14	37·26	75	189·75	135	339·75	195	489·75	255	639·75	315	789·75	375	939·75	435	1089·75
15	39·75	76	192·27	136	342·27	196	492·27	256	642·27	316	792·27	376	942·27	436	1092·27
16	42·27	77	194·76	137	344·76	197	494·76	257	644·76	317	794·76	377	944·76	437	1094·76
17	44·76	78	197·25	138	347·25	198	497·25	258	647·25	318	797·25	378	947·25	438	1097·25
18	47·25	79	199·77	139	349·77	199	499·77	259	649·77	319	799·77	379	949·77	439	1099·77
19	49·77	80	202·26	140	352·26	200	502·26	260	652·26	320	802·26	380	952·26	440	1102·26
20	52·26	81	204·75	141	354·75	201	504·75	261	654·75	321	804·75	381	954·75	441	1104·75
21	54·75	82	207·27	142	357·27	202	507·27	262	657·27	322	807·27	382	957·27	442	1107·27
22	57·27	83	209·76	143	359·76	203	509·76	263	659·76	323	809·76	383	959·76	443	1109·76
23	59·76														

27	69·75	87	219·75	147	369·75	207	519·75	267	669·75	327	819·75	387	969·75	447	1119·75
28	72·27	88	222·27	148	372·27	208	522·27	268	672·27	328	822·27	388	972·27	448	1122·27
29	74·76	89	224·76	149	374·76	209	524·76	269	674·76	329	824·76	389	974·76	449	1124·76
30	77·25	90	227·25	150	377·25	210	527·25	270	677·25	330	827·25	390	977·25	450	1127·25
31	79·77	91	229·77	151	379·77	211	529·77	271	679·77	331	829·77	391	979·77	451	1129·77
32	82·26	92	232·26	152	382·26	212	532·26	272	682·26	332	832·26	392	982·26	452	1132·26
33	84·75	93	234·75	153	384·75	213	534·75	273	684·75	333	834·75	393	984·75	453	1134·75
34	87·27	94	237·27	154	387·27	214	537·27	274	687·27	334	837·27	394	987·27	454	1137·27
35	89·76	95	239·76	155	389·76	215	539·76	275	689·76	335	839·76	395	989·76	455	1139·76
36	92·25	96	242·25	156	392·25	216	542·25	276	692·25	336	842·25	396	992·25	456	1142·25
37	94·77	97	244·77	157	394·77	217	544·77	277	694·77	337	844·77	397	994·77	457	1144·77
38	97·26	98	247·26	158	397·26	218	547·26	278	697·26	338	847·26	398	997·26	458	1147·26
39	99·75	99	249·75	159	399·75	219	549·75	279	699·75	339	849·75	399	999·75	459	1149·75
40	102·27	100	252·27	160	402·27	220	552·27	280	702·27	340	852·27	400	1002·27	460	1152·27
41	104·76	101	254·76	161	404·76	221	554·76	281	704·76	341	854·76	401	1004·76	461	1154·76
42	107·25	102	257·25	162	407·25	222	557·25	282	707·25	342	857·25	402	1007·25	462	1157·25
43	109·77	103	259·77	163	409·77	223	559·77	283	709·77	343	859·77	403	1009·77	463	1159·77
44	112·26	104	262·26	164	412·26	224	562·26	284	712·26	344	862·26	404	1012·26	464	1162·26
45	114·75	105	264·75	165	414·75	225	564·75	285	714·75	345	864·75	405	1014·75	465	1164·75
46	117·27	106	267·27	166	417·27	226	567·27	286	717·27	346	867·27	406	1017·27	466	1167·27
47	119·76	107	269·76	167	419·76	227	569·76	287	719·76	347	869·76	407	1019·76	467	1169·76
48	122·25	108	272·25	168	422·25	228	572·25	288	722·25	348	872·25	408	1022·25	468	1172·25
49	124·77	109	274·77	169	424·77	229	574·77	289	724·77	349	874·77	409	1024·77	469	1174·77
50	127·26	110	277·26	170	427·26	230	577·26	290	727·26	350	877·26	410	1027·26	470	1177·26
51	129·75	111	279·75	171	429·75	231	579·75	291	729·75	351	879·75	411	1029·75	471	1179·75
52	132·27	112	282·27	172	432·27	232	582·27	292	732·27	352	882·27	412	1032·27	472	1182·27
53	134·76	113	284·76	173	434·76	233	584·76	293	734·76	353	884·76	413	1034·76	473	1184·76
54	137·25	114	287·25	174	437·25	234	587·25	294	737·25	354	887·25	414	1037·25	474	1187·25
55	139·77	115	289·77	175	439·77	235	589·77	295	739·77	355	889·77	415	1039·77	475	1189·77
56	142·26	116	292·26	176	442·26	236	592·26	296	742·26	356	892·26	416	1042·26	476	1192·26
57	144·75	117	294·75	177	444·75	237	594·75	297	744·75	357	894·75	417	1044·75	477	1194·75
58	147·27	118	297·27	178	447·27	238	597·27	298	747·27	358	897·27	418	1047·27	478	1197·27
59	149·76	119	299·76	179	449·76	239	599·76	299	749·76	359	899·76	419	1049·76	479	1199·76
60	152·25	120	302·25	180	452·25	240	602·25	300	752·25	360	902·25	420	1052·25	480	1202·25

Figure 19.4   Tax-due table from Inland Revenue

TABLE B

TAX DUE ON TAXABLE PAY FROM £721 TO £1080

Total TAXABLE PAY to date	Total TAX DUE to date	Total TAXABLE PAY to date	Total TAX DUE to date	Total TAXABLE PAY to date	Total TAX DUE to date	Total TAXABLE PAY to date	Total TAX DUE to date	Total TAXABLE PAY to date	Total TAX DUE to date	Total TAXABLE PAY to date	Total TAX DUE to date
£	£	£	£	£	£	£	£	£	£	£	£
721	216.30	781	234.30	841	252.30	901	270.30	961	288.30	1021	306.30
722	216.60	782	234.60	842	252.60	902	270.60	962	288.60	1022	306.60
723	216.90	783	234.90	843	252.90	903	270.90	963	288.90	1023	306.90
724	217.20	784	235.20	844	253.20	904	271.20	964	289.20	1024	307.20
725	217.50	785	235.50	845	253.50	905	271.50	965	289.50	1025	307.50
726	217.80	786	235.80	846	253.80	906	271.80	966	289.80	1026	307.80
727	218.10	787	236.10	847	254.10	907	272.10	967	290.10	1027	308.10
728	218.40	788	236.40	848	254.40	908	272.40	968	290.40	1028	308.40
729	218.70	789	236.70	849	254.70	909	272.70	969	290.70	1029	308.70
730	219.00	790	237.00	850	255.00	910	273.00	970	291.00	1030	309.00
731	219.30	791	237.30	851	255.30	911	273.30	971	291.30	1031	309.30
732	219.60	792	237.60	852	255.60	912	273.60	972	291.60	1032	309.60
733	219.90	793	237.90	853	255.90	913	273.90	973	291.90	1033	309.90
734	220.20	794	238.20	854	256.20	914	274.20	974	292.20	1034	310.20
735	220.50	795	238.50	855	256.50	915	274.50	975	292.50	1035	310.50
736	220.80	796	238.80	856	256.80	916	274.80	976	292.80	1036	310.80
737	221.10	797	239.10	857	257.10	917	275.10	977	293.10	1037	311.10
738	221.40	798	239.40	858	257.40	918	275.40	978	293.40	1038	311.40
739	221.70	799	239.70	859	257.70	919	275.70	979	293.70	1039	311.70
740	222.00	800	240.00	860	258.00	920	276.00	980	294.00	1040	312.00
741	222.30	801	240.30	861	258.30	921	276.30	981	294.30	1041	312.30
742	222.60	802	240.60	862	258.60	922	276.60	982	294.60	1042	312.60
743	222.90	803	240.90	863	258.90	923	276.90	983	294.90	1043	312.90
744	223.~~	804	241.20	864	259.20	924	277.20	984	295.20	1044	313.20
745	~~	~~5	241.50	865	259.50	925	277.5~	985	295.50	1045	313.50
			~~90	866	259.80	926			~~5 80	1046	313.80
				867	260.10					1047	314.10
				~~	26~~						314.40

Figure 19.5   Deductions and net pay (the second part of a payslip)

Gross pay to date for tax purposes	1695.50
Tax free pay	654.75
Taxable pay to date	1040.75
Tax due to date	312.00
Refund due (if any)	—
Deductions:	
Tax PAYE	23.50
NI contribution	49.32
TU	1.50
Dr. Barnardo	.20
Total deductions	74.52
Net pay	445.51
Refund (see above)	—
Other 1	—
2	—
Amount payable	445.51
Employers NI Contribution	62.75
Total due to NI	112.07

(e) The words 'Other 1' and 'Other 2' refer to other moneys which might be put in the pay packet; for example, refunds of travelling expenses, car mileage allowances, refunds of expenses incurred etc. The final amount payable is the amount in the pay packet (or, more likely these days, transferred into the employee's bank account).

19.9 Exercises: calculating take-home pay

Using the same layout as the sample payslips provided in Figures 19.2 and 19.5 above, calculate the take-home pay of the four people named below. The details of their pay that you require are given below. They are all concerned with Month 3, so both Table A (Figure 19.3) and Table B (Figure 19.4) can be used.

Figure 19.6 Extract from the National Insurance
contributions booklet

National Insurance contributions

Gross pay	Total NIC	Employee's contribution	Employer's contribution
525.00	107.57	47.34	60.23
527.00	107.98	47.52	60.46
529.00	108.38	47.70	60.68
531.00	108.79	47.88	60.91
533.00	109.20	48.06	61.14
535.00	109.61	48.24	61.37
537.00	110.02	48.42	61.60
539.00	110.43	48.60	61.83
541.00	110.84	48.78	62.06
543.00	111.25	48.96	62.29
545.00	111.66	49.14	62.52
547.00	112.07	49.32	62.75
549.00	112.47	49.50	62.97
551.00	112.88	49.68	63.20
553.00	113.29	49.86	63.43
555.00	113.70	50.04	63.66
557.00	114.11	50.22	63.89
559.00	114.52	50.40	64.12
561.00	114.93	50.58	64.35
563.00	115.34	50.76	64.58

Hint: In each case you have to do the following things:

(a) Start off the payslip and find 'gross pay'.
(b) Deduct superannuation to find 'pay for tax purposes'.
(c) Add this 'pay for tax purposes' to the pay in the previous two months to get 'gross pay to date for tax purposes'.
(d) Look up the tax free pay in Table A (Figure 19.3) and hence find 'taxable pay to date'.
(e) Look up 'tax due to date' in Table B (Figure 19.4).
(f) Now work out the tax to be deducted (or refunded) this month to get the tax correct for the three-month period. Write the tax due in the deductions section (or the refund on the refund line).
(g) Write in the rest of the deductions and find the total.

(h) Take this total from the 'pay for tax purposes'.
(i) Add on the refund, if there was one, and any other amounts to be paid.
(j) Work out the amount payable.
(k) Work out the total due to National Insurance.

1 R. Lyons (code no. 156): salary £485.50; commission £136.50; superannuation £49.76. Gross pay to date for tax purposes up to the end of Month 2: £842.76. Up to last month, R. Lyons had paid £282.50 tax. National Insurance contributions were: R. Lyons £55.98, employer £68.42. R. Lyons pays £2.38 trade union contribution and 40p to a local charity. He is also due to receive fares of £18.45 for the previous month.

2 M. Davies (code no. 284): salary £525.60; overtime £32.68; superannuation £33.50. Gross pay to end of Month 2 for tax purposes: £1220.44. Up to last month, M. Davies had paid £340 in tax. National Insurance contributions were: M. Davies £50.25, employer £61.41. M. Davies saves in a Save As You Earn scheme £10 per month, and also gives 50p to Dr Barnardo's Homes. She is not due to receive any other payments from her employer.

3 M. Brogan (code no. 195): salary £724.75; commission £32.50; superannuation £75.73. Gross pay to end of Month 2 for tax purposes: £852.23. Up to last month, M. Brogan had paid £290 in tax. National Insurance contributions were: M. Brogan £68.15, employer £83.30. M. Brogan pays trade union subscription £2.25 and fees to a professional body £1.55 as voluntary deductions. He is not due any other payments from his employer.

4 L. Patient (code no. 256): salary £420.25; overtime £80.75; superannuation £40.88. Gross pay to end of Month 2 for tax purposes: £1220. Up to last month, L. Patient had paid £188.60 in tax. National Insurance contributions were: L. Patient £45.99, employer £56.21. L. Patient pays £1.52 trade union contributions, 50p to a local charity, and is due to receive a tax-free award of £25 as a prize for success in passing examinations.

20

Hire Purchase

20.1 What is hire purchase?

Hire purchase (HP) is a way of purchasing expensive domestic items like cars, washing machines, refrigerators, gas stoves, electrical appliances etc. in small payments called **instalments**.

Almost all families use hire purchase for some of these items, especially the family car. As families might easily over commit themselves to hire purchase if there were no controls, and suppliers might also treat the poorer families (who are most likely to get into difficulties) harshly, the whole system is controlled by the Office of Fair Trading and the Consumer Credit Act 1974. The Act requires certain standards of behaviour from suppliers; it states that goods can only be repossessed in special ways which require a Court Order, and so on.

The basic idea is that the goods sold on hire purchase are still sold at exactly the same price as they would cost if the consumer was paying cash. To prevent families getting into difficulties, the Government usually insists that a part of the purchase price (the **deposit**) must be paid at once, though this does not apply to one or two items that are essential to every family, such as gas cookers and electric cookers. These are available without deposit, and spread over several years to enable even the poorest family to obtain them. Disregarding these items, and considering something on which there is a deposit (a small family car for example) we have the calculation as follows:

	£	
Cash price of car	3900	
Less deposit	1300	(one-third of £3900)
Balance to pay	£2600	

You will notice that £1300 is a large deposit to save up, even to buy the smallest car, but once we

have a car we can always get a 'trade-in' value on it. The dealer might give us £1000 for the old car, so we only have to find £300 extra for the deposit. In hire purchase the first item we buy is the difficult one, after which we may get a trade-in value on the old item to help with a new deposit.

Once the deposit is deducted from the price there is a balance to be paid by hire purchase. To this balance a rate of interest is added on a *flat-rate basis*. Supposing the interest is 10% per annum for three years, this means that 30% must be added to the balance payable. In the example given above we have:

	£	
Balance to pay	2600	
Add interest	780	(30% of £2600 =
Hire purchase payable	£3380	3 × £260)

There are two points to note here. First, the flat rate of interest is convenient, but it is not a true rate of interest. The reason is that we are paying 10% on £2600 borrowed for three years but as we start to repay at once, each month, the money is not being borrowed for three years, but for an average of $1\frac{1}{2}$ years. The only part that will be borrowed for the full three years is the very last instalment. Really the interest rate is much higher than 10%: almost 20%, although the calculation is quite difficult. For this reason the Office of Fair Trading requires the supplier to state what the **Annual Percentage Rate** (APR) is. You will see these APRs displayed in many shops. APRs do not make any difference to the calculations, but they do let customers know the rate of interest they are really paying on the goods they buy.

The second point is that people must be told the cash price of the item, so that they can see the amount they can save if they wait for a while and save up enough to buy the article for cash. In this case we have to pay £3380 + the deposit £1300 for the item, i.e. £4680 for a car that really costs £3900. Before this requirement came into force, dealers often quoted the price on hire purchase only, and gave no idea of the cash price.

The final part of the calculation is to work out the amount payable for each instalment. As this is over a three-year period, we have the following instalments to pay:

(a) If we pay monthly over 36 months £3380 ÷ 36
$$= £93.89 \text{ per month}$$

```
        £
       93.89
  36)3380
     324
     140
     108
     320
     288
     320
     320
       £
```

(b) If we pay weekly over 156 weeks (3 × 52 weeks) £3380 ÷ 156
$$= £21.67 \text{ per week}$$

```
       21.666
 156)3380
     312
     260
     156
    1040
     936
    1040
```

Clearly a car is a considerable expense in any family's budget, even when purchased on HP.

The following example illustrates this type of calculation.

Example: A refrigerator selling at a cash price of £124.80 is offered for a deposit of 20% and 24 monthly instalments. The interest rate is 15% per annum. What will the monthly instalment be? (Answer correct to the nearest penny.)

```
                        £
Cash price      =   124.80
Less deposit    =    24.96  (⅕ of £124.80)
Balance to pay  =    99.84
Add interest    =    29.95  (30% of £99.84)
Hire purchase   =  £129.79
  payment
```

Therefore: Monthly instalment = £129.79 ÷ 24

$$= £5.41 \text{ per month}$$

```
        5.407
  24)129.79
     120
      97
      96
     190
```

20.2 Exercises: simple hire purchase calculations

1 What will the monthly instalments be in each of the hire purchase agreements listed below? (Answer correct to the nearest penny.)

	Cash price of goods	Deposit payable	Rate of interest per annum	Number of years
(a)	£100	£25	15%	1
(b)	£240	£48	10%	2
(c)	£375	£125	10%	2
(d)	£375	£37.50	15%	2
(e)	£180	£36	10%	2

2 Motorists wishing to buy the motor cars whose cash price is listed below must in each case pay one-third of the cash price as deposit. Interest will then be added at a flat rate of 10 per cent per annum for three years, payment being made in 36 monthly instalments. What will (a) the deposit, and (b) the monthly instalment be in each case? (Answer where necessary correct to the nearest penny.)

(a) £3900   (b) £4500
(c) £4800   (d) £7580
(e) £5218

3 Find the weekly instalment payable in each of the hire purchase agreements summarised in the table below. (Answer correct to the nearest penny, where necessary.)

	Cash price (£)	Deposit payable	Rate of interest (%)	No. of years	Instalments payable
(a)	390	£40	12½	2	monthly
(b)	450	£35	10	2	monthly
(c)	480	£30	15	1	monthly
(d)	1500	£50	12½	2	monthly
(e)	2100	£30	15	2	monthly
(f)	690	10%	12½	2	monthly
(g)	1460	20%	15	2	monthly
(h)	1245	20%	10	2	weekly
(i)	1295	20%	12½	2	weekly
(j)	1960	25%	15	2	weekly

4 A family preparing for a camping holiday buys the goods below on hire purchase. The deposit is fixed at 20% and the interest rate is $12\frac{1}{2}\%$, the goods being paid for in weekly instalments in one year.

Tent	£156.00
Cooking utensils	£35.80
Sleeping equipment	£84.50
Tables, chairs etc.	£45.00
Roof-rack for car	£13.30

What is the deposit payable? How much is payable in each instalment? (Answer correct to the nearest penny where necessary.)

5 A sailing dinghy is priced at £950, payable by a 25% deposit and 24 monthly instalments. Find, correct to the nearest penny, the amount payable each month. The rate of interest is $12\frac{1}{2}\%$ per annum.

21

Business Accounts: The Work of the Cashier

21.1 Business accounts

The study of business accounts is a specialist subject in its own right and we can only touch upon the subject in this Business Calculations book. We all open up bank accounts as soon as we leave school, so the word 'account' is in common use. A business might have thousands, even millions, of accounts. What is an 'account'? It is a page in a book called 'the ledger', which is consequently called 'the main book of account'. Today, instead of a book, we may keep our accounts on a disk in a computer, or on a floppy disk on the desk near a computer, but if you think of it as a page or leaf in a book (or, rather, a double page in a book), you will get the right idea.

When I say 'I have an account at Lloyds' Bank', I mean that I have a leaf in Mr Lloyd's ledger; although, of course, the original Mr Lloyd is long dead, and it is a company called 'Lloyds PLC' that keeps the ledger these days. Every page has a number called the **folio number** (from the Latin *folium*, meaning 'a leaf'), so if I go to the bank to make an enquiry about my account they are sure to ask me the account number, and when they key it into the computer the account will appear on a visual display unit (VDU).

All businesses have many accounts. They have accounts for cash, money at the bank, premises, furniture, typewriters and other assets, for their suppliers (creditors) and their customers (debtors), for expenses such as light and heat, telephones, advertising, wages etc. There might be several thousand pages in their ledger.

Suppose we own a business. Two of the most important accounts are our Cash Account and our Bank Account. These accounts are where we keep a record of our money. If we receive or pay out cash, we record it in the Cash Account; if we receive and pay out cheques, we record them in the Bank Account. The person who keeps these accounts is called the **cashier**, or in large businesses, the **chief cashier**. Every Bank of England note is signed by the chief cashier of that bank. (Have a look at a banknote and see whose name appears on it.)

21.2 Cash Accounts and Bank Accounts

These two accounts are very similar. A Cash Account keeps a record of cash money moving in or out of the business; a Bank Account keeps a record of receipts and payments by cheque, although we can pay cash into a Bank Account (in fact, that is how we 'open' an account with a bank). However, as explained below, there is one difficulty about accounts with banks that causes a lot of confusion, and gives many students a totally wrong idea.

Look at the following Cash Account, and read the notes below it. As you do, you will learn the basic rule about *every* account that is ever kept. This rule is:

Debit the account that receives goods, or services or money.
Credit the account that gives goods, or services or money.

Naturally, Cash Accounts and Bank Accounts only deal with money, not goods or services, so we can simply say that when they receive money (or cheques) we debit them, and when they give away money (or cheques), we credit them. The left-hand side of an account is the debit side and the right-hand side is the credit side, so when we say we debit the account we mean we make the entry on the left-hand side, and when we credit the account we make the entry on the right-hand side. Now look at the Cash Account and read the notes following it.

and is the opposite of 'Sales'. It is very important, because later we find our profits by finding the difference between purchases and sales.

CASH ACCOUNT

19. .	Details (Debit side)	Folio	£	19. .	Details (Credit side)	Folio	£
Jan. 1	Capital	L1	250.00	Jan. 2	Postage	L9	4.50
1	Sales	L10	56.85	4	Purchases	L11	28.25
2	,,	L10	72.65	5	Sundry Expenses	L12	1.95
3	,,	L10	132.80	6	Cleaning Materials	L13	7.32
4	,,	L10	140.52	7	Bank	L8	795.26
5	,,	L10	236.25	7	Travelling Expenses	L14	7.65
6	,,	L10	325.80	7	Balance	c/d	378.19
7	R. Deeping	L15	8.25				
			£1223.12				£1223.12

19. .			£
Jan. 8	Balance	b/d	378.19

(a) When the account receives cash we make the entry on the debit side and when it gives cash away we make the entry on the credit side.

(b) The business started on 1st January and £250 cash was contributed as part of the capital subscribed by the proprietor. This is debited in the account.

(c) On the 1st, 2nd, 3rd, 4th, 5th and 6th we had cash sales to enter on the debit side because the cash was received in the tills.

(d) The only other debit entry was cash received from R. Deeping, who must have been a debtor who settled a debt in cash.

(e) On the credit side are the expenses which we paid in cash. On 2nd January, postage; on 6th January, cleaning materials; on 7th January, travelling expenses.

(f) The words 'Sundry Expenses' refer to a general account where many small expenses can be collected together. Such things as string, wrapping paper, refreshments for the typists etc., might be collected together in this way.

(g) 'Purchases' is a rather special account because it refers to all the things we buy to sell again. Thus postage stamps are not 'Purchases' even though we do purchase them. 'Purchases' has a special meaning in business,

(h) The only other item on the credit side is the item 'bank'. This refers to the banking of surplus cash to reduce the chances of theft. Most firms bank every day, and most supermarkets bank every hour, to give the maximum safety. It is never wise to keep too much 'takings' in the tills or in a safe in the office.

(i) Notice that, where possible, ditto marks are used to save time.

(j) Later if you learn book-keeping properly you will learn that all entries appear in two accounts, which gives rise to the term 'double-entry' book-keeping. The other entry is always in a second account, for example, the Capital coming into the Cash Account on 1st January has also to appear in the Capital Account. Each word written in the details account is also the name of a second account where the double-entry will be recorded.

(k) The numbers in the folio column are the page numbers of these accounts. Thus stamps go into the Postage Account, so we write 'Postage' in the details column and the folio number of this account is L9. 'Taking' is the money we take when we sell things and the entry would be made in the Sales Account, which is L10. You will gradually get used to the sort of words used for account headings.

(l) At the end of the day we 'balance off' the account. To do this we add up the debit side and add up the credit side. The debit side will always be larger, because you cannot take more out of a cash box than you have in it. Find the difference between the two and this is the 'balance' of cash in hand. (At this point in a real office you would check your cash box or till to make sure you really had this cash in hand.) Enter this balance on the credit side, which makes the two totals the same (£1223.12 in the example). Then bring the balance down on the left-hand side to start a new week on 8th January.

21.3 Exercises: simple Cash Accounts

1 For the first day of A. J. Smith's business his Cash Account had the following entries. Make these entries in his account. Some suggested names of accounts for the details column have been put in brackets to help you.

19. .
July 1 Starting contribution of capital £100.00
Paid for key cutting £3.85 (Sundry Expenses)
Paid for goods for re-sale £27.25 (Purchases)
Paid for rent £25.00 (Rent)
Paid for minor repairs £6.95 (Repairs)
Paid to delivery man £10.00 (Gratuities)
Paid to M. Layside £14.72 (M. Layside)
Paid for cleaning materials £4.26 (Cleaning)
Received for sales for the day £138.25 (Sales)

Balance off the account at the end of the day and bring down the balance ready for July 2nd.

2 For the first day of M. Astroseal's business his Cash Account had the following entries. Make these entries in his account.

19. .
Aug. 1 Starting contribution of capital £85.00
Paid for repairs to door £10.50

Paid for goods for re-sale £32.25 (Purchases)
Sales for the day £162.25
Paid for minor office equipment £8.20 (Office Equipment)
Paid to delivery man £3.50 for goods for re-sale
Paid for postage stamps £3.20
Paid for goods for re-sale £17.38

Balance off the account at the end of the day and bring down the balance ready for August 2nd.

3 Enter the following items in the Cash Account of Peter Lewis, a builders' merchant. The names of some suggested accounts are given at the end of the exercise.

19. .
July 1 Began business with capital of £300.00. Paid for account book (stationery) £6.50, office equipment £27.30, stamps £3.20.
Takings in cash £85.00.
2 Takings in cash £163.00. Purchases for re-sale £132.50, paid for cleaning materials £7.25.
3 Paid for stationery £4.25, paid R. Levinson £22.85, paid for repairs to front steps £13.50. Cash takings £133.40.
4 Paid for sundry expenses £3.60, paid to charity £1.50, paid M. Green £42.50. Cash takings £133.25.
5 Paid rent £18.50, paid to bank £500. Daily takings £198.20.

Balance off Peter Lewis's account and bring down the balance ready for the start of business on Monday 8th July. (Suggested accounts: Capital Account, Sales Account, Stationery Account, Office Equipment Account, Postage Account, Purchases Account, Sundry Expenses Account, R. Levinson Account, Repairs Account, M. Green Account, Rent Account, Bank Account.)

21.4 A simple Bank Account

You should now consider the Bank Account shown over the page.

BANK ACCOUNT

19. .			£	19. .			£
Jan. 1	Balance	b/d	1275.97	Jan. 1	R. Barber		127.24
1	R. Salmon		155.29	1	Office Equipment		174.25
3	Cash		1325.60	2	M. Blackburn		55.30
5	Cash		1475.60	3	Cambridgeshire C.C.		230.55
6	Dividends Rec'd		27.25	4	M. Brandon		426.25
				5	R. Knight		72.70
				6	Deposit A/c		2000.00
				6	Balance	c/d	1173.42
			£4259.71				£4259.71

			£
Jan. 8	Balance	b/d	1173.42

(a) At the start of this week we have a balance in the Bank Account of £1275.97.

(b) R. Salmon paid us £155.29 on 1st January.

(c) The items of cash on 3rd and 5th were moneys banked from the Cash Account.

(d) The item 'Dividends Rec'd' is the receipt of a cheque from a firm with whom we have invested money by buying shares. The dividend is a receipt of profits from the firm.

(e) Money was paid to creditors on the 1st, 2nd, 3rd, 4th and 5th. Creditors are people to whom we owe money for goods or services supplied.

(f) The item 'Office Equipment' on 1st January is the purchase of an asset.

(g) The item 'Deposit A/c' is the transfer of £2000 to a separate account which will earn interest (interest is not earned on ordinary current accounts).

(h) The account is balanced off and brought down to start the new week (assuming that the 7th is a Sunday). Note that it is absolutely wrong to fail to bring the balance down, leaving the impression that the account is clear. We will usually have a debit balance on a Bank Account.

21.5 Why some people get the wrong idea about Bank Accounts!

When we have an account with a bank it always appears from any conversation with our banker that when we have money in the bank we are in credit. 'I see your account has a credit balance', says the bank manager, 'Well done!' It leads us to think that when we have money in the bank it is a credit balance, whereas we can see from 1st January above, that when we have money in the bank we have a debit balance.

The reason is that the bank keeps our account from its point of view: we are in credit because we have given the bank our money, and we are a creditor of the bank because we are a person to whom the bank owes money. When the bank manager says 'Well done', he means: 'Thank you for giving us this money, it is very kind of you'. So do be clear, as far as *our* Bank Account is concerned, in *our* books, money in the bank is a *debit* balance, the bank is a debtor; that is, the bank owes us our money back again.

21.6 Exercises: simple Bank Accounts

1 P. Hammersley has a Bank Account, the folio number of which is L12. On 17th March 19. . it has a balance in the bank (a debit balance) of £1705.39. Enter this balance and then make the following subsequent entries.

(a) Paid T. Hall £42.50 by cheque.

(b) Paid City Council £195.80 by cheque for rates due.

(c) Eclipse & Co. paid us £45.00 by cheque for work undertaken in February.

(d) Paid H. Ecott £176.50 by cheque for supplies delivered in February.

(e) Cash takings paid into bank £480.75.

(f) Bank notified us that they had deducted £52.50 for interest and charges.

Balance off the account at the end of the day and bring down the balance for 18th March.

2 B. L. Hamilton has a Bank Account, the folio number of which is L2. On 25th June 19. . it has a balance in the bank of £1385.20. Enter this balance and then make the following subsequent entries. Then balance off the account and bring down the balance ready for 26th June.

(a) Paid P. King £175.50 by cheque.
(b) Paid A. Landlord £120.00 by cheque for rent due.
(c) P. Knebworth paid us £456.00 for work undertaken in May.
(d) Paid M. Kirk £176.50 for supplies delivered in May.
(e) Cash takings paid into bank £680.85.
(f) Bank notified us that they had credited us with £72.50 interest on a gilt-edged security. (Be careful: if the bank says they have credited us, it is a *debit* in our account.)

3 J. Rix's Bank Account has a debit balance on Monday 1st December 19. . of £4275.32. Enter the following items and balance off the account at the end of the week bringing down the balance for the following week. The folio number of this account is L19.

Dec. 1 Paid by cheque to B. Howlett £196.85. Paid by cheque to F. Roach £27.72. Banked takings £842.50 from tills.

Dec. 2 C. Ridley paid us £242.25 by cheque. Paid City Council by cheque for rates £384.46. Banked takings from tills £796.80.

Dec. 3 Paid to M. Roberts £42.95 by cheque. A. H. Ripley paid us £27.98. Banked takings from tills £1427.55.

Dec. 4 Paid N. Robertson £416.50 by cheque. Paid T. Logan £27.84 by cheque. F. Robertson paid us £173.25 by cheque. Banked takings from tills £848.28.

Dec. 5 Paid M. Childs £42.65 by cheque. Paid Royal Hotel Ltd £129.25 by cheque. Banked takings from tills £1127.26. Bank notified receipt of dividend from United Coal Supplies Ltd £143.63. Transferred to Deposit Account £5000.00.

22
Petty Cash

22.1 The work of the petty cashier

While the cashier is responsible for the main Cash Account and Bank Account for any business, there are many items of expenditure too trivial for such an important member of staff. To handle tiny payments such as bus fares, postage, and other minor expenses it is usual to appoint a petty cashier, frequently in the Post Department.

A sum of money, called the **imprest**, is allocated to the petty cashier by the chief cashier, and is usually enough money to last one week. Suppose this sum is £100; the petty cashier draws the imprest and enters it on the debit side of a specially ruled book, the Petty Cash Book. Because the petty cashier does not receive money very often (once a week from the cashier and very occasionally from other people), the debit side is not printed in full, and the entries made on the debit side (debit the account which receives goods, or services or money) are written in a cash column only. The 'centre' of the page for the Petty Cash Book is therefore displaced to the left-hand side, which means the credit side of the book can have much more room. This room is used for a number of analysis columns, the use of which will be made clear.

Look at Figure 22.1 and read the notes below so that you fully understand the ruling of a Petty Cash Book kept under the **Imprest System**.

(a) The 'centre' of the page is offset towards the left-hand side.
(b) The debit side is reduced to a single money column, and the details about the debit entries are written in the details column on the credit side. Consequently on these lines there are no entries in the money columns on the credit side.

(c) The credit side is extended to include several **analysis columns**. Only the first column headed 'Total' is the real credit side of the account, in which all money paid out (credit the giver) is entered. Each amount is then analysed off into columns where the various expenses can be collected together, Postage, Travelling Expenses etc. The last column, 'Ledger A/cs', is different from the rest, and has a separate column for folio numbers alongside it.
(d) On 4th April the cashier gives the petty cashier the imprest of £100, which is entered on the debit side. The PCV column (PCV means 'petty cash voucher') is a column where we record the number of the documents used to authorise the payments (see below). There is no document in this case, instead we write the page of the Cash Book from which the £100 came (CB 179).
(e) As payments are made they are entered on the credit side, and analysed off as well into an analysis column, so each figure has to appear twice: once in the total column, and once in the analysis column.
(f) Certain items cannot be collected with other items, for example we paid T. Smith £11.24. This could not be muddled in with other items, and consequently there is a separate folio column so that it can be posted to T. Smith's account separately.
(g) The only other item of cash received was £18.42 collected from staff for private telephone calls. This appears on the debit side and would be cleared to the Telephone A/c, which we can see is page 42 in the ledger (L42).
(h) At the end of the week a line is drawn right across the credit side and all the columns are added. We then cross-total the analysis

Figure 22.1 The ruling of a Petty Cash Book

| Debit Side | | | | | | | | | | | | | | | Credit Side | PCB 17 | |
£	p	Date	Details	PCV	Total £	p	Postage £	p	Travelling £	p	Stationery £	p	Sundry Expen. £	p	F	Ledger A/cs £	p
100	=	19.. Apr 4	Imprest Received	CB17/4													
		4	Postage Stamps	1	27	30	27	30									
		5	Train Fares (Reading)	2	9	65			9	65							
		5	Envelopes	3	13	65					13	65					
		6	Recorded Delivery Leaflets	4	4	25	4	25									
		6	Cleaning Materials	5	3	65							3	65			
		6	Bus Fares	6	=	68			=	68							
		7	Refreshments/Visitors	7	8	26							8	26			
		7	T. Smith	8	11	24									L17	11	24
18	42	8	Telephone Cash Received	L42													
		8	Gratuity (Rubbish Clearance)	9	1	=							1	=			
		9	Postage Stamps	10	14	25	14	25									
					93	93	45	80	10	33	13	65	12	91		11	24
		9	Balance	c/d	24	49	(L3)		(L33)		(L45)		(L73)				
£118	42				£118	42											
24	49	11	Balance	b/d													
75	61	11	Imprest Restored	CB18/7													

columns to make sure they total to the same figure as the total column, as it is easy to forget to analyse one of them off.

(i) The balance on the book is now found by taking the total on the credit side from the total on the debit side. The balance in this case is £24.49 which is entered in the usual way on the credit side, and then carried down to the debit side. Note that c/d means 'carried down' and b/d means 'brought down'.

(j) The imprest is then restored by the cashier after checking that the book has been properly kept. Note that the cashier does not provide another £100; only enough money to make the balance up to £100. The actual figure is what was spent: £93.93 minus £18.42 collected for telephone calls = £75.51.

(k) Finally, the totals of the analysis columns are posted to the various ledger accounts, and the folio numbers L25 etc. written in a circle below the column. The petty cash vouchers obtained when money was spent are numbered, 1, 2, 3 etc., and entered in the PCV column.

Although this sounds rather complicated it is, in fact, a very simple procedure and it is easy to keep such a book and take employment as a petty cashier.

22.2 Exercises: the Petty Cash Book

In examinations you are sometimes provided with specially-ruled petty cash paper. At other times you have to draw up paper quickly in your own format. Stick to the design given above in Figure 22.1 for the exercises below.

1 A petty cashier keeps a book with an initial imprest of £75, and analysis columns for Petrol, Fares, Office Expenses, Postage and Ledger Accounts. On 4th July 19.., she starts by drawing the full imprest from the chief cashier. Expenses are then as follows:

July 4 Paid postage £4.50; stationery £12.60 (office expenses).
,, 5 Paid for petrol £9.95; postage £1.32; to R. Longhurst £12.50.
,, 6 Paid bus fares £1.20; office expenses £3.25.

,, 7 Paid postage £3.25; collected telephone charges from staff (private calls) £18.25.
,, 8 Paid train fares £7.25. Paid M. Haworth £14.25.

Make the necessary entries, balance off the book at the end of the week and bring the balance down. Invent suitable folio numbers and petty cash voucher numbers.

2 Draw up a Petty Cash Book with columns for Travelling Expenses, Postage, Stationery, Carriage, Sundries and Ledger Accounts. Then enter the following:

May 1 Balance b/d was £4.60 and imprest was restored to £70.00.
,, 2 Paid for stamps £3.20; rail fares £6.45.
,, 3 Paid for envelopes £2.85; postage on parcels £5.50, tea, sugar etc. £2.90 (sundries).
,, 4 Stamps £1.60. Received £0.50 for phone call from member of staff.
,, 5 Paid a creditor Mr Charles £12.25; postage for parcels £4.80; taxi fare £3.75; labels £2.35 (stationery).
,, 6 Postage for parcels £5.10. Office cleaner was paid £9.30 (sundries).
,, 6 Balance off on this date, and collect new imprest to restore the imprest to £70.00. Invent suitable folio numbers and PCV numbers.

3 Draw up a Petty Cash Book with columns for Travelling Expenses, Postage, Stationery, Carriage, Sundries and a Ledger Accounts column, then enter the following:

May 1 Balance b/d was £24.60 and imprest was restored to £100.00.
,, 2 Paid for stamps £13.20; rail fares £6.45.
,, 3 Paid for envelopes £12.85; postage on parcels £5.90.
,, 4 Stamps £1.60. Received £19.50 for phone calls from members of staff.
,, 5 Paid a creditor Mr Marshall £12.45; postage for parcels £2.80; taxi fare £3.95; envelopes £12.85.
,, 6 Postage for parcels £5.60. The office cleaner was paid £10.

,, 6 Balance off on this date, and collect cash from the cashier to restore the imprest to £100.00. Invent suitable folio numbers and PCV numbers.

4 Enter transactions in a Petty Cash Book having analysis columns for Postage, Advertising, Part-time Staff Wages, General Expenses and Ledger Accounts. The opening balance is £10.55.

Apr. 24 Received £89.45 to restore imprest to £100.00.

,, 25 Paid for office flowers £2.75; £8.80 for repairs to office cabinet.

,, 26 Paid for ad. in local paper £4.60; received £6.50 for postage stamps taken by staff; paid Box Pack Co. £15.15; £12.80 for part time wages.

,, 27 Paid for tea etc. £3.35.

,, 28 Wages £10.50; purchased postage stamps £9.60; a member of the staff paid Petty Cashier £3.60 for private phone call.

,, 29 Window cleaning £3.90; paid wages £16.30; for advert £2.90.

,, 30 Balance off the book on this date, bring down the balance and have the imprest restored to £100.00. Invent suitable folio numbers and PCV numbers.

5 Enter the following in a Petty Cash Book with six analysis columns: Stationery, Postage, Fares, Hotel Expenses, General Expenses and a Ledger Accounts column.

Mar. 1 Balance b/d £45.50 and imprest of £54.50 restored (to bring to £100).

,, 4 Stationery expenses £4.25; paid for coffee, tea etc. £2.10.

,, 6 Paid for stamps £1.60; staff fares £8.60.

,, 9 Paid traveller's hotel expenses £15.50; collected £4.75 from a staff member for an international call (Telephone A/c); paid Contract Cleaning Ltd £12.30.

,, 12 £3.80 spent on stamps.

,, 13 Staff fares £8.60; plant for office £3.00.

,, 16 Settled traveller's hotel bill £17.25.

,, 20 Paid staff their fares £8.60; paid for tea etc. £3.75; stationery expenses £1.30.

,, 26 Balance off on this date and restore imprest to £100.00. Invent suitable folio numbers and PCV numbers.

23

Depreciation

23.1 What is depreciation?

Everything wears out with use. The car I buy today loses value year by year and will be on the scrap heap ten years from now. Today's brand new typewriter is next year's hard-worked typing pool model and in ten years it is a museum specimen. This presents two problems to the business:

(a) How shall we charge the cost of the motor vehicle or the typewriter to the business?
(b) What value shall we place on it at any given time?

Suppose a car costs £5000. If we include the price of this car as one of the costs of the business, it will reduce the profits for the year by £5000. It will also reduce the value of the car on our books to zero, because when we write a cost off the profits we must reduce the cost of the asset on our books by the same amount. As the car will still be valuable next year it is silly to have it on our books at zero value, and if we reduce the profits drastically in this way the investors in our company will not be able to have any dividends and, even more important, the Government will not be able to obtain its taxes to run the social services, armed forces etc.

The solution is to write off only a fair share of the value of each asset we own, so that the value on our books only declines by a 'fair' amount, and the profits only reduce by a 'fair' amount. This is called 'depreciating the asset'. The question is: 'How much is fair?' Business people answer this question in many different ways, but here we only need to learn three methods.

(a) The straight-line method
(b) The diminishing balance method
(c) The revaluation method

23.2 The straight-line method of depreciation

By this method we reduce the value of the asset by the same amount each year. The formula for how much to write off is as follows:

$$\text{Depreciation} = \frac{\text{cost price} - \text{residual value}}{\text{lifetime in years}}$$

The residual value is the final value (the residue of value) left at the end of the lifetime of the asset. Suppose we believe that our cars in general use will last five years, and will then be unreliable, so that we prefer to buy a new car. Although less reliable they will not be worthless, and can probably fetch £500 trade-in value. So depreciation each year will be:

$$\text{Depreciation} = \frac{£5000 - £500}{5}$$

$$= \frac{£4500}{5}$$

$$= £900$$

So every year we will write off £900 for this car from the profits and reduce the car's value by £900. The car will fall in value as shown below:

Day 1	Day 1	Day 1	Day 1	Day 1	Day 1
Year 1	Year 2	Year 3	Year 4	Year 5	Year 6
£5000	£4100	£3200	£2300	£1400	£500

The car is now unreliable and we will trade it in and buy a new car. Of course, we might get £800 or £700 or only £200 when we actually try to trade it in. This will mean either a profit on sale or a loss on sale of the old car, which we will have to take into account in Year 6. It is impossible to get depreciation exactly right, as it is only an estimate (or, as one joker said, a guesstimate).

23.3 Exercises: depreciation by the straight-line method

1 Work out the straight-line depreciation per annum on each of the following items. (Answer correct to the nearest pound where necessary.)

Asset	Cost price (£)	Residual value (£)	Expected lifetime (years)
(a) Car	8 600	1600	5
(b) Lorry	26 500	4500	4
(c) Computer	8 250	1250	5
(d) Typewriter	1 900	—	8
(e) Copier	2 450	450	10

2 Work out the straight-line depreciation per annum on each of the following items. (Answer correct to the nearest pound where necessary.)

Asset	Cost price (£)	Residual value (£)	Expected lifetime (years)
(a) Car	12 500	2 500	6
(b) Light aircraft	96 000	16 000	10
(c) Industrial plant	38 850	1 200	30
(d) Pipeline	7 350 000	—	50
(e) Crude-oil carrier	£29 million	£4.5 million	15

23.4 The diminishing-balance method of depreciation

The straight-line method of depreciation has one disadvantage: it writes off the same amount every year. Unfortunately there is another expense involved with assets: they need occasional repairs and servicing. The trouble is that these costs are generally low in the first few years and then rise in the later years. This gives a bigger write-off (when depreciation and repairs are put together) in later years than in earlier years, which some people argue is unfair.

Their solution is to adopt the diminishing balance method. Here we write off the **same percentage** every year of the **diminishing balance** on the Asset Account. Consider the car described earlier, which cost £5000. Depreciation is to be written off at the rate of 25% on the diminishing balance.

			£
Day 1 Year 1	Cost	=	5000
End of Year 1	Depreciation =		1250 ($\frac{1}{4}$ of £5000)
Day 1 Year 2	Balance	=	3750
End of Year 2	Depreciation =		938 ($\frac{1}{4}$ of £3750, correct to nearest £1)
Day 1 Year 3	Balance	=	2812
End of Year 3	Depreciation =		703 ($\frac{1}{4}$ of £2812)
Day 1 Year 4	Balance	=	2109
End of Year 4	Depreciation =		527 ($\frac{1}{4}$ of £2109)
Day 1 Year 5	Balance	=	1582
End of Year 5	Depreciation =		396 ($\frac{1}{4}$ of £1582)
Day 1 Year 6			1186

Each year the amount of depreciation is less, but the cost of repairs will be rising, making a fair share of costs applied to each year.

23.5 The revaluation method of depreciation (or appreciation)

The third possible method of depreciation is the revaluation method. With some assets it is impossible to say that the value depreciates by a certain amount each year, or a fixed percentage each year. Take a zoo, with an asset, an elephant. Can we say 'Jumbo has depreciated by 30 per cent this year' or 'Jumbo will have a residual value of £1000'? Clearly, it is difficult. Similarly, a cow may have a calf and the two animals be worth more, not less, at the end of the year. This is called **appreciation**, an increase in value over the year. Machine tools are another asset that is treated in this way. Many firms make jigs and presses that stamp out part for all sorts of assembly work. These tools are added to each year, and some are scrapped from time to time. A single press tool for a toy plastic motor car may cost £10 000 to make. The only way to value what you have in this sort of area, is to revalue the stock each year.

Consider a farmer's herd of prize cattle. Suppose in Year 1 they are worth £100 000. In Year 2 they are valued at £140 000. There has been an appreciation, not a depreciation. We need to take a profit into account, not write off a loss. In Year 3 the herd is wiped out by foot-and-mouth disease. We have a depreciation of £140 000, offset by a Government grant in compensation for the slaughter of the herd of £45 000, therefore:

$$\text{Depreciation} = £140\,000 - £45\,000$$
$$= \underline{\underline{£95\,000}}$$

23.6 Exercises: more about depreciation

1 (a) Calculate the depreciation each year, for the first three years, on each of the following items, which are depreciated by $33\frac{1}{3}\%$ per annum. (b) What is the final value on the books of each of these assets? (All calculations to be made correct to the nearest £1.)

Items	Cost on 1st January, Year 1
(a)	£740
(b)	£3 670
(c)	£5 540
(d)	£18 900
(e)	£26 920

2 (a) Calculate the depreciation to be deducted each year for the first three years, on each of the assets below, which are purchased on 1st January in Year 1, and are depreciated at the rate shown. (b) What is the value of each asset on 1st January in Year 4? (All calculations to be made correct to the nearest £1.)

Asset	Cost price (£)	Depreciation rate (%)
(a)	550	20
(b)	880	20
(c)	1 250	25
(d)	2 750	25
(e)	55 000	30

3 The assets in the following list were not purchased at the start of the financial year, and only a fair proportion of the depreciation is to be deducted in the first year. In subsequent years a full year's depreciation will be deducted. (a) Calculate the depreciation on each for the first three years of each asset. (b) What is the value on 1st January in Year 4, in each case? (Calculate correct to the nearest £1.)

Asset	Date of purchase, Year 1	Cost price (£)	Rate of depreciation (%)
(a)	July 1	460	25
(b)	July 1	2 300	25
(c)	October 1	5 700	$33\frac{1}{2}$
(d)	October 1	9 200	$33\frac{1}{2}$
(e)	April 1	15 670	$33\frac{1}{2}$

4 A herd of cows is valued at £146 550 on 1st January 19.., and at the end of the year it is valued at £132 750. What is the depreciation for the year?

5 A circus values its animals at £478 000 on 1st January 19... On 31st December of the same year they are valued at £531 000, and an insurance claim has also been admitted for £5200 for the death of a lion which had to be shot after being set free by vandals. How would you treat the change in value, and what is the final figure on the Animals Account at 31st December?

24

Measuring Lengths, Areas and Volumes

24.1 The art of measuring in a three-dimensional world

Lengths, areas and volumes are an important part of business calculations. They are of great importance in trade and transport; for example, containers of a certain size only can be carried through railway tunnels without jamming the train in the tunnel. Many aircraft will only take packages of a certain size and there are limits to the **dimensions** of postal packages acceptable to the Post Office. When selling goods to householders we find that the **area** to be covered, for example of floors or walls, is often of crucial importance, while the **volume** of rooms and cupboards and corridors may be vital in the building trades.

The United Kingdom has still not quite completed the change to the metric system, but the advantages of using a simple decimal system are such that nearly all measurements today are given in metres and centimetres rather than the old imperial measures. The basic unit for lengths, areas and volumes is thus the metre.

We live in a three-dimensional world, though time is sometimes referred to as the fourth dimension. The first dimension of anything is the **length**, which is always taken to be the longest measurement. When measuring the next dimension we speak of the **breadth** (how broad a thing is) or the **width** (how wide it is). The third dimension is the **height**, though if the height is not very great we often speak of the **thickness**. Thus we do not speak of the height of floor-covering or carpet, we speak of its thickness.

In geometrical terms, an **area** is the space enclosed by a two-dimensional shape, whereas a **volume** is the space enclosed by a three-dimensional figure, or **solid.**

Square measure and cubic measures

When measuring area (a two-dimensional space), we have to use square measure. The basic unit is a square metre, which is written by the symbol m^2. For smaller areas less than $1\,m^2$ (one square metre) we usually use square centimetres, written cm^2. For measuring very large areas of land we do not use acres (the old imperial measure for land), but hectares. A hectare is a piece of land 100 metres by 100 metres, i.e. $10\,000\,m^2$. The full metric table of square measure is given below. You will understand it best if you set down one square centimetre on a piece of scrap paper and mark in the millimetres along the edge. If you join up the marks to give a grid you will find there are 100 square millimetres in a square centimetre.

Square measure

100 square millimetres = 1 square centimetre
100 square centimetres = 1 square decimetre
100 square decimetres = 1 square metre
100 square metres   = 1 are (pronounced 'air')
100 ares   = 1 hectare
100 hectares   = 1 square kilometre

In symbol form this reads:

$$100\,mm^2 = 1\,cm^2$$
$$100\,cm^2 = 1\,dm^2$$
$$100\,dm^2 = 1\,m^2$$
$$100\,m^2 = 1\,are$$
$$100\,a = 1\,ha$$
$$100\,ha = 1\,km^2$$

The same system applies to cubic measures. There will be $10 \times 10 \times 10$ cubic millimetres in a cubic centimetre, written:

$$1000\,mm^3 = 1\,cm^3$$

In real life we usually only meet cubic centimetres and cubic metres. For example, freight forwarders have to measure crates with cubic metres (m^3) because they have to pay for the transport of goods according to the volume of the space the goods occupy in a ship's hold or an aircraft's luggage hold. Thus on every export document a written statement of volume (m^3) is required, and the freight forwarder must state the volume of the package or crate in transit. Cubic metres is also used in building work; for example, schools, colleges and hospitals must have rooms large enough to give each pupil, student or patient a certain volume of air, and the architect must meet these planning requirements if the planning authority is to pass the plans.

24.2 Perimeters and areas (squares and rectangles)

A geometric figure with only two dimensions is called a plane figure. If the corners of the figures are right angles the figure is said to be a rectangle, while if all the sides are the same length it is called a square. Consider Figure 24.1 and read the notes (a) to (d) below it.

Figure 24.1 A square and a rectangle

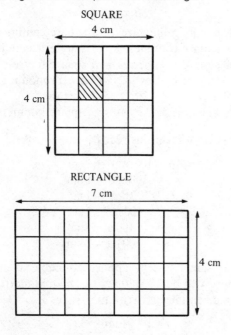

SQUARE

4 cm

4 cm

RECTANGLE

7 cm

4 cm

(a) A rectangle is a four-sided figure with all its angles right angles (90°).

(b) A square is a special case of a rectangle, it is a rectangle with all four sides the same length.
(c) The perimeter of a plane figure is the distance all the way round the edge. Thus the perimeter of the square is $4 \times 4\,cm = 16\,cm$, while the perimeter of the rectangle is 22 cm. The perimeter of the rectangle may be found by adding the two sides together and doubling the answer: $(4\,cm + 7\,cm) \times 2 = 11\,cm \times 2 = 22\,cm$; or by taking $2 \times 4\,cm$ and $2 \times 7\,cm$, and adding the results together.
(d) The formula for the area of the figures is: Area = length × breadth. So the area of the square is $4\,cm \times 4\,cm = 16\,cm^2$, and the area of the rectangle is $7\,cm \times 4\,cm = 28\,cm^2$.

After studying Figure 24.1 we are ready to answer such simple questions as those given below.

24.3 Exercises: perimeters and areas

1 Find the perimeter of squares having sides measuring as follows.

(a) 7 cm
(b) 12 cm
(c) 15 cm
(d) 1.5 m
(e) 4.25 m
(f) 100 m

2 Find the perimeter of rectangles measuring as follows.

(a) 7 cm × 10 cm
(b) 12 cm × 18 cm
(c) 4 m × 9 m
(d) 22 m × 12 m
(e) 100 m × 120 m
(f) 85 m × 65 m

3 What is the breadth of a rectangular playground which is 120 metres long and has a perimeter of 380 metres?
4 What is the length of a rectangular playing field which is 200 metres broad and has a perimeter of 1 kilometre?
5 Find the area of the squares whose sides are given below.

(a) 5 cm
(b) 9 cm
(c) 13 cm
(d) 20 cm
(e) 4.2 metres
(f) 5.8 metres

6 Find the area of the rectangles whose dimensions are given below.

	Length	*Breadth*
(a)	62 cm	15 cm
(b)	36 cm	12 cm
(c)	90 cm	33 cm
(d)	77 cm	45 cm
(e)	$3\frac{1}{2}$ m	1 m
(f)	4 m	$2\frac{1}{2}$ m
(g)	13 m	8 m
(h)	16 m	10 m
(i)	250 m	196 m
(j)	360 m	480 m

24.4 Areas of irregular rectangular figures

Many rooms and pieces of land have irregular shapes that are still based upon rectangular figures. Consider the room illustrated in Figure 24.2.

Such a shape can be divided up into two parts by continuing the line BC to meet the side FE at the point T. We are then left with two parts to the room, a large square ABTF of side 2.5 metres and a rectangle CDET. Because the opposite sides of a rectangle must be equal, it is possible to discover the missing measurement for the rectangle CDET. DE measures 1.35 metres, but what is the length of CD? The answer is 2 metres, because the full side FE is 4.5 metres, and the left-hand end FT must be the same length as AB, that is 2.5 metres. Therefore the remaining part TE must be 2 metres. Therefore the area of CDET is $2\,m \times 1.35\,m = 2.70\,m^2$.

The calculation of the area of such irregular figures is therefore done in parts:

$$\text{Area of Part (i)} = 2.5\,m \times 2.5\,m$$
$$= 6.25\,m^2$$
$$\text{Area of Part (ii)} = 2\,m \times 1.35\,m$$
$$= 2.7\,m^2$$
$$\text{Therefore total area} = 6.25\,m^2 + 2.7\,m^2$$
$$= 8.95\,m^2$$

```
 2.5
 2.5
 ----
 12 5
 50 0
 ----
 6.25
```

Another type of irregular figure is the type we get when a flower bed is surrounded by footpaths, or a picture is framed. Consider the illustrations in Figure 24.3, where we have to find the area of paths, lawns and flower beds.

In the garden layout we can find the area of the lawn and the paths in the following ways.

The area of the lawn is easy. Its dimensions are $26\,m \times 21\,m$ (2 metres must be deducted on each side from the overall dimensions of $30\,m \times 25\,m$).

$$\text{Area of lawn} = 26\,m \times 21\,m$$
$$= 546\,m^2$$

```
   26
   21
  ----
   26
  520
 ----
 546 m²
```

For the area of the paths, we can use either of two methods, (a) or (b):

(a) Find the area of the whole garden and deduct the area of the lawn.

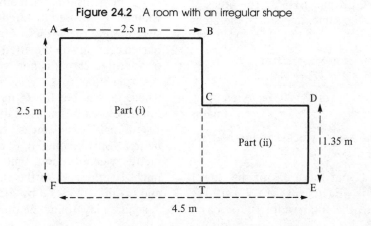

Figure 24.2 A room with an irregular shape

Figure 24.3 Garden and courtyard layouts

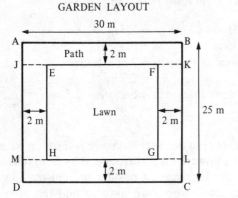

GARDEN LAYOUT

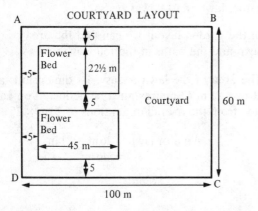

COURTYARD LAYOUT

Area of whole garden $= 30\,\text{m} \times 25\,\text{m}$
$$= 750\,\text{m}^2$$
Deduct the area of the lawn
$$= 750\,\text{m}^2 - 546\,\text{m}^2$$
$$= 204\,\text{m}^2 \text{ (area of paths)}$$

(b) Treat each part separately. The dotted lines indicate two long paths ABKJ and CDML, and two short paths FGLK and EHMJ. The areas of the long paths are the same, and so are the areas of the short paths.

Long paths $= 30\,\text{m} \times 2\,\text{m} \times 2 = 120\,\text{m}^2$
Short paths $= 21\,\text{m} \times 2\,\text{m} \times 2 = \underline{84\,\text{m}^2}$

Total $= \underline{204\,\text{m}^2}$ Area of paths

The answer is the same whichever method we use.

In the courtyard layout the areas of the flower beds are the same. Each is $45\,\text{m} \times 22\frac{1}{2}\,\text{m}$. We know this because the total width BC is 60 m.

Three paths of 5 m (15 m in all) and a flower bed of $22\frac{1}{2}\,\text{m}$ make $37\frac{1}{2}$ metres in all. Therefore the other flower bed must be $22\frac{1}{2}$ metres wide. Therefore:

Area of flower beds $= 45 \times 22\frac{1}{2} \times 2$
$$= 45 \times 45$$
$$= 2025\,\text{m}^2$$

$$
\begin{array}{r}
45 \\
45 \\
\hline
225 \\
1800 \\
\hline
2025 \\
\end{array}
$$

Area of whole figure is $100\,\text{m} \times 60\,\text{m}$
$$= 6000\,\text{m}^2$$
Area of courtyard and paths $= 6000\,\text{m}^2 - 2025\,\text{m}^2$
$$= 3975\,\text{m}^2$$

Of course, we could have found the area of the courtyard and paths by working out the area of each separate piece. The reader might like to do this for himself or herself and check that the result is the same.

24.5 Exercises: the areas of irregular figures

In the following exercises it is nearly always helpful to do a rough diagram in your exercise book, and mark in the dimensions. (Do not mark the textbook unless it is your own property.)

1 Find the areas of each of the irregular figures (i) to (iv) in Fig 24.4 below. All the measurements are in metres.
2 A room measuring 7 metres by 4 metres is completely covered by fitted carpet. An expensive oriental rug $4\frac{1}{2}$ metres by $3\frac{1}{2}$ metres is then placed centrally on the fitted carpet. How much of the fitted carpet is now visible?
3 A carpet $3\frac{1}{2}$ metres by $2\frac{1}{2}$ metres is laid in a room whose dimensions are $6\frac{1}{2}$ metres by $3\frac{1}{2}$ metres. Find the area of floor left uncovered.
4 A football pitch measures 80 metres $\times$ 60 metres. Surrounding it is a spectator area 6 metres wide all round. Find (a) the area of the pitch, (b) the area of the whole piece of land, and (c) the area used by spectators.
5 A square playground measures 32 m along each

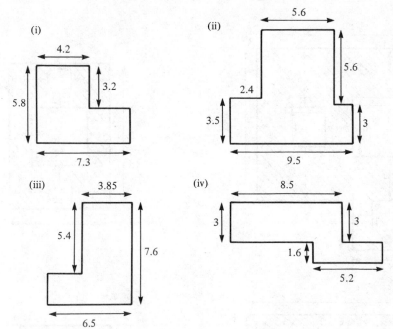

Figure 24.4 Four irregular figures

edge. Surrounding it is a path $2\frac{1}{2}$ m wide, and beyond the path are flower beds which are $1\frac{1}{2}$ m wide all round. What is the area of (a) the playground itself, (b) the paths, and (c) the flower beds?

6 What is the perimeter of a field 100 metres × 160 metres?

7 What is the perimeter of a hockey pitch 60 metres × 70 metres?

8 Using the measurements of Question 5 above, what is the external perimeter of (a) the playground, (b) the playground and path combined, and (c) the complete playground, park and gardens?

9 In each of the recreation areas (i) to (iv) in Figure 24.5 below, ornamental gardens are set in a courtyard area. You are asked to find the area of the courtyard (the shaded section) in each case. The simplest way is to find the area of the whole figure in square metres and deduct the areas of the gardens, in each case. All measurements are in metres.

24.6 Floors, walls and ceilings

One of the most common measuring problems in real life is concerned with redecorating our homes. Most houses have at least five or six rooms, and each needs redecorating every few years, so that the problem constantly recurs. The chief problems are:

(a) Covering the floor, either with fitted carpet, or with plastic floor-covering, or with tiles (which may be plastic or carpet tiles).

(b) Covering the ceilings, usually with emulsion paint or similar material, though occasionally a bad ceiling may be papered, or coated with a plastic material.

(c) Covering the walls, either with emulsion paint or similar material, or with wallpaper.

All these present simple calculation problems. These can be illustrated by considering the following example.

Example: A room is to be redecorated. It is 5.5 metres long by 4.5 metres wide, and 2.7 metres high. It is proposed to cover the floors with carpet tiles which are $\frac{1}{2}$ metre square. These are sold in packs of 10, which cost £8.50 per pack. The ceiling is to be given two coats of an emulsion paint which covers 15 m^2 per litre tin. These litre tins cost £2.25 each. The walls are to be papered with wallpaper. Each roll of wallpaper covers

Figure 24.5 Four exercises on irregular figures

(i)

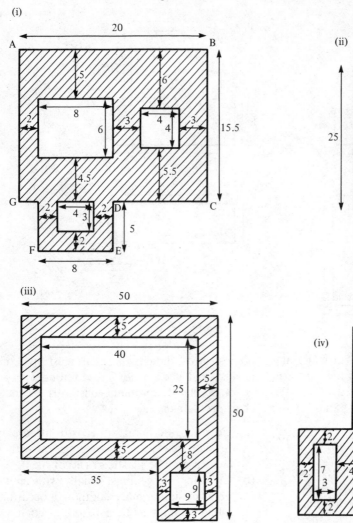

(ii)

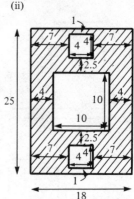

(iii)

(iv)

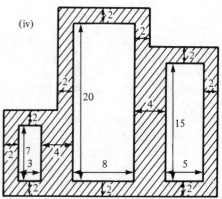

6.5 m² and costs £3.25. The doors and windows have a total area of $5\frac{1}{2}$ m². Find:

(a) The cost of the carpet tiles
(b) The cost of the paint for the ceiling
(c) The cost of the wallpaper
(d) The total cost, given that special paint for the doors and window frames cost £6.50

(*Note:* In all such exercises small quantities of paint, paper etc. are left over and can only be used for patching and improving later, when damage occurs.)

(a) *Covering the floor with carpet tiles*. The dimensions of the floor are 5.5 metres by 4.5 metres. To cover the floor with tiles measuring $\frac{1}{2}$ metre square we need to work out how many tiles are required. Along the $5\frac{1}{2}$ metre side we shall have a row of 11 tiles; and along the $4\frac{1}{2}$ metre side, 9 tiles will be required. We therefore need 11×9 tiles $= 99$ tiles. We should therefore have to buy 10 packs, costing £85.

(*Note:* There is an important point here. There is a difference between tiles which are $\frac{1}{2}$ metre square (meaning half a metre along each edge) and tiles which are $\frac{1}{2}$ m² (half a square metre). A tile which is $\frac{1}{2}$ metre square has an area of $\frac{1}{2}$ m $\times \frac{1}{2}$ m $= \frac{1}{4}$ m². It is important not to confuse these two measurements. Tiles are always $\frac{1}{2}$ metre square or $\frac{1}{4}$ metre square; the latter has an area of $\frac{1}{16}$ m^2.)

(b) *Painting the ceiling.* The dimensions of the ceiling are the same as the floor: 5.5 m × 4.5 m. The area is therefore:

$$\text{Area} = 5.5\,\text{m} \times 4.5\,\text{m}$$

$$\begin{array}{r} 5.5 \\ 4.5 \\ \hline 27\ 5 \\ 220\ 0 \\ \hline \end{array}$$

$$= 24.75\,\text{m}^2 \qquad 24.75$$

The number of tins required for 2 coats, if each tin of paint covers 15 m^2:

$$\text{No. of tins} = \frac{24.75 \times 2}{15}$$

$$= \frac{49.50}{15}$$

$$= 3.3\,\text{tins}$$

$$\begin{array}{r} 3.3 \\ 15\overline{)49.5} \\ 45 \\ \hline 4\ 5 \\ 4\ 5 \\ \hline \end{array}$$

We must therefore buy 4 tins of paint at £2.25 per tin = £9.

(c) *The area of the walls of a room.* When dealing with the areas of the walls of a room it is usual to regard the walls as laid out flat, rather as if a cardboard model had been prepared. We then have a figure like Figure 24.6, in which the length of the rectangle is the perimeter of the room, i.e. two lengths and two breadths. The width of the rectangle is the same as the height of the room. The dimensions are therefore 20 metres by 2.7 metres. The doors and the windows, we are told, measure $5\frac{1}{2}$ square metres.

Figure 24.6 The area of the walls of a room

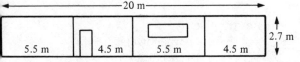

Area of walls to be papered
$$= 20\,\text{m} \times 2.7\,\text{m} - 5\tfrac{1}{2}\,\text{m}^2 \text{ (doors and windows)}$$
$$= 54\,\text{m}^2 - 5\tfrac{1}{2}\,\text{m}^2$$
$$= 48\tfrac{1}{2}\,\text{m}^2$$

As one roll of paper covers 6.5 square metres, we need:

No. of rolls
$$= 48\tfrac{1}{2}\,\text{m}^2 \div 6\tfrac{1}{2}\,\text{m}^2$$
$$= \tfrac{97}{2}_1 \times \tfrac{2^1}{13}\,\text{m}^2 \text{ (Cancelling by 2)}$$
$$= 7\tfrac{6}{13}\,\text{rolls} \ (7 \times 13 = 91)$$

We therefore need to buy 8 rolls at £3.25 per roll
$$\text{Cost} = 8 \times £3.25$$
$$= £26$$

The final total cost is as follows:

	£
Carpet	85
Ceilings	9
Walls	26
Door and windows	6.50
Total	£126.50

24.7 Exercises: floors, walls and ceilings

1 A room is 7 metres long, 5 metres wide and 3 metres high. Find the area of the walls after deducting 7 square metres for the area of the doors and windows.

2 A room is 3 metres square and $2\frac{1}{2}$ metres high. The door and window together have an area of 3 square metres. Find the area of (a) the ceiling, and (b) the walls.

3 What will be the area of the walls of a room 5.5 metres long, 3.5 metres wide and 3 metres high if the area of the doors and windows total 10 square metres?

4 What will be the area of the walls of a room 7 m long, 6 m wide and 4 m high if doors and windows have a total area of 14 m^2?

5 A squash court measures 7 metres by 12 metres and the room is 6 metres high. What will it cost to paint the walls (no doors or windows to deduct) with 3 coats of paint with a coverage of 15 square metres per litre? The paint costs £2.85 per 2 litre can.

6 A school hall is 18 metres long by 16 metres wide. The floor is to be sealed with a sealer costing £3.30 per tin. Each tin covers 12 m^2. (a) How many tins will be required? (b) What will be the total cost?

7 A room is 7 metres long, 6 metres wide and 3

metres high. The doors and windows have a total area of 6.25 square metres.

(a) What will it cost to carpet the floor with carpet tiles each $\frac{1}{2}$ metre square (not $\frac{1}{2}$ m^2) sold in packs of 10 for £9.45 per pack?

(b) What will it cost to paint the ceiling with 2 coats of emulsion at £2.75 per litre? One litre of paint covers 14 square metres.

(c) What is the area of the walls?

(d) What will it cost to cover the walls in paper, given that each roll covers 6.5 m^2 and costs £4.25?

8 A room is $5\frac{1}{2}$ metres long and $3\frac{1}{4}$ metres wide. The floor is to be tiled with square tiles, each side measuring $\frac{1}{4}$ metre, and costing 38p each. The walls, which are 3 metres high, are to be papered with wallpaper costing £3.45 per roll, giving a coverage of 6.5 m^2 each roll. The ceiling is to be painted with paint giving a coverage of 15 m^2 per tin, and each tin costing £2.50. Two coats of paint will be required. The doors and windows have an area of 5.5 square metres. They will cost £8 to paint. Find the total cost of this redecoration, if labour charges are £85.

24.8 Areas of triangles

Every triangle can be considered as half a rectangle. This is very easy to see in the case of a right-angled triangle (as in Figure 24.7 (i)), for the third side becomes the diagonal of the rectangle (in this case, a square) that completes the triangle. With triangles which are not right-angled triangles it is necessary to use two rectangles to complete the two parts of the triangle (as in Figure 24.7 (ii)). The explanation for the area of a triangle is as follows:

(a) In each case the triangle is half the area of the rectangle which can be constructed to surround it.

(b) The dimensions of these rectangles are found by the usual formula:

Area = length × breadth

(c) Note that in these cases it is the base of the triangle that can be taken as the length, and the perpendicular height (the height when

Figure 24.7 The area of a triangle

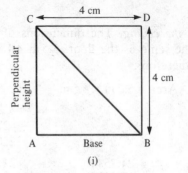

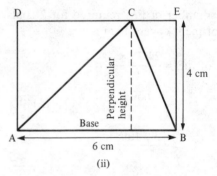

drawn at right angles to the base, passing through the apex of the triangle) that can be taken as the breadth. The formula for the area of the rectangles could therefore be re-written:

Area = base × perpendicular height

(d) The area of the triangle is therefore half of this:

Area of triangle = $\frac{1}{2}$ (base × perpendicular height)

The areas of the two triangles (i) and (ii) in Figure 24.7 are calculated as follows.

Area of triangle (i)
$= \frac{1}{2}$ (base × perpendicular height)
$= \frac{1}{2}$ (4 cm × 4 cm)
$= \frac{1}{2}$ (16 square centimetres)
$= 8$ cm^2

Area of triangle (ii)
$= \frac{1}{2}$ (6 cm × 4 cm)
$= \frac{1}{2}$ (24 cm^2)
$= 12$ cm^2

24.9 Exercises: areas of triangles

1 Find the areas of the following triangles whose dimensions are given below.

	Base	Perpendicular height
(a)	5 cm	4 cm
(b)	7 cm	9 cm
(c)	12 cm	8 cm
(d)	15 cm	12 cm
(e)	18 cm	15 cm

2 Find the areas of the following triangles whose dimensions are given below.

	Base	Perpendicular height
(a)	3 metres	2.5 metres
(b)	5 metres	3.6 metres
(c)	8 metres	8.4 metres
(d)	10 metres	6.5 metres
(e)	12 metres	9.5 metres

24.10 Volumes of cubes and cuboids

Three-dimensional objects that have all their sides the same length are known as **cubes**. Rectangular solids whose sides are not all the same length are called **cuboids**. The volume of cuboids is expressed in cubic measures, such as cubic centimetres (cm^3), cubic metres (m^3) etc.

The formula for the volume of a regular cuboid is:

$$\text{Volume} = \text{length} \times \text{breadth} \times \text{height}$$

Consider the cuboids in Figure 24.8. One of them is a regular cuboid (i) and the other an irregular cuboid (ii). (Actually (ii) is a box-like set of steps to be used to reach a raised dais in an assembly hall.) Note that just as irregular areas can be split up into a series of simple regular areas, this irregular cuboid can be split up into two regular cuboids.

(a) The first figure (i) is a regular cuboid, such as a packing case.

(b) The second figure (ii) can be made into two regular cuboids by drawing in the line DL. We then have a regular cuboid FEDLGHIM and another regular cuboid ABCLMJKN. (M and N, the other points of these regular cuboids, are hidden from view.)

Figure 24.8   A regular and an irregular cuboid

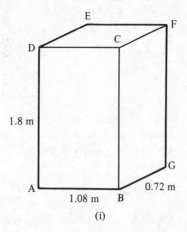

(i)

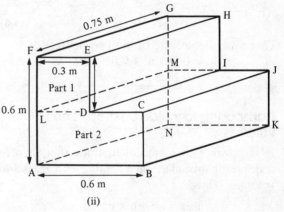

(ii)

The volumes of these two figures are calculated as follows:

Volume of cuboid (i) = length × breadth × height
= 1.08 m × 0.72 m × 1.8 m
= 1.39968 m^3

```
        1.08
        0.72
        ────
         216
        7560
        ──────
      0.7776 m²
         1.8
        ──────
       62208
       77760
       ──────
      1.39968
```

Volume of cuboid (ii)
= volume of Part 1 + volume of Part 2

Volume of Part $1 = l \times b \times h$
$$= 0.75\,m \times 0.3\,m \times 0.3\,m$$
$$= 0.75 \times 0.09\,m^2$$
$$= 0.0675\,m^3$$

```
    0.09
    0.75
  ─────
    45
   630
  ─────
  0.0675
```

Volume of Part $2 = l \times b \times h$
$$= 0.75\,m \times 0.6\,m \times 0.3\,m$$
$$= 0.75\,m \times 0.18\,m^2$$
$$= 0.135\,m^3$$

```
    0.75
    0.18
  ─────
   600
   750
  ─────
  .1350
```

Therefore the volume of the two figures
$$= 0.135\,m^3 + 0.0675\,m^3$$
$$= 0.2025\,m^3$$

Transposing formulae on areas and volumes

It is possible to meet calculations that involve transposing formulae when dealing with areas and volumes. Thus:

$$area = length \times breadth$$

Suppose we know the area and the length, but not the breadth. Rearranging the formula we have:

$$\frac{area}{length} = breadth \quad \text{(dividing both sides by the length)}$$

or

$$breadth = \frac{area}{length} \quad \text{(any equation may be reversed and it is still true)}$$

A similar formula can be produced to find the length, as in the first example below.

Example: (a) The area of a tea tray is 1500 sq. cm. If the tray is 30 cm broad, how long is it?

$$length = \frac{area}{breadth}$$
$$= \frac{1500\,cm^2}{30\,cm}$$
$$= 50\,cm$$

Similarly if we know the volume of a crate and the length and breadth (i.e. the area), we can calculate the height:

$$volume = l \times b \times h$$
$$\frac{volume}{l \times b} = h$$
$$h = \frac{volume}{l \times b}$$

Example: (b) A crate is 1.44 cubic metres in volume. The length is 1.2 metres and the width 0.8 metre. How high is it?

$$h = \frac{volume}{l \times b}$$
$$= \frac{1.44\,m^3}{1.2\,m \times 0.8\,m}$$
$$= \frac{1.44\,m^3}{0.96\,m^2}$$
$$= 1.5\,metres$$

```
        1.5
   96)144
       96
      ───
      480
      480
      ───
```

24.11 Exercises: volumes of cubes and cuboids

1 Export cargoes are packed in crates with the dimensions shown below. What will be the volume marked in the box headed 'Vol m³' on the export document?

	Length	Breadth	Height
(a)	60 cm	40 cm	30 cm
(b)	120 cm	90 cm	60 cm
(c)	100 cm	70 cm	50 cm
(d)	2.4 metres	1.6 metres	0.6 metre
(e)	1.3 metres	1.2 metres	0.8 metre
(f)	1.4 metres	0.6 metre	1.2 metres
(g)	1.6 metres	0.5 metre	1.7 metres
(h)	1.5 metres	0.8 metre	1.2 metres
(i)	2.6 metres	0.9 metre	1.5 metres
(j)	3.2 metres	1.1 metres	0.9 metre

2 How many packets $4\,cm \times 4\,cm \times 3\,cm$ can be packed into each of the following crates?

	Length	Breadth	Height
(a)	2 m	1 m	1.2 m
(b)	2.8 m	1 m	1.05 m

Figure 24.9   Irregular cuboids

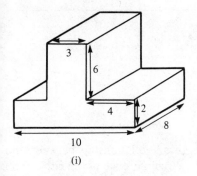

(i)

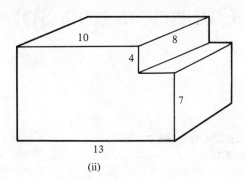

13

(ii)

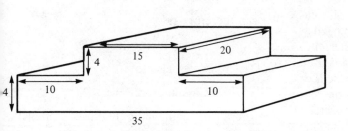

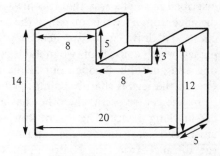

(c)	1.5 m	1.6 m	1.2 m
(d)	1.4 m	1.2 m	0.9 m
(e)	1.4 m	1.2 m	0.75 m

3 Find the volume of each of the cuboids in Figure 24.9. The dimensions are given in centimetres.

4 The volume of a rectangular crate is 4.2 m³. If the area of the base is 2.8 m², how high is it?

5 The volume of a rectangular stage is 54 m³. If it measures 9 metres by 12 metres, how high is it raised above the ordinary flooring?

25
Circles, Cylinders and Spheres

25.1 The Radius, Diameter and Circumference

A circle is a round, plane figure enclosed by a line inscribed in such a way that it is always the same distance from a fixed point called the **centre** of the circle. To draw circles we need a **pair of compasses**, which consists of two metal legs, hinged at one end and able to open out at the other end. One of the legs is sharply pointed, which is used to fix the centre point; the other has a pencil- or ink-marking device. The extent to which the legs are pulled apart decides the **radius** of the circle: the distance from the centre point to the line drawn, which is called the **circumference**. An infinite number of radii can be imagined as drawn in the circle; but where two radii are opposite one another to form a continuous line across the circle, they form the **diameter**. These parts of a circle have been illustrated in Figure 25.1.

Figure 25.1 The parts of a circle

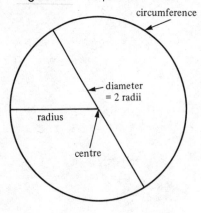

As we can see, a diameter equals two radii, or using abbreviations:

D (diameter) = 2r (radii)

There is an important relationship between the diameter and the circumference of the circle. The circumference is just over three times as long as the diameter, in fact about $3\frac{1}{7}$ times the diameter. This awkward figure is given the Greek letter π (pi) as a symbol.

We can therefore say:

$$\text{Circumference} = \pi \times D$$

As D = 2r, we can also say:

$$\text{Circumference} = \pi \times 2r$$

In algebra (the mathematics that uses symbols) it is usual to leave out multiplication signs. If two symbols are written alongside one another, they are deemed to be multiplied together. It is also usual to put any coefficients (whole numbers) first. So:

$$\text{Circumference} = \pi D$$

and

$$\text{Circumference} = 2\pi r$$

Consider the following three examples.

Example: (a) What is the circumference of a circle whose diameter is 14 cm?

$$\begin{aligned}
\text{Circumference} &= \pi D \\
&= 3\tfrac{1}{7} \times 14 \\
&= \frac{22}{7_1} \times 14^2 \quad \text{(cancelling by 7)} \\
&= \underline{\underline{44\,\text{cm}}}
\end{aligned}$$

Example: (b) What is the circumference of a circle radius 10.5 cm?

$$\begin{aligned}
\text{Circumference} &= 2\pi r \\
&= 2 \times \frac{22}{7_1} \times 10.5^{1.5} \quad \text{(cancelling by 7)} \\
&= \underline{\underline{66\,\text{cm}}}
\end{aligned}$$

π is often written as 3.14, or more accurately 3.1416, instead of $3\frac{1}{7}$, but even so, these expressions of the relationship between the diameter of a circle and the circumference are approximations.

Example: (c) A cyclist whose wheels have a diameter of 66 cm makes a journey in which the wheels revolve 3500 times. How far does he go?

The wheels revolve on their circumference. So the journey = 3500 × circumference.

Circumference = πD

$$\frac{22}{7} \times 66 \text{ cm per revolution}$$

$$\therefore \text{journey} = \frac{\overset{5}{\cancel{3500}}}{\underset{1}{\cancel{100}}} \times \frac{22}{\underset{1}{\cancel{7}}} \times 66 \text{ metres}$$

(changing to metres; cancelling by 7 and 100)

$$= 110 \times 66$$
$$= 7260 \text{ metres}$$
$$= 7.26 \text{ km}$$

110
66
——
660
6600
——
7260

(*Note:* Had we been given the distance travelled, we could have found how many revolutions of the wheels were required by *dividing* the circumference into the total distance.)

25.2 Exercises: the circumference of circles

1 Find the circumference of the circles whose diameters are given below. (Use $\pi = 3\frac{1}{7}$, and answer correct to one decimal place.)

(a) 7 cm   (b) $3\frac{1}{2}$ cm
(c) 5 cm   (d) 9 cm
(e) 14 metres   (f) 10 metres
(g) $10\frac{1}{2}$ m   (h) 28 m
(i) 49 cm   (j) 0.7 metre

2 Find the circumferences of the circles whose radii are given below. (Use $\pi = 3\frac{1}{7}$, and answer correct to one decimal place.)

(a) 4 cm   (b) 6 cm
(c) 12 cm   (d) 18 cm
(e) 21 metres   (f) 55 metres

(g) 24.5 metres   (h) 35 metres
(i) 70 metres   (j) 84 metres

3 A cyclist whose wheels have a diameter of 70 cm goes on a journey in which the wheels revolve 6400 times. How far did he actually travel? (Use $\pi = 3\frac{1}{7}$.)

4 A motor vehicle's wheels have a diameter of 56 cm. The car makes a journey of 52.752 kilometres. How many times did the wheels revolve on the journey? (Use $\pi = 3.14$.)

5 A tractor ploughing a major field has wheels measuring 0.7 metre in radius. (a) How far does it go in one revolution of the wheels? (b) If it travelled 35.796 km up and down the field, how many times (to the nearest complete revolution) did the wheels revolve? (Use $\pi = 3.14$.)

6 An aeroplane whose wheels are 2 metres in diameter starts to roll up the runway on take-off. Before it is airborne the wheels revolve 1271 times. What is the length of its take-off run, correct to the nearest *ten* metres? (Use $\pi = 3.14$.)

25.3 The areas of circles and rings

As areas have to be measured in square measure, and it is not very easy to see how this can be arranged as far as a circle is concerned, we have to adopt a little device to 'square' the circle or, rather, rectangularise it.

The method adopted is to cut the circle up into pieces and rearrange them as a rectangle. To produce a perfect rectangle we would need to cut the circle up into millions of pieces, but the illustrations in Figure 25.2 illustrate the problems. In part (i) the circle has been cut up into quarters, with one quarter divided into eighths. In part (ii) it has been divided into eighths, with one eighth divided into sixteenths.

(a) In (i) the circle is reassembled into a roughly rectangular shape with two very wavy sides. The length of these sides is each $\frac{1}{2}$ of the circumference. As the circumference = $2\pi r$, each side must be $1\pi r$.

(b) In (ii) the rearrangement gives a smoother long side to a final figure, because the circle has been cut up into eighths.

Figure 25.2 Finding the area of a circle

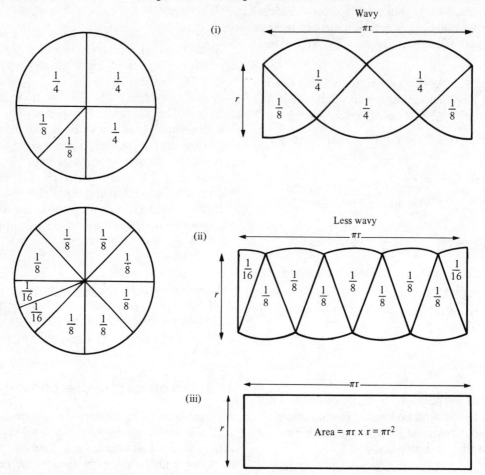

(c) In (iii) we imagine the circle cut up into a million parts, although this would be physically impossible. In such circumstances the wavy line would be reduced to an infinitely small ripple, and we finish with a rectangle which is r wide and πr long. The area of this rectangle is $\pi r \times r$. For convenience this is written πr^2 (pi r squared).

Now consider the following two examples.

Example: (a) What is the area of a circle radius 7 cm?

Area $= \pi r^2$

$$= \frac{22}{\not{7}_1} \times 7\,\text{cm} \times \not{7}^1\,\text{cm} \quad \text{(cancelling by 7)}$$

$= 154\,\text{cm}^2 \quad (154 \text{ square centimetres})$

Example: (b) What is the area of a circle diameter 42 cm?

Diameter $= 2r$ so $r = 21$ cm

Area $= \pi r^2$

$$= \frac{22}{\not{7}_1} \times \not{21}^3\,\text{cm} \times 21\,\text{cm (cancelling by 7)}$$

$= 66 \times 21\,\text{cm}^2$

$= 1386\,\text{cm}^2$

$$\begin{array}{r} 66 \\ 21 \\ \hline 66 \\ 1320 \\ \hline 1386 \\ \hline \end{array}$$

The area of rings

A ring consists of two concentric circles (i.e. two circles with the same centre). If we say the larger circle has a radius R and the smaller circle a radius r (as in Figure 25.3), the area of the ring will be as follows:

Area of ring = area of large circle
— area of small circle
$$= \pi R^2 - \pi r^2$$

Figure 25.3 The area of a ring

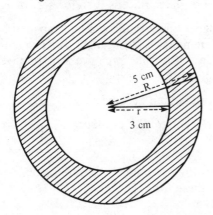

We could calculate the area of the ring by doing two area calculations, but it can be simplified by using some elementary algebra:

$$\pi R^2 - \pi r^2$$

As π is common to both, we can remove π as a common factor. So:

$$\pi R^2 - \pi r^2 = \pi(R^2 - r^2)$$

$(R^2 - r^2)$ is the difference of two squares, which may be rewritten as $(R+r)(R-r)$.

Therefore:

$$\pi R^2 - \pi r^2 = \pi(R^2 - r^2) = \pi(R+r)(R-r)$$

Using this formula we can solve problems as in the example below.

Example: What is the area of a ring, the external circle of which is 5 cm in radius and the internal circle 3 cm in radius? (Use $\pi = \frac{22}{7}$)

$$\text{Area} = \pi(R+r)(R-r)$$
$$= \tfrac{22}{7}(5+3)(5-3)\,\text{cm}^2$$
$$= \tfrac{22}{7}(8 \times 2)\,\text{cm}^2$$
$$= \tfrac{22}{7} \times 16\,\text{cm}^2$$
$$= \tfrac{352}{7}\,\text{cm}^2$$
$$= 50\tfrac{2}{7}\,\text{cm}^2$$

$$\begin{array}{r} 22 \\ \times\,16 \\ \hline 132 \\ 220 \\ \hline 352 \\ \hline \end{array}$$

25.4 Exercises: the areas of circles and rings

1 Find the areas of the circles whose radii are as shown below. (Use $\pi = 3\tfrac{1}{7}$.)

(a) 7 cm   (b) 14 cm
(c) 35 cm   (d) 10.5 cm
(e) 21 cm   (f) 12 cm
(g) 33 cm   (h) 46 cm
(i) 27 cm   (j) 52 cm

2 Find the area of the circles whose diameters are as shown below. (Use $\pi = 3\tfrac{1}{7}$, and calculate the area correct to one decimal place.)

(a) 7 cm   (b) 14 cm
(c) 24 cm   (d) 28 metres
(e) 30 metres   (f) 6 metres
(g) 15 metres   (h) 60 metres
(i) 75 metres   (j) 280 metres

3 Using the formula, area of a ring = $\pi(R+r) \times (R-r)$, find the areas of rings whose external and internal radii are as shown below. (In each case use $\pi = 3.14$, and calculate the area correct to one decimal place.)

	External radius (r)	Internal radius (r)
(a)	7 cm	5 cm
(b)	14 cm	12 cm
(c)	$10\tfrac{1}{2}$ cm	$7\tfrac{1}{2}$ cm
(d)	15 metres	10 metres
(e)	120 metres	90 metres

25.5 Cylinders and spheres

A cylinder is a solid object. Geometrically it is the shape described by the movement of a straight line moving parallel to itself, in such a way as to describe a circle at both ends.

Paradoxically the most common cylinders used in real life today are not solid at all, but hollow. These are the cylinders in the cylinder block of an internal combustion engine, in which controlled explosions of inflammable vapour drive the pistons of the engine to provide driving power to the wheels. Thousands of cylinder blocks are turned out every day.

Calculations concerned with cylinders involve two chief calculations: (a) what is the volume of the cylinder, and (b) what is the surface area of the cylinder? The first of these is important both in engineering and in the food industry, e.g. how much meat is in a tin of canned meat? The surface area of the cylinder is important in actually making the tin cans in which canned foods and canned drinks are sold. Figure 25.4 illustrates the calculations.

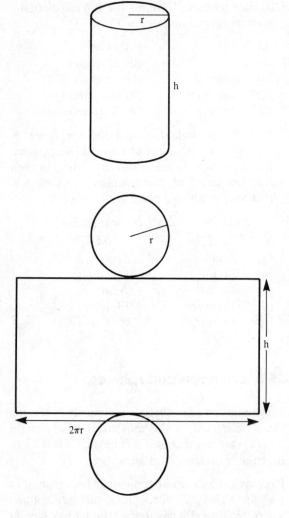

Figure 25.4 The volume and surface area of a cylinder

(a) The volume of a cylinder reflects the size of the circle at the end and the height (or length) of the cylinder. It is therefore made up of $\pi r^2 h$ (the area of the end cylinder multiplied by the height of the cylinder).

(b) The surface area consists of the area of the two circles at the ends and the area of the rectangle that makes up the walls of the cylinder. When opened out flat, this becomes a rectangle whose width is the height of the cylinder and whose length is the circumference of the circle at the ends, i.e. $2\pi r$. The area is, therefore, $2\pi r h$ (i.e. $2\pi r \times h$). The area of the surface is therefore: $2\pi r h + 2\pi r^2$.

Once again this formula can be simplified by the use of elementary algebra. As $2\pi r$ is a common factor in $2\pi r h$ and $2\pi r^2$, we can remove this common factor.

The formula then becomes:

$$\text{Surface area of a cylinder} = 2\pi r h + 2\pi r^2$$
$$= 2\pi r(h + r)$$

The following examples illustrate calculations involving these formulae.

Volumes of cylinders

Example: Find the volume of a cylinder of radius 5 cm and length 15 cm. (Use $\pi = 3.14$.)

$$
\begin{aligned}
\text{Vol} &= \pi r^2 h \\
&= 3.14 \times 5 \times 5 \times 15 \\
&= 15.70 \times 5 \times 15 \\
&= 1177.5 \text{ cm}^3
\end{aligned}
$$

$$
\begin{array}{r}
15.70 \\
75 \\
\hline
7850 \\
109900 \\
\hline
1177.50
\end{array}
$$

Note that the volume finishes up as a measure in cubic centimetres, which are written cm³ in the SI system. Many magazines (particularly motoring magazines) quote cylinder volumes in cc, 980 cc for example. This is the old-fashioned way of writing cubic centimetres. The SI system uses cm³: the 3 standing for 'three dimensions', which can only be a volume.

Surface areas of cylinders

Example: How much tinplate will be required to make a can for baked beans, if the can measures 3.5 cm in radius and 11.5 cm in height? (Use $\pi = 3\frac{1}{7}$.)

Surface area $= 2\pi r(h+r)$

$\qquad = 2 \times \frac{22}{7} \times 3.5(11.5+3.5)\,\text{cm}^2$

$\qquad = 22(15) \quad$ (7 cancels with

$\qquad\qquad\qquad 2 \times 3.5)$

$\qquad = 330\,\text{cm}^3$

$$\begin{array}{r} 22 \\ 15 \\ \hline 110 \\ 220 \\ \hline 330 \end{array}$$

Volume of a sphere

The formula for the volume of a sphere is as follows:

$$\text{Volume of a sphere} = \tfrac{4}{3}\pi r^3$$

A sphere is a three-dimensional solid figure created when a semicircle rotates about a diameter. Every point on the surface of the sphere is the same distance from the centre of the sphere.

Example: What is the volume of a sphere of 5 cm radius? (Use $\pi = 3\frac{1}{7}$.)

Volume $= \frac{4}{3}\pi r^3$

$\qquad = \frac{4}{3} \times \frac{22}{7} \times 5 \times 5 \times 5$

$\qquad = \dfrac{88 \times 5 \times 25}{21}$

$\qquad = \dfrac{440 \times 25}{21}$

$\qquad = \dfrac{11000}{21}$

$\qquad = 523\frac{17}{21}\,\text{cm}^3$

$$\begin{array}{r} 523 \\ 21)\overline{11000} \\ 105 \\ \hline 50 \\ 42 \\ \hline 80 \\ 63 \\ \hline 17 \end{array}$$

25.6 Exercises: cylinders and spheres

1 Find the volume of each of the cylinders whose dimensions are given below. (In each case use $\pi = 3.14$ and find the volume correct to the nearest cubic centimetre.)

	Radius (cm)	Height (cm)
(a)	2.5	8
(b)	3	10
(c)	4.5	10.5
(d)	5	12
(e)	7.5	13.5
(f)	9	15

2 Find the volume of each of the cylinders whose dimensions are given below. (Use $\pi = 3.14$ and give your answer correct to one decimal place)

	Radius (metres)	Height (metres)
(a)	0.65	5
(b)	0.85	12
(c)	1.25	10.5
(d)	1.75	14
(e)	3.85	15.5

3 What area of metal will be necessary to make each can for the food processing industry, if the cylindrical cans measure as shown below? (Use $\pi = 3.14$, and answer correct to one decimal place.)

	Radius (cm)	Height (cm)
(a)	2.4	5
(b)	3.6	10
(c)	4.2	12
(d)	7.5	24
(e)	8.4	30

4 Cylindrical storage tanks at a tank farm measure as shown below. What is the volume of the tank, in cubic metres? (Use $\pi = 3.14$, and answer correct to the nearest m³.)

	Radius (metres)	Height (metres)
(a)	5	6
(b)	8	12
(c)	10	18
(d)	12	20
(e)	15	24

5 What is the volume of spheres whose radii are as shown below? (Use $\pi = 3\frac{1}{7}$. Answer correct to one decimal place.)

(a) radius $= 3\,\text{cm}$
(b) radius $= 7\,\text{cm}$
(c) radius $= 15\,\text{cm}$
(d) radius $= 1.4\,\text{metres}$
(e) radius $= 3.5\,\text{metres}$

26
Introduction to Business Statistics

26.1 What are statistics?

The term statistics can mean two different things. In many cases people refer to statistics when they mean **'facts given in a numerical form'**. For example, people say they are talking about statistics if they refer to the number of people who are unemployed in the United Kingdom or the amount we spend on imports and earn on exports. This is the first meaning.

The second meaning given to the word 'statistics' is a **body of knowledge, or a subject where we collect and analyse numerical facts**. All such information is called **data** and as we often use computers to help us analyse the data there is a whole area of business calculations called **data processing**.

In almost every firm, statistics will be collected and used. How do we collect data? We can obtain figures from our own sources, for example, the amounts and types of sales achieved by the firm (so much of this product and so much of that). We can collect data by special research programmes, for example market research **questionnaires** and **interviews**. We can also obtain data from other organisations. Trade associations may collect statistics on the average efficiency in our industry. The Government will also publish data which may be of interest to the firm, for example demands of foreign firms for British manufacturers, or details of the incomes of families at home. These may help us direct our selling efforts to those with the right sort of incomes.

In this chapter we look at some of the methods of collecting data, and how the mass of data is then processed so that we can understand it and make use of it. Although in doing so we shall refer to subjects which might not appear to be of major interest to businessmen (traffic surveys, for example) we usually find that all such investigations lead to conclusions of value to business.

26.2 Censuses and samples

One of the commonest sources of data is a **census**. A census is an enquiry in which we seek the opinion of the whole **population**. Once every ten years, in the first year of every decade, the United Kingdom holds a census. On a certain night every householder, hotel keeper, lodging house, etc. has to record every person present in the building. There are penalties for not keeping a proper record (some people do not like to say where they spent the night). Equally there are heavy penalties for revealing what was on a census form to any one who is not involved in the statistical work (for we wish to interfere with the people's private lives as little as possible). The figures collected give us the population figures for the whole country.

In addition to these facts, every tenth house has to fill out a lot more detailed information, such as whether they have a colour television set, a motor car, a telephone, double glazing etc. This is a sample survey, not a census, because we are not asking the whole population. The data enables the Government statisticians to estimate how many people have these sorts of facilities.

A simple census to organise is a traffic census. We do this using the five-barred gate system of counting. This is illustrated in Figure 26.1. Study the illustration now, and read the notes (a) to (e) below it.

Figure 26.1 A traffic census

Traffic Census : Station Road
Half-hour period from 09.00 - 09.30 Tues. 7 May 19 ...

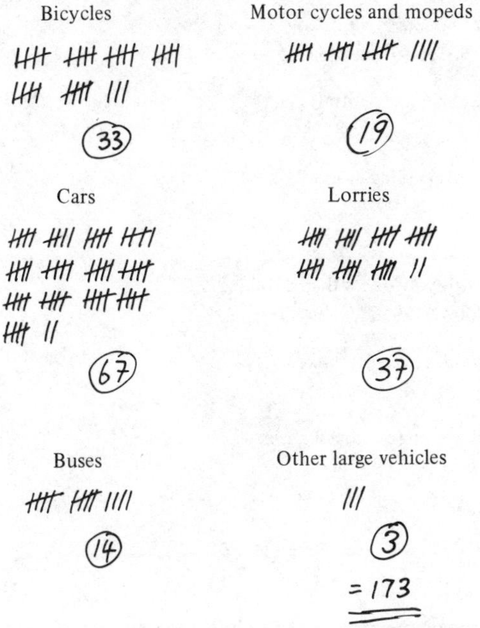

Bicycles   Motor cycles and mopeds

HHT HHT HHT HH   HHT HHT HHT ////
HH HHT ///

(33)   (19)

Cars   Lorries

HHT HHl HHT HHl   HHT HHl HHT HHT
HHT HHl HHT HHT   HHT HHT HHT //
HHT HHT HHT HHT
HHT //

(67)   (37)

Buses   Other large vehicles

HHT HHT ////   ///

(14)   (3)

                           = 173

(a) We have six classes of vehicles of which one is a general class to include any we find difficult to classify under the other headings.

(b) We record each one with a little stroke 1 but when we have reached four we put the fifth one in as the cross-bar on a five-barred gate. We can easily count in fives.

(c) The person recording the vehicles is called an **enumerator** (one who numbers). As enumerators get tired, we usually change them every fifteen minutes or, as in this case, every half-hour.

(d) The totals are counted and written in a circle and the grand total for the half-hour is recorded.

(e) Later in the day, when the census is complete, we would add the data on the small slips together to give us the grand total (explained in Section 26.4).

26.3 Questionnaires

A traffic census collects data by **observation**: the enumerator stands by the roadside or on a bridge over a busy road and records what he or she sees. Another way to collect data is by distributing questionnaires. These are commonly used in market research, and to investigate such matters as expenditure of household income. Drawing up a questionnaire is a skilled business, and frequently test-runs are carried out with only a few people to see what sort of mistakes creep into the data when the questionaires are completed. A typical questionnaire is illustrated in Figure 26.2, and discussed in the notes (a) to (c) below.

(a) Wherever possible, the questions are arranged so that they can be answered by a simple tick. Such answers are easily sorted out by the investigators.

(b) Where the individual is asked to write something in, it is more difficult to sort the results, but greater detail is revealed. For example, Question 2 might reveal that a substantial number of people went to the USA for their summer holiday in the year in question.

(c) The stages of such an inquiry are: (i) preparation of the questionnaire, (ii) distribution, (iii) analysis of the responses (the raw scores), (iv) tabulation of the data (putting it in the form of a table), (v) deriving other data from it, particularly percentages, and (vi) writing the report.

Sorting the data from a questionnaire

Once again the five-barred gate device is used to sort the answers from a questionnaire. The responses would be recorded on a chart; for example, Question 4 in Figure 26.2, below, would be recorded against a list such as in Figure 26.3.

26.4 Tabulation

To tabulate data is to arrange it in the form of a table, which is simple to understand. Consider the data collected in the traffic census on Station Road. Suppose the final figures for the complete working day 7 a.m.–7 p.m. were: bicycles 632, motor cycles and mopeds 395, cars 1739, lorries 845, buses 148, other large vehicles 27. Arranged in tabulated form these would appear as follows:

Figure 26.2 A questionnaire

Please tick one space in each line, or write in the answer where asked.

Summer Vacation 19....

1. Did you take a holiday this summer?   Yes......... No.........
    If you answered 'Yes' please continue. If 'No' go to Question 12.

2. Where did you go? UK......... France......... Spain......... Italy.........
    Other (please specify) ....

3. How much did your holiday cost, apart from spending-money?
    Less than £99.........; £100 - £199.........; £200 - £299.........;
    £300 - £399.........; £400+.........

4. How much spending-money did you take with you? Less than £100.........;
    £100 - £199.........; £200 - £299.........; £300 - £399.........; £400+.........

5. Was the weather (a) splendid.........; (b) good.........; (c) mixed.........
    (d) bad.........

6. Was the food (a) splendid.........; (b) good.........; (c) mixed.........
    (d) bad.........

7. What was the best thing about your holiday?...
    ....

8. What was the worst thing about your holiday?...
    ....

9. If you used a travel agent would you (a) recommend your travel agency
    heartily?......... (b) give them qualified approval?......... (c) not recommend
    them to others?.........

10. Did you experience any tummy trouble on your holiday? Yes......... No.........

11. Did you drink the tap water? Yes......... No.........

___

To be answered only by those who did not take a holiday.

12. What was the chief reason why you did not take a holiday this year?
    (a) Could not afford to......... (b) Job uncertainty......... (c) Family
    event......... (d) Other reason (please give brief explanation).........................
    ....
    ....
    ....

Figure 26.3 Recording data from responses to a questionnaire

£0-£99	///
£100 - £199	₩₩ //
£200 - £299	₩₩ ₩₩ ₩₩ ////
£300 - £399	₩₩ //
£400 and over	//

Table 1 Station Road traffic

(7 a.m.–7 p.m., Tuesday, 7 May 19..)

Type of vehicle	Number observed
Bicycles	632
Motor cycles and mopeds	395
Cars	1739
Lorries	845
Buses	148
Other large vehicles	27
Total	3786

Classes in tabulations

When we draw up a table of data, we have to have the separate classes that form the basis of the table. In Table 1, above, the classes (bicycles, motor cycles and mopeds etc.) were given to us, and they formed the basis of the observations made. In other investigations we may have to choose the classes for ourselves. Consider the following mass of data which records the sales made by 20 commercial travellers in the week of 1–7 July 19...

Sales (£)

1729	9516	8612	1957
1345	2475	2134	2836
4629	1382	1349	7912
7314	6146	7384	1425
8162	7587	2000	8416

In sorting out these data we can see that no traveller sold less than £1000 of goods, or as much as £10 000. Between 5 and 10 classes is usually the best for any table, so we could classify them as follows:

Class	Number
£0–£1999	6
£2000–£3999	4
£4000–£5999	1
£6000–£7999	5
£8000–£9999	4
	20

The rules about classifying data are:

(a) Try to have between 5 and 10 classes.
(b) Do not allow classes to overlap. Thus if we have the classes £0–£2000 and £2000–£4000, we have an overlap and we are not sure which class should be given an item of exactly £2000.

Derived statistics

Although the relatively simple figure of this traffic census can be easily understood, we do not instantly have a complete understanding of the data just by looking at the table. We can improve our understanding by *deriving* other data from the *raw data* (untreated data) of the enquiry. The usual form taken by derived data is the percentage format. Each of the figures can be calculated as a percentage of the total, for example:

Bicycles as a percentage

$$= \frac{632}{3786} \times 100$$

$$= \frac{63200}{3786}$$

$$= 16.7\%$$

```
         16.69
3786)63200
      3786
      25340
      22716
      26240
      22716
      35240
      34074
```

These calculations are, of course, very simple with an electronic calculator.

The whole set then becomes:

Table 1 Station Road traffic

(7 a.m.–7 p.m., Tuesday, 7 May 19..)

Type of vehicle	Number observed	%
Bicycles	632	16.7
Motor cycles and mopeds	395	10.4
Cars	1739	45.9
Lorries	845	22.3
Buses	148	3.9
Other large vehicles	27	0.7
Total	3786	99.9

Note that the percentages given correct to one decimal place do not quite add up to 100%. This is because the tiny fractions discarded in the rounding process do not always cancel one another out. The total can be left as 99.9 (sometimes it will be 100.1). If preferred, the total can be written 100.0 and the sentence, '% do not sum to 100% because of rounding', can be written below the table.

Rounding

In Chapter 5 reference was made to **rounding** as a method of simplifying decimal answers by giving them correct to a required number of decimal places. In the last example above, the percentages of vehicles were rounded in this way correct to

one decimal place. Rounding is used very frequently in statistics, because we can eliminate much of the unnecessary detail in a set of statistics by rounding the figures off in a tabulation. In Figure 26.4 a copy of the weekly 'Return' of the Bank of England is reproduced. It shows the value of the notes in circulation on the day in question.

In giving these figures the Bank has given the full details, which can be seen as running into thousands of millions of pounds. By rounding the figures off (say, to the nearest million pounds in each case), a statistician not required to give the full details could convey the same impression. The figures would then be as shown in Table 26.1. Note that the figures have been rounded to the

Figure 26.4 The weekly 'Return' of the Bank of England

Bank of England

Wednesday the 2nd day of April 19....

Issue Department

	£		£
Notes Issued:		Government Debt	11 015 100
In Circulation	10086 487 814	Other Govt. Securities	7678 034 756
In Banking		Other Securities	2410 950 144
Department	13 512 186		
	10100 000 000		10100 000 000

Banking Department

	£		£
Capital	14 553 000	Govt. Securities	663 546 810
Public Deposits—		Advances and Other	
Including Exchequer, National		Accounts	352 160 339
Loans Fund, National Debt		Premises, Equipment	
Commissioners and		and Other Securities	361 649 038
Dividend Accounts	44 621 613	Notes	13 512 186
Special Deposits	131 835 000	Coin	254 762
Bankers Deposits	550 789 203		
Reserves and Other			
Accounts	649 324 319		
	1391 123 135		1391 123 135

Dated the 3rd day of April 19--

J.G.DRAKE, Deputy Chief Cashier

Reproduced by courtesy of the Bank of England

	£m		£m
Notes Issued:		Government Debt	11
In Circulation	10 086	Other Govt. Securities	7 678
In Banking Department	14	Other Securities	2 411
	10 100		10 100

Banking Department

	£m		£m
Capital	15	Govt. Securities	664
Public Deposits	45	Advances and Other Accounts	352
Special Deposits	132	Premises, Equipment and Other	
Bankers Deposits	551	Securities	362
Reserves and Other Accounts	649	Notes	14
		Coin	—
	1391		1391

Table 26.1

(*Note:* Banking Department figures do not sum correctly due to rounding.)

nearest million. Where a number ends with a figure of less than half a million we 'round down' to the millions figure below, by simply discarding the extra figures. Where a number ends with a figure of over half a million, as with 'Other Securities' £2410 950 144, we 'round up' to the next million above, in this case £2411 million. If a figure had exactly 500 000 (half a million) we should round to the nearest even number of millions: £2413 500 000 becomes £2414 m, because £2413 is an odd number. Similarly, £2412 500 000 becomes £2412 m, not £2413 m.

Note also that in the rounding process the £254 762 of coins in circulation becomes zero. So, we see that in eliminating the detail by rounding, we may also make the figures slightly less sensible than the full details provided by the Bank of England.

26.5 Exercises: tabulation and derived statistics

1 Sales of the four products of a motor manufacturer in the year 19 . . were as follows:

Model 1: £23 742 526; Model 2: £12 327 436; Model 3: £8 249 815; Model 4: £5 500 000.

Present this data in tabulated form (correct to the nearest million pounds). Show the total sales, and the percentage sales in each group as given by the rounded figures. Do not attempt the percentage calculations using the full figures.

2 Population figures for an African country in a recent year were given as follows: Persons under the age of 5 years 2 674 812; 5–13.9 years 4 271 834; 14–49 years 19 821 243; over 50 years 7 382 500. You are asked to present this data in tabular form (correct to the nearest thousand ('000)), and to bring out the total population (correct to the nearest thousand).

3 The take-home pay of twenty young secretaries in the month of July 19 . . was noted as follows:

£176	£216	£154	£256	£248
£184	£222	£196	£184	£216
£172	£195	£238	£178	£222
£204	£185	£220	£192	£208

Arrange these in six classes: less than £160; £160–£179; £180–£199; £200–£219; £220–£239 and £240 and over. Present them in tabular form, and show the percentage of secretaries in each class.

4 Draw up a questionnaire and conduct a survey among class students about the pocket money and earnings they receive each week, and how they spend it. Make it clear in the introduction that completion of the questionnaire is voluntary but their co-operation would be appreciated. Names need not be given on the form at all if privacy is desired. Draw up a questionnaire listing likely sources of *weekly* income and likely items of expenditure. Other relevant questions, such as whether they live at the parental home or in lodgings or other accommodation, should be included.

5 Figures for live births in a recent year were as follows: England 635876; Wales 37635; Scotland 74397; Northern Ireland 29194. Give these figures (rounded to the nearest thousand) in a tabular presentation to bring out the total United Kingdom population. Show in an additional column the percentages of total live births in each country.

6 Activity at civil aerodromes is measured in 'set down' and 'picked up' terms. In one recent year the figures were: (a) passengers set down 41220460, passengers picked up 40484792; (b) freight set down 323947 tonnes, freight picked up 396105 tonnes; (c) mail set down 24316 tonnes, mail picked up 33891 tonnes. Round the data in (a) to the nearest thousand passengers, and in (b) and (c) to the nearest thousand tonnes, and present them to show the total movements under each of the three headings.

7 In a recent year retail trade figures were as follows: 197884 small retail shops did a total trade of £18117295644; 191 co-operative societies did £3868584221 of trade; 28932 small multiples £8451726284; and 1070 large multiples £28046925737. Arrange these figures in tabular form under three headings: retail outlets; sales £ millions (to the nearest million); and % share of retail trade. Calculate the percentages correct to one decimal place using the rounded figures of your table, not the full figures. Bring out the totals in each column.

8 Calls handled by 40 telephone operators in an 8-hour shift are as follows:

239	195	301	242	195
186	186	248	273	187
144	172	132	138	228
194	198	276	255	239
133	143	285	264	186
243	123	127	126	256
285	283	243	197	301
273	286	291	281	149

Classify these in groups of 20, beginning 120–139, 140–159 etc. up to 300–319. Then calculate what percentage of operators fall into each group and show these derived statistics in a separate column in the table.

27

The Pictorial Representation of Statistics: Graphs

27.1 Displaying data

We have seen that data can be presented in tabular form, and that in this way the figures are fairly easy to understand. However, many people are not very numerate (i.e. good at numbers) and understand data much more easily if presented in picture form.

Sometimes we do actually draw little pictures to illustrate data. These are called **pictograms**. Another type of drawing is the **bar chart**, which compares statistics by showing the data as a length of bar. It is easy to see that a long bar must mean a bigger figure (or a more frequent occurrence) than a short bar, and we can even split a bar up into parts to show various elements in the statistics. This is called a **component bar chart**. For example, with data about a diet, we could show how much fat, carbohydrate and protein entered into the diet by shading parts of the bar.

Other data can be presented as a **pie chart**: a circular diagram resembling a pie or cake cut up into slices to show the relative importance of parts of the data. All these methods are explained in Chapter 28, but first we must consider the commonest type of pictorial representation, the **graph**.

The word 'graph' comes from the Greek word *graphos*, meaning 'writing', but it also has come to mean drawing. One device that helps us draw easily is a paper with a square grid pattern, such as the early map-makers used, called 'graph' paper. If we draw two lines on graph paper (which are called the axes of the graph) so that they intersect at right angles, we can fix any position on the paper by reference to the two axes. We call the two axes the x-axis and the y-axis, and any point on the graph can be defined by its position relative to the axes. This is explained in Figure 27.1 and the notes (a) to (f) below.

(a) The x-axis is the horizontal line and the y-axis is the vertical line.
(b) They intersect at 0 which is called the **origin** of the graph.
(c) The horizontal axis is labelled with the name of the independent variable; which is, in this case, sales in thousands of units.
(d) The vertical scale is labelled with the name of the dependent variable; in this case, money in thousands of pounds. How much money we get depends upon how many units we sell, so it is the dependent variable.
(e) Any point in the area between the axes (the two arms) can be explained by reference to the axes, simply by dropping a perpendicular on to them. Thus the point A is the point where $x = 3000$ units and $y = £1500$. Similarly, the point B is the point where $x =$ sales of 6000 units and y shows income from sales of £3000. Work out for yourself what the point C represents!
(f) Lay a ruler along the paper as if you were going to join up A, B and C and you will find it is a straight line. This is because the money received for every item is the same, 50p. This might not have been so: we might have had to cut our prices to sell larger quantities, in which case we should have finished up with a curve instead of a straight line.

One important point about drawing graphs is the question of the **scale** of the graph. Scale means size, and it is always necessary to choose a scale that will fit the information on the paper. For example, in Figure 27.1 the items sold were 50p each, and sales went up to 10 000 units. Therefore we could easily put on the graph paper the

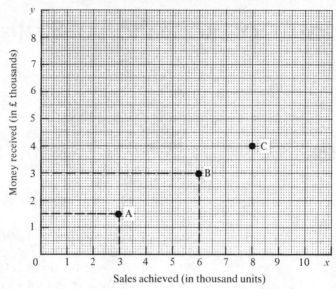

Figure 27.1 Plotting points on a graph

Money received (in £ thousands) (y-axis)

Sales achieved (in thousand units) (x-axis)

information about money received, using a scale of 1 centimetre = £1000.

Suppose the items had been £75 each, in which case the income from the sales of 10 000 would have been £750 000 and we could not have fitted this information on a scale that only shows £8000 as the highest figure. We should have had to make the scale 1 centimetre = £100 000 to get the total of £750 000 into the diagram. We cannot change the size of the paper, but we can change the scale of the graph. Similarly, if the number of units likely to be sold had been 1 000 000, not 10 000, we should have had to change the scale to 1 centimetre = 100 000 units.

27.2 Plotting simple graphs

One of the commonest uses of graphs is to show such figures as factory output, sales achieved by commercial travellers, temperatures of hospital patients etc. Over a period of time the graph becomes a record of a variable, and consequently is often known as a 'time series'. The figures may be plotted weekly, or monthly, or hourly (in the case of temperatures). The scale must be chosen appropriately, so that the data can be clearly represented on the charts.

Consider the following data of output recorded in a small manufacturing plant.

Units produced, 19..

Jan.	425	July	830
Feb.	480	Aug.	760
Mar.	530	Sept.	660
Apr.	695	Oct.	580
May	724	Nov.	520
June	850	Dec.	405

First notice that the smallest output is 405 units in December, so that any display of output from 0–400 in Figure 27.2 would be a waste of graph paper. For this reason the scale can be made to start at 400. The highest output figure is 850 units in June so that there is little point in showing any scale for 900 and above. Consequently the scale used runs from 400–900, with a break in the y-axis below 400 to indicate that the scale is not shown below 400.

The actual output figures can either be plotted as tiny points, or, for greater clarity, small crosses (as in Figure 27.2). If the lines do not actually join up at the points, the cross is displayed more clearly.

The product appears to have a summer demand, output rising to a peak in June and falling away to a low point in midwinter (northern hemisphere, of course). The axes are labelled and the whole chart can be captioned in a convenient space. In this case we will imagine the units are greenhouses.

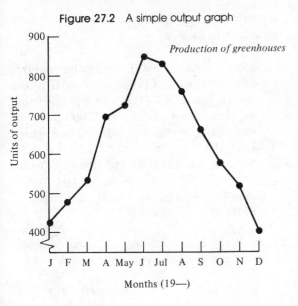

Figure 27.2 A simple output graph

Production of greenhouses

Units of output (y-axis: 400, 500, 600, 700, 800, 900)

Months (19----) — J F M A May J Jul A S O N D

27.3 Exercises: simple graphs

1 A group of salesmen achieve the following sales in the 13-week period from 1st April. Plot these sales on a simple graph using an appropriate scale. The dates are the Saturdays in the week concerned.

Week	Sales (£ thousands)	Week	Sales (£ thousands)
7 Apr.	11	26 May	17.5
14 Apr.	12.5	2 June	17
21 Apr.	14	9 June	16.5
28 Apr.	17.5	16 June	19.5
5 May	21	23 June	21.5
12 May	19.5	30 June	22
19 May	18		

2 The sales of two commercial travellers Mr A and Miss B are as follows throughout the year. Plot the two sets of data on the same graph, one in pencil and one in ink (or use different coloured pencils if you prefer).

	Sales (£ thousands) Mr A	Sales (£ thousands) Miss B
Jan.	6.5	4.2
Feb.	7.3	4.9
Mar.	8.2	6.8
Apr.	8.6	9.5
May	9.5	5.9
June	11.0	10.6
July	11.8	10.8
Aug.	12.8	8.9
Sept.	10.7	12.6
Oct.	8.6	13.5
Nov.	7.5	14.7
Dec.	7.3	12.2

3 Record the following temperatures on a temperature chart, in degrees Celsius. The scale runs from 35 °C to 41 °C. Temperatures are taken every 2 hours from the time the patient was admitted at 8 p.m. on Tuesday until the temperature became normal two days later. The readings were:

Tuesday
8 p.m.	39.1°
10 p.m.	39.4°
midnight	39.6°

Wednesday
2 a.m.	39.6°
4 a.m.	39.8°
6 a.m.	39.8°
8 a.m.	40°
10 a.m.	40°
noon	40.2°
2 p.m.	40.2°
4 p.m.	39.8°
6 p.m.	39.6°
8 p.m.	39.4°
10 p.m.	39.4°
midnight	39.4°

Thursday
2 a.m.	38.6°
4 a.m.	38.4°
6 a.m.	38.2°
8 a.m.	38.1°
10 a.m.	38.0°
noon	37.8°
2 p.m.	37.6°
4 p.m.	37.4°
6 p.m.	37.4°
8 p.m.	37.2°
10 p.m.	37.0°
midnight	37.0°

4 Your firm collects circulation statistics for an advertising agency to justify the use of various magazines. Two magazines, *Family Matters* and *Family Affairs*, have circulations (in millions) as follows:

Month	Family Matters	Family Affairs
Jan.	3.0	4.1
Feb.	3.1	4.2
Mar.	3.3	4.2
Apr.	3.5	3.9
May	3.8	3.7
June	4.2	3.6

(continued)

Month	Family Matters	Family Affairs
July	4.6	3.8
Aug.	4.8	3.9
Sept.	4.9	3.5
Oct.	5.0	3.2
Nov.	5.1	3.4
Dec.	5.2	3.1

Plot these data on a simple graph to display the trend in the magazines' circulations over the year.

27.4 Z charts

A Z chart is a graph that plots three sets of figures at the same time over a period of 12 months, to show clearly what is happening to sales. The three sets of figures are as follows:

(a) The monthly sales.
(b) Cumulative monthly sales, i.e. the sales for the year added together.
(c) Total sales for the preceding 12 months. In order to prepare this set of figures we need to know at the start of each year what the preceding twelve months sales were.

Suppose sales in Year 1 for a particular firm have been as follows:

Sales in Year 1 (£ thousands)
Jan.	17
Feb.	19
Mar.	21
Apr.	22
May	24
June	27
July	30
Aug.	33
Sept.	37
Oct.	39
Nov.	42
Dec.	48
Total	359 (that is, £359 000)

Now suppose the sales for January of Year 2 are £36 000, while for February they are £41 000 (in £ thousands, 36 and 41 respectively).

The three sets of figures we require for these months are as follows:

Jan. Monthly sales £36 000, cumulative monthly sales for Year 2 £36 000, total sales in last twelve months £378 000. (To find this figure we deduct last January's £17 000 from the total of £359 000 and add on this year's £36 000.)

Feb. Monthly sales £41 000, cumulative sales for year £77 000, total sales in last twelve months £400 000 (£378 000 − £19 000 + £41 000).

As the year continues we add each month's figures to give us in the end, figures as follows:

	Year 1 (£ thousands)	Year 2 (£ thousands)	Cumulative Year 2 (£ thousands)	Total for previous 12 months (£ thousands)
Jan.	17	36	36	378
Feb.	19	41	77	400
Mar.	21	43	120	422
Apr.	22	47	167	447
May	24	51	218	474
June	27	53	271	500
July	30	54	325	524
Aug.	33	56	381	547
Sept.	37	58	439	568
Oct.	39	59	498	588
Nov.	42	60	558	606
Dec.	48	62	620	620

When presented as a Z chart, we get a result as shown in Figure 27.3, over the page.

27.5 Exercises: Z charts

1 A firm's sales in Years 1 and 2 were as follows (in £ thousands).

Month	Year 1	Year 2
Jan.	30	28
Feb.	31	34
Mar.	32	36

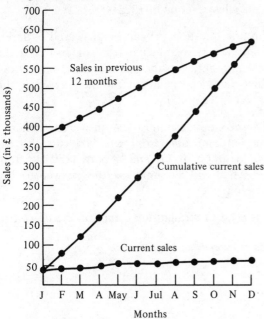

Figure 27.3 A Z chart of sales for the year 19..

Month	Year 1	Year 2
Apr.	34	39
May	42	45
June	39	48
July	36	43
Aug.	32	41
Sept.	29	33
Oct.	24	29
Nov.	19	28
Dec.	18	28
	366	432

Draw a Z chart for Year 2.

2 Imports of washing machines from a certain country over a two-year period were as follows:

Month	Year 1 (thousands of units)	Year 2 (thousands of units)
Jan.	33	37
Feb.	34	38
Mar.	28	32
Apr.	28	31
May	31	36
June	33	37
July	37	39
Aug.	38	41
Sept.	39	43
Oct.	40	44
Nov.	41	46
Dec.	42	50
	424	474

Draw a Z chart for Year 2 from these data.

3 Imports of electric showers from a certain country were as follows over a two-year period. The figures for November and December in Year 2 reflect the fact that a quota of 50 000 showers was imposed to prevent excessive imports. Draw a Z chart for Year 2 from these data.

Month	Year 1 (hundreds of units)	Year 2 (hundreds of units)
Jan.	26	33
Feb.	28	35
Mar.	30	33
Apr.	27	36
May	34	40
June	29	51
July	32	58
Aug.	35	59
Sept.	38	66
Oct.	33	67
Nov.	34	22
Dec.	40	—
	386	500

27.6 Straight-line graphs

When the relationship between sets of data is direct, so that a variation in one set of data produces the same sort of change every time in the other set of data, they produce a straight-line graph when plotted. For example, if items are sold at a price of £25 there is a **direct variation** in sales income with every extra unit sold. Thus the sales of the item and the income from sales should be as follows:

The Pictorial Representation of Statistics: Graphs 139

Items sold (units)	0	1	2	3	4
Sales income (£)	0	25	50	75	100

Items sold (units)	5	6	7	8	9	10
Sales income (£)	125	150	175	200	225	250

When plotted on a graph, the result will be a straight-line graph through the origin. Strictly speaking, to plot such a graph we only need one pair of matching figures. For example, in Figure 27.4 the figure used is 10 000 items, which bring an income of £250 000. As such a graph must go through the origin, we have only to join up the point plotted with the origin to give us the straight line which joins all points where the constant relationship $y = 25x$ applies.

(b) What sales would have to be achieved to yield a sales revenue of £325 000?

The first question (a) can be answered by interpolation: a perpendicular from the x-axis at the 8000 unit mark cuts the graph at the point P, from which point a perpendicular to the y-axis finds the answer of £200 000.

The second question (b) is answered similarly. The perpendicular from £325 000 cuts the extended graph at Q, and a perpendicular from there finds 13 000 units as the answer to the question.

This type of straight-line graph is therefore fre-

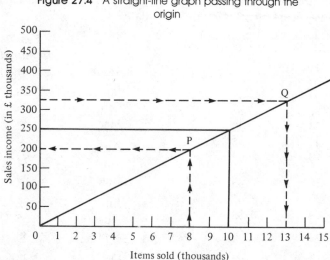

Figure 27.4 A straight-line graph passing through the origin

Interpolation and extrapolation

The word 'pole' means point of reference, as with the North Pole and the South Pole. If we have two points of reference, as in Figure 27.4 (the origin of the graph, and the point found by sales of 10 000 units bringing in a sales income of £250 000), it is possible to read off other values from the graph. This is called **interpolation** if we are seeking the meaning of a point on the graph in between the known points of reference, or **extrapolation** if we seek the meaning of a point beyond the largest (or, in some cases, latest) data available. In Figure 27.4 two questions have been answered:

(a) What income will sales of 8000 units bring in?

quently used as a 'ready reckoner'. In the days before the electronic calculator, graphs of this sort were frequently set up over the desks of invoice typists so that they could read off from the graph the value of the items ordered by a customer, and could type them onto the invoice.

27.7 Straight-line graphs not through the origin

Straight-line graphs do not always go through the origin. For instance, a graph can be drawn to show the relationship between the Fahrenheit and Celsius thermometer systems. For every 5 degrees Celsius there are 9 degrees Fahrenheit. In addition, the Fahrenheit scale has freezing point at 32° F. Expressed in mathematical terms, if the Fahrenheit scale is shown on the y-axis and Celsius on the x-axis.

$$y = 32 + \tfrac{9}{5}x$$

We can use freezing point 0° C and boiling point 100° C as our reference points. In these cases

$$y = 32 + \tfrac{9}{5}x$$

The Fahrenheit freezing point $= 32 + (\tfrac{9}{5} \times 0°)$
$$= 32° \text{F}$$

The Fahrenheit boiling point

$$= 32 + \left(\frac{9}{\underset{1}{\cancel{5}}} \times \cancel{100}^{20} \right) \text{(cancelling by 5)}$$

$$= 32 + 180$$

$$= 212° \text{F}$$

The result is shown on Figure 27.5 and discussed in the notes (a) to (c) which follow.

Figure 27.5   A straight-line graph not passing through the origin

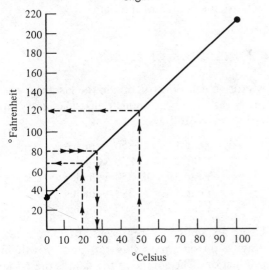

(a) The graph does not pass through the origin but intercepts the y-axis at 32° F.
(b) Any temperature in °F can be converted to °C by interpolation, e.g. 80° F = 27° C.
(c) Any temperature in °C can be converted to °F by interpolation, e.g. 20° C = 68° F and 50° C = 122° F as shown on the graph, but it is not easy to read off accurate figures on a graph and the answers can only be approximate, unless the scale is very large.

27.8 Exercises: straight-line graphs

1 A factory employee is paid on an hourly basis, at a rate of £3.25 per hour. Draw a graph which can be used as a 'ready reckoner' for any number of hours between 0 hour and 80 hours (this employee does a good deal of overtime).

2 On a journey a motorist averages 60 km per hour. Draw a graph to show the expected distance travelled in an 8-hour driving day. Read off from your graph: (a) the time taken to go 320 kilometres; and (b) distance travelled in 2 hours 45 minutes.

3 Draw a graph for use as a 'ready reckoner' for the cost of up to 100 items at £1.75 each. From the graph read off: (a) the cost to a customer of 65 items; and (b) the number of items a customer could buy for £77.

4 A man works a 42-hour week for £84 and is then paid overtime at £3.20 an hour. Draw a graph to show his overtime earnings and his basic pay. The graph will start with the basic earnings of £84 with no overtime, and then with extra pay for 5, 10, 15, 20, 25 and 30 hours of overtime. Read off from your graph: (a) the man's gross pay after working 18 hours overtime; and (b) the number of hours worked overtime to earn a total pay of £106.40.

28

The Pictorial Presentation of Data: Other Methods

28.1 Pictograms

Sometimes data can be displayed very simply by the use of small illustrations called **pictograms**. Thus a tiny telephone symbol could be devised to display data comparing the utilisation of telephones in different countries. There are some rules about such symbols:

(a) Choose a symbol that is appropriate to the data concerned; for example, a glass of wine might be appropriate to illustrate the consumption of wine in the United Kingdom. What symbol might be used for each of the following: graduate teachers, aircraft landings at London Airport, and deaths due to road accidents?
(b) Choose an appropriate scale for use in the diagram. For example, if we have to represent 9000 telephones in a particular country we might need to use a scale where we show one telephone symbol for each thousand appliances.
(c) Decide how you will show 500 telephones, or 250, or 750. We usually cannot divide a symbol up into more than four parts, so it may

be necessary to give the figures to the nearest 250 if the full symbol represents 1000.
(d) To help the reader of our reports it may be helpful to put the actual figure in at the end of the line of pictures, as shown in Figure 28.1.

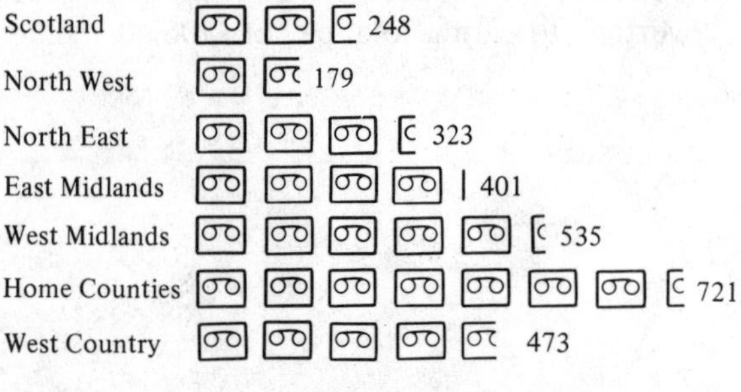

Notes to Figure 28.1:

(a) Each hundred machines sold is represented by a cassette.
(b) Part cassettes indicate 50, 25, or 75 machines sold.
(c) The actual sales figure is shown for each area to reinforce the data.
(d) A suitable heading shows the scale used (1 cassette = 100 dictation machines) and also shows the source of the data.

28.2 Exercises: pictograms

1 Motor vehicle construction in the last five years in Nicasia (newly industrialised country in Asia) was as follows:

Year 1	17 856 vehicles
Year 2	29 820 vehicles
Year 3	45 350 vehicles
Year 4	55 380 vehicles
Year 5	67 500 vehicles

Using a small car to represent 10 000 vehicles, draw a pictogram to illustrate the growth in production. The source of the data is the *Nicasian Annual Abstract of Statistics*.

2 A small survey shows that in a particular town the probability is that the following numbers of bedrooms are available to families in the town. The results of the survey, carried out at every tenth house, have been multiplied by ten to give the figures.

Figure 28.1 A pictogram showing sales of dictation machines

Sales (in hundreds) of Executive Dictation Machines, 19----

(Source: Sales reports)

Number of bedrooms	Number of occupied premises
1	2370
2	5950
3	7260
4	3170
5	1810

Draw a pictogram to represent these data, which resulted from the City Shelter Research Project.

3 A manufacturer of home computers who is proposing to extend a factory by 50 per cent, asks you for a report on the home computer market and the wisdom of the proposed expansion. Your investigations reveal the following figures for sales in the last six years.

Year	Sales (£ million)
1	16
2	22
3	38
4	64
5	56
6	45

Choose a suitable symbol, and a suitable scale, and draw a pictogram to display the data. Is the expansion wise, or not?

4 An industrial company employs the following staff: (a) 110 senior-management staff; (b) 495 middle-management staff; (c) 1495 clerical staff; and (d) 4250 shop-floor workers. Using a *different* symbol for each type of employee, illustrate these data with a pictogram. The source of the data is the Personnel Department.

28.3 Bar charts

A bar chart is similar to a pictogram but easier to draw. Instead of using symbols to represent the data, we use the length of a bar to compare different magnitudes. Information is related to the horizontal or vertical length of a bar or thick line.

The idea is illustrated in Figure 28.2, below. The largest piece of data is shown as the maximum length of the bar possible on the piece of paper to be used, and smaller items are given a length in proportion. In Figure 28.2, for example, the Bombay factory's output (20 000 units) is shown as a bar 10 cm long. This is a scale of 1 cm = 2000 units. The London factory, the output of which is 16 000 units, is represented by a bar 8 cm long. This is found by the calculation:

$$\frac{16\,000}{2000} = 8\,\text{cm}$$

as every 2000 units is represented by 1 centimetre.

Figure 28.2 A bar chart: units of output in a multinational company's factories

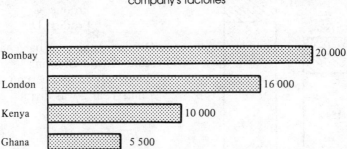

28.4 Component and percentage bar charts

Sometimes a set of data may be divided up into component parts, which can be easily displayed to show how the components build into the total. For example, in Figure 28.3, below, the proportions of wealth created by a particular company are shown in such a way as to display the proportions enjoyed by various groups over a period of ten years, the situation in Year 1, Year 5 and Year 10 being compared.

In each case we have to calculate that part of the height of the bar which would correctly be allocated to each group. On the original drawing the Year 1 figures were allocated a height of 3 cm, and this height therefore represents £150.2 millions. Wages and salaries paid to employees took £91.4 millions. The height of this section of the data should therefore be:

$$\frac{91.4}{150.2} \times 3\,\text{cm} = \frac{274.2}{150.2}$$
$$= \underline{1.8\,\text{cm}} \text{ (correct to one decimal place)}$$

A similar type of bar chart is a **percentage bar chart**. Here the components of the data are shown as a percentage of the total length of the bar. Thus, in the following set of data about motor vehicles licensed in the United Kingdom in 19.., the original data have been calculated as percentages of the total data.

Motor vehicles licensed in the United Kingdom, 19..

Type of vehicle	Number of vehicles (thousands)	Percentage of vehicles
Private cars and vans	15 685	79.3
Motor cycles, scooters etc.	1 370	6.9
Farm vehicles	458	2.3
Goods vehicles	1 616	8.2
Public service vehicles	111	0.6
Other licensed vehicles	92	0.5
Exempt vehicles	438	2.2
Total	19 770	100.0

These percentages could then be shown as component parts of a bar, to give a percentage bar chart.

28.5 Exercises: bar diagrams

1 A certain factory makes four products. Output in the year 19.. is as follows.

Product A	8 500 units
Product B	6 250 units
Product C	9 000 units
Product D	15 000 units

Display these in a bar chart, using a suitable scale of your choosing.

2 Cargo carried by a certain shipping line in Year 1 and Year 2 was divided as follows.

	Year 1 (million tonnes)	Year 2 (million tonnes)
Bulk cargo	11	14
Heavy manufactures	5	7
Other manufactures	2	2.5
Motor vehicles (by weight)	4.5	6.5

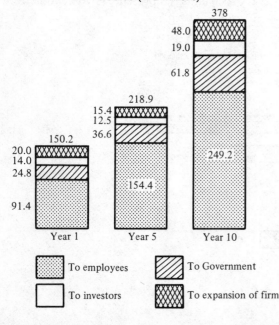

Figure 28.3 A component bar chart: division of wealth created (in £ millions)

Key:
To employees
To investors
To Government
To expansion of firm

Show these cargoes in the form of a bar chart, the four bars for Year 1 separate from the four bars for Year 2, so that it is possible to compare (a) the cargoes carried in each year, and (b) the changes in volumes carried over the two years.

3 Sales in a two-year period by a certain department store were as follows.

Department	Year 1 (£ thousands)	Year 2 (£ thousands)
Furniture	60	100
Soft furnishings	30	60
Glassware etc.	30	40
Fashions	80	100
Total	200	300

Display these figures in two component bar charts to show the changes in sales over the two years.

4 A firm makes profits of £182 000. Of this, £40 500 is paid to the shareholders, £72 800 is paid in taxation, £20 250 is paid as bonuses to staff, and the rest is used to expand the firm's organisation. Display these data in the form of a component bar chart.

5 A Government department shares up a fund of £120 000 in the following way: assistance to students in financial difficulty £18 000; development of tennis facilities £24 000; university exploration projects £15 000; development of small businesses £42 000; research into child welfare problems £9000. The balance is devoted to capital equipment for a workshop for the disabled. Show the expenditure as a percentage bar chart.

28.6 Pie diagrams

A pie diagram is circular in shape, like a round apple pie. The component parts of the data are shown as slices cut from the pie. In order to present a correct picture, it is necessary for the data to be calculated as parts of a circle, i.e. parts of 360 degrees.

Refer to the table, 'Exports of the United Kingdom, 19..', below. Data for each export has been calculated as parts of the total. Before drawing the pie diagram, the value of each export had to be calculated as a part of the value of total exports.

For example, if we take the value of finished manufactures, £21 000 m, as part of the value of total exports, £50 000 m (360°):

$$\text{degrees required} = \frac{21\cancel{000}}{50\cancel{000}} \times 36\cancel{0}$$

$$= \frac{756}{5}$$

$$= 151.2°$$

$$\frac{21}{36}$$
$$\frac{126}{630}$$
$$\frac{756}{}$$

Exports of the United Kingdom, 19.. (in £ millions)

Type of export	Value	Degrees in diagram
Finished manufactures	21 000	151.2
Fuels	7 500	54
Semi-manufactures	14 000	100.8
Basic raw materials	2 500	18
Food, drink and tobacco	3 500	25.2
Other items	1 500	10.8
Total	£50 000	360.0

The resulting pie diagram is shown in Figure 28.4.

Figure 28.4 A pie diagram

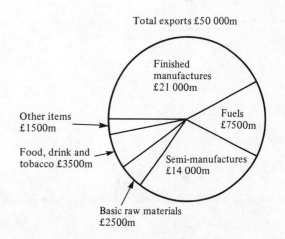

Total exports £50 000m

Finished manufactures £21 000m

Fuels £7500m

Semi-manufactures £14 000m

Basic raw materials £2500m

Food, drink and tobacco £3500m

Other items £1500m

28.7 Exercises: pie diagrams

1 A charity collection of £5400 in a certain school is made up in the following ways: proceeds of a fun-run £1800; sales of food items made by the domestic science department £450; donations by parents, £1350; donations by local business £540. The rest was raised by a 'bring-and-buy' sale. Draw a pie chart to illustrate the above data.

2 Imports into the United Kingdom in one recent year were as follows.

	Value (£ millions)
Finished manufactures	16 000
Semi-manufactures	12 000
Fuels	6 000
Basic raw materials	4 000
Food, drink and tobacco	6 000
Other items	1 000
	£45 000

3 Heavy goods vehicles on the roads number 48 000. Of these, 3000 are less than 6 tonnes in weight; 12 000 are between 6 tonnes and $8\frac{1}{2}$ tonnes; 6000 are between $8\frac{1}{2}$ tonnes and 16 tonnes; and 15 000 are between 16 and 28 tonnes. 12 000 are over 28 tonnes in weight. Draw a pie chart to show the distribution of heavy goods transport over the various sizes.

4 A social survey reveals that families have the following incomes in Africairia (an African country) with a population of 40 million and averaging five members to a family.

Income per annum (shillings)	Number of families (thousands)
Less than 1000	3600
1000 and under 1500	2400
1500 and under 2000	800
2000 and under 3000	600
3000 and under 4000	400
over 4000	200

Draw a pie diagram to show the proportions of the population in each income band.

29

More about Averages: the Mean, Median and Mode

29.1 Averages in statistics

An inquiry provides a mass of information (data) about the subject matter of the inquiry, and enables us to draw conclusions from the information we have collected. Part of the decision-making process is to describe the set of data we have collected, so that we can understand the general pattern of results. The process of describing the set of data begins with finding the central position, called the **average** of the data. For example, if we take the three numbers 1, 51 and 101, the average is 51; or the three numbers 49, 51 and 53, the average is again 51.

The averages quoted above (51 in each case) were the arithmetic averages. Their statistical name is 'the arithmetic mean', which means the central position found by simple arithmetic. We learned about these calculations in Chapter 10.

There are two other common averages that we meet in statistics: the **median** and the **mode**. We will learn about these later in this chapter. First let us revise what we know about the arithmetic mean.

29.2 The arithmetic mean

The arithmetic mean of a simple set of numbers is found by adding the numbers together, and then dividing by the number of numbers.

Thus the mean of 26, 32, 40 and 54 is found by adding them together and dividing their total by 4 (as there are four numbers).

$$\frac{26 + 32 + 40 + 54}{4} = \frac{152}{4} = 38$$

Similarly, the mean of 125, 135, 150, 175 and 195

$$= \frac{780}{5}$$

$$= 156$$

More difficult examples of the calculation of arithmetic means require us to consider weighted averages and frequency distributions.

Weighted averages

Sometimes an average involves more than one example of each value. For example, suppose 20 students score in an examination as follows:

1	scores	100
2	score	91
1	scores	87
3	score	77
2	score	75
1	scores	69
2	score	53
4	score	47
3	score	41
1	scores	27
20		

What is the mean score? Clearly some of the numbers are weighted; that is, they have to be counted more than once. There are 4 students who scored 47, for example, which means we must add in 188 for this group. We can complete the calculation by multiplying the weights by the scores to give a series of products. This series of products can then be added to give the total scores. The arithmetic mean will be found by dividing this total by the number of students (20).

Number of students	Examination score		Products
1	100	=	100
2	91	=	182
1	87	=	87
3	77	=	231
2	75	=	150
1	69	=	69
2	53	=	106
4	47	=	188
3	41	=	123
1	27	=	27
20			1263

$$\text{Mean score} = \frac{1263}{20}$$

$$= \frac{126.3}{2}$$

$$= 63.15$$

Averages of frequency distributions

A frequency distribution is a set of data that shows the data grouped into classes, with the number of items in each class (the frequency) shown. Consider the following monthly wage packets earned by young people employed in the London area.

Wage per month	Frequency
Under £100	24
£100 and under £150	42
£150 and under £200	56
£200 and under £250	164
£250 and under £300	98
£300 and over	16
	400

It is impossible to find the average wage unless we make certain assumptions. The first of these is that the items in a group are evenly spread throughout the group. Of course we cannot know whether this is so on the evidence available to us. Are the 56 people in the £150–£200 group actually earning an average of £175? They might not be, but we assume they are evenly spread throughout the group and so earn an average of £175.

The other assumption we make is that any open-ended group (the first group and the last group) has twice as large a range inside it as the other groups. Thus since the class intervals are usually £50 we assume the end groups to be £100. This makes the mid-point of these end groups £50 for the first group and £350 for the last group. We are now ready to work out the average using the mid-points of all these groups. To some extent these assumptions can vary with the circumstances of an inquiry and the results obtained in (for example) the open-ended groups.

Frequency (f)	Mid-point of group (x)	Products (f × x)
24	£50	1 200
42	£125	5 250
56	£175	9 800
164	£225	36 900
98	£275	26 950
16	£350	5 600
400		85 700

$$\therefore \text{Average} = \frac{85\,700}{400}$$

$$= \frac{857}{4}$$

$$= 214.25$$

You will see that the method is similar to the weighted average method, except that we use the mid-points of the groups as being the wages earned by each member of the group.

29.3 Exercises: the arithmetic mean

1 Find the arithmetic mean of 3, 5, 8, 7, 11, 14 and 15.
2 Find the arithmetic mean of 21, 24, 27, 35, 36 and 43.
3 In an examination 30 students score as follows: 2 score 91 marks each, 1 scores 89, 3 score 79, 2 score 76, 1 scores 71, 3 score 62, 1 scores 61, 3 score 58, 2 score 54, 3 score 51, 2 score 50, 1 scores 47, 2 score 44, 3 score 39 and 1 scores 28. Find the average score. (Answer correct to one decimal place.)

4 If 7 bricklayers are paid £2.80 per hour for a 40 hour week, and 5 bricklayers are paid £2.15 per hour for a 40 hour week, what is the average wage packet? (Answer correct to the nearest penny.)

5 A statistical inquiry reveals that monthly salary cheques for factory staff are as follows:

Wage per month	Number of staff
Under £300	48
£300 and under £350	82
£350 and under £400	56
£400 and under £450	84
£450 and under £500	26
£500 and over	4
	300

What is the average monthly salary? (Answer correct to the nearest penny.)

29.4 The median

Another average that is frequently used in statistics is the **median**. The median is the value of the central item in a distribution that has been arranged in order of size. Consider the following group of numbers:

$$4, 5, 7, 11, 13, 15, 17, 29, 41$$

The group is arranged in ascending order of value and the median value is the value of the central item in the array. This is found by the formula:

$$\text{Median} = \frac{n+1}{2}$$

where n is the number of numbers.

As there are nine numbers

$$\frac{n+1}{2} = \frac{9+1}{2} = 5,$$

so the median is the value of the 5th item, which is 13. There are four numbers below 13 and four above.

$$4, 5, 7, 11, \quad 13, \quad 15, 17, 29, 41$$

Note that the median (13) is very different from the arithmetic mean, which is calculated as $\frac{142}{9} = 15.\dot{7}$.

Where the number is even, we do not find the median to be the value of an actual item in the array. For example:

$$4, 5, 7, 11, 13, 15, 17, 29, 41, 60$$

There are now ten numbers. Therefore,

$$\text{Median} = \frac{n+1}{2} = \frac{10+1}{2} = \frac{11}{2} = 5\tfrac{1}{2}$$

So the median is the $5\tfrac{1}{2}$th item and must be the average of the 5th and 6th items in the array. Therefore the median is the average of 13 and $15 = \frac{28}{2} = 14$. Once again the median (14) is not the same as the mean ($\frac{202}{10} = 20.2$).

It might seem strange to use an average that is quite different from the arithmetic average (the mean), but sometimes it gives a better answer. Consider a dog that loses a leg in an accident. If this dog joins a group of 9 dogs (each with four legs apiece), so that there are now 10 dogs, the mean number of legs is reduced to 3.9 legs per dog; but the median says there are 4 legs per dog, which is the more sensible answer. We shall see later that the mode also gives the same result.

If a class of forty students each 16 years old is joined by two 80-year-old students, the mean age of the class is:

$$\text{Mean age} = \frac{(40 \times 16) + (2 \times 80)}{42}$$

$$= \frac{640 + 160}{42}$$

$$= \frac{800}{42}$$

$$= 19.05 \text{ years}$$

The median age is calculated as follows:

$$\text{Median age} = \frac{n+1}{2} = \frac{42+1}{2} = 21\tfrac{1}{2}\text{th item}$$

The $21\tfrac{1}{2}$th item is a 16-year-old person, as there are 40 of them in the array. The median answer of 16 years is a more sensible average age, as it describes the vast majority of the group, while no one in the group has the mean age of 19 years.

Elementary questions about the median require us to arrange the data in ascending order of value and then apply the formula to find the median.

Example: Lap times in a sports car race in minutes and seconds are as follows: 2 mins 38 sec; 2 mins 45 sec; 3 mins 5 sec; 3 mins 3 sec; 2 mins 54 sec; 2 mins 59 sec; 3 mins 16 sec. What is the median time?

There are seven cars, so n = 7. Therefore the median time is the

$$\frac{n+1}{2} = \frac{8}{2} = \text{4th time in ascending order}$$

Lap times are: 2.38, 2.45, 2.54, 2.59, 3.3, 3.5, 3.16. The median time is therefore 2 minutes 59 seconds.

29.5 Exercises: the median

1 Electric light bulbs tested to destruction in a quality control experiment burned out after the following times. What is the median life of a bulb?

(a) 500 hours (b) 1242 hours (c) 749 hours
(d) 22 hours (e) 184 hours (f) 3052 hours
(g) 476 hours (h) 44 hours (i) 72 hours

2 Sales by the ten salesmen of a pharmaceutical firm for the month of July are as follows. What is the median sales value?

(a) £8264   (b) £7381
(c) £18 716   (d) £14 295
(e) £27 384   (f) £5894
(g) £14 925   (h) £3875
(i) £16 386   (j) £11 582

3 The tonnage of cargo vessels in a deep-sea fleet are as follows. What is the median tonnage?

(a) 124 700 tonnes   (b) 77 850 tonnes
(c) 165 600 tonnes   (d) 140 000 tonnes
(e) 368 500 tonnes   (f) 138 900 tonnes
(g) 12 854 tonnes   (h) 427 250 tonnes
(i) 18 750 tonnes   (j) 37 500 tonnes
(k) 125 280 tonnes

4 The salaries earned by employees of Grow and Pack Ltd are as follows in the month of October. What is the median salary?

£185 £205 £208 £430 £210 £215 £442 £219
£424 £188 £205 £416 £192 £205 £198 £185
£188 £484 £192 £550

29.6 The mode

The mode is an average that tells us which item occurs most frequently in a set of data. Just as fashions can be 'a la mode' in Paris (meaning everyone in Paris is wearing them), the mode in statistics simply records the most 'popular' statistic, the one occurring most often.

Consider the following scores made by a football team in a series of matches:

0, 5, 2, 1, 1, 4, 3, 1, 2, 0, 5, 4, 1, 3, 1, 0

Set down to bring out the frequencies of the particular scores we have:

0, 0, 0
1, 1, 1, 1, 1
2, 2
3, 3
4, 4
5, 5

Clearly 1 is the modal score, as 1 goal was scored on five occasions. Note that the mode is very far from the mean in this case, the mean being 2.06.

Bi-modal and tri-modal series

One of the disadvantages of the mode as an average is that it is possible to have two modes, or even three modes. As in the series shown below:

1, 0, 1, 5, 5, 3, 4, 7, 1, 2, 2, 5, 4, 3

This is a bi-modal series, as 1 goal and 5 goals occur with equal frequency.

1, 1, 5, 2, 3, 2, 5, 1, 4, 5, 0, 3, 0, 4, 3

This is a tri-modal series, as the team scored 1 goal, 3 goals and 5 goals with equal frequency.

29.7 Exercises: the mode

1 Three football teams score as follows in a series of 12 matches. What was the modal score for each team?

Team A 1, 2, 3, 1, 4, 3, 5, 2, 2, 3, 2, 1
Team B 0, 1, 0, 2, 0, 0, 0, 3, 0, 1, 0, 1
Team C 2, 2, 3, 1, 0, 3, 1, 0, 5, 5, 4, 2

2 Houses in Playa Spiritosa, where it is customary to welcome paying guests in vacation periods, have guest rooms as follows.

Number of guest rooms	1	2	3	4	5
Houses concerned	242	387	1459	1684	477

If each guest room accommodates 2 persons on average, what is the modal number of guests catered for in Playa Spiritosa?

3 Four bowlers have the following record for wickets taken in a certain season. What is the modal number of wickets taken for each bowler?

Bowler A 4, 3, 2, 0, 2, 3, 1, 5, 8, 3, 2, 1, 2, 4, 2
Bowler B 7, 8, 2, 2, 3, 4, 4, 5, 4, 3, 5, 2, 1, 0, 8
Bowler C 2, 4, 2, 2, 2, 4, 3, 3, 0, 1, 0, 4, 4, 5, 5
Bowler D 1, 1, 3, 7, 7, 2, 6, 8, 4, 3, 3, 2, 8, 7, 7

4 Lorries passing under a continental motorway bridge are recorded as follows.

5-tonne vehicles	8-tonne vehicles	16-tonne vehicles	32-tonne vehicles	44-tonne vehicles
328	758	1248	3858	1364

What is the modal weight for vehicles using the motorway?

29.8 Which average should we use?

Any average has its advantages and disadvantages, but the most widely used average is the arithmetic mean. This is because it is simple to calculate, takes account of all the items in the data (because they are all added together when it is calculated), and above all, because it is susceptible to mathematical manipulation. This means that it can be used to calculate further statistics, such as standard deviations, correlation data, etc. Why then bother with the others? The answer is that in certain circumstances they do give a better picture of the mass of data than the mean. We have already referred to the three-legged dog, which in any group of dogs affects the mean number of legs in the group. The mode tells us that dogs normally have four legs, and the median gives the same result.

In any set of data where there are extreme items, either very large items or very small items, these will affect the arithmetic mean and falsify it as a measure of centrality for the set. Thus the numbers 1, 2, 3, 4, 5 and 1000 have an average of 169.16, which is not a very good description of the whole series. The median, 3.5, would in some ways be a 'better' average. The mode is not much help at all, for it is a six-modal series.

30
Stocks and Shares

30.1 Introduction

Stocks and shares are paper securities issued to investors in companies and nationalised corporations or in local and central Government bond schemes. The modern world's enterprises are too vast to be financed by any one person or family, and the risks of failure are too great for most people to 'put all their eggs in one basket' as used to happen in earlier times.

Today thousands, even millions of people subscribe capital to a limited company and thus become part-owners of (i.e. shareholders in) the company, or lend money to the company and thus become debenture-holders. Other people lend money to local authorities by purchasing bonds. 'Bonds' can be defined as 'promises to repay in the future'. Similarly, central Governments borrow money against bonds, and even the World Bank does the same sort of thing. The British Government funds were recorded many years ago in an official book with gilt-edged pages and became known as 'gilt-edged securities'. We therefore have the following types of securities.

Shares

These are shares in the capital of a company. They are usually based on £1, but 50p and 10p shares are quite common. Shares can be issued at the nominal price or par value of £1, 50p etc., but they are often issued at a premium, which means a higher price. This is not a commerce book, so we cannot go into a full explanation, but the higher price reflects the hard work done by the original shareholders in which the new shareholders are being invited to share. They have to pay a premium to get into the company.

Once shares are issued they do not stay at the par value, but vary in price on the market according to the success of the company. Thus you might need to pay £3.20 for £1 share if the company is doing particularly well, while lots of shares (called penny shares) are only worth about 1p or 2p because the company is doing so badly.

Debentures

These are issued when money is loaned to a company, rather than invested in it. The debenture-holder is not a shareholder, but earns interest on the debentures rather than a share of the profits. This interest has to be paid whether the company makes profits or not; and if a company fails, the debenture-holders have a prior right of repayment. Hence the investment is safer than an ordinary shareholding.

Stocks

These are of two kinds.

(a) Company stocks are created when shares are amalgamated into stock, to make dealings easier. Most nationalised corporations, local authorities and Governments issue stocks. The most famous stock of all is 'Old Consols', originally issued in 1745 when all Government debt was consolidated into one stock called Consolidated Stock. Today you can buy £100 of Old Consols for about £24, but of course they vary in price every day.

Dealings in shares can take place privately, but the vast majority change hands on an official exchange called a Stock Exchange. The major United Kingdom Stock Exchange is in Throgmorton Street in the City of London, and visitors can call in at any time and watch the dealings from a secluded balcony overlooking the floor of the Exchange. The dealers who buy and sell for the general public are called stockbrokers, and their charges are called brokerage charges. If you telephone a stockbroker and ask to purchase shares or stock for you, he or she will go down to the floor of the house, find the stock-jobber offering the best bargain for the shares you require, and purchase them for you. You are bound to honour the bargain the stockbroker has made for you. Stock-jobbers, like any other market trader, have parcels of shares for sale at any time, or know where to get them.

(b) You may feel that you have no interest in stocks and shares, and that it is a game only rich people play! Nothing could be further from the truth. Many people of average income in the United Kingdom have shares bought and sold for them every day. This is because many people have some sort of savings: they insure their motor vehicles, their homes etc.; they buy houses. All this money is collected by insurance companies, building societies etc., and is invested on the Stock Exchange in every kind of firm. These organisations are called 'financial institutions' and the institutional investors buy and sell shares on behalf of every person who insures, saves money etc. The financial institutions build huge portfolios of stocks and shares which they can sell later to pay out pensions, or compensate accident victims etc.

(*Note*: The description of Stock Exchange procedures given above is to change in a year or two if new methods of working, under discussion at present, are finally agreed.)

30.2 Dealings in shares

When we buy and sell shares there are certain basic situations we need to understand. It may seem a little confusing at first, but practice makes perfect, and answering the questions at the end of each section in this chapter will help you follow the procedures. Consider the following examples.

Example: (a) Mr M buys 500 £1 shares in a firm called ABCD Ltd. These shares are priced at £1.97 on the market, and the stockbroker's charges are £7.25. How much will he have to pay?

Each share costs £1.97, and we must add on the charges to be paid.

$$
\begin{array}{lr}
 & \text{£} \\
\text{500 shares cost £1.97} \times 500 = \text{£197} \times 5 = & 985 \\
\text{Add broker's charges} \hspace{2em} = & 7.25 \\
\hline
 & \text{£992.25}
\end{array}
$$

Example: (b) Mrs B sells 650 shares in Welshgold Mining Ltd. The broker sells them at a price of 38p each, and his charges are £6.25. What does Mrs B receive?

Each share sells for 38p, and we must deduct the broker's charges.

$$
\begin{aligned}
\text{650 shares sell for 38p} \times 650 \\
= \text{£38} \times 6\tfrac{1}{2} \\
= \text{£228} + \text{£19} \\
= \text{£247}
\end{aligned}
$$

Deducting brokerage charges Mrs B received £247 − £6.25

$$= \text{£240.75}$$

Example: (c) Miss H sells 17 500 shares in Universal Markets Ltd for £1.82 per share (brokerage charges £38.50). Some time earlier she had purchased the shares at 97p (brokerage charges £23.50). What profit did she make on the sale?

Sale realises (£1.82 × 17 500) − £38.50

$$
\begin{array}{lr}
= (\text{£182} \times 175) - \text{£38.50} & 182 \\
= \text{£31 850} - \text{£38.50} & 175 \\
= \text{£31 811.50} & \\
\hline
 & 910 \\
 & 12\,740 \\
 & 18\,200 \\
\hline
 & 31\,850
\end{array}
$$

Cost price earlier was

(97 pence × 17 500) + £23.50

$$
\begin{array}{lr}
= (\text{£97} \times 175) + \text{£23.50} & 175 \\
= \text{£16 975} + \text{£23.50} & 97 \\
= \text{£16 998.50} & \\
\hline
 & 1\,225 \\
 & 15\,750 \\
\hline
 & 16\,975
\end{array}
$$

Therefore profit

$$
\begin{aligned}
&= \text{£31 811.50} - \text{£16 998.50} \\
&= \text{£14 813}
\end{aligned}
$$

The same answer could have been arrived at in a different way, by taking the profit on a single share:

$$£1.82 - 97p = 85p$$

Therefore profit on 17 500 shares

$$
\begin{aligned}
&= 85p \times 17\,500 \\
&= £85 \times 175 \\
&= \underline{\underline{£14\,875}}
\end{aligned}
$$

$$
\begin{array}{r}
175 \\
85 \\
\hline
875 \\
14\,000 \\
\hline
14\,875 \\
\hline
\end{array}
$$

As the charges have to be paid on both occasions, this means we have to deduct both lots of charges:

$$
\begin{aligned}
\text{Profit} &= £14\,875 - (£38.50 + £23.50) \\
&= £14\,875 - £62 \\
&= \underline{\underline{£14\,813}}
\end{aligned}
$$

This is the same answer as before.

30.3 Exercises: dealings in shares

1 Find the cost of the following sets of shares. In each case brokerage charges are as shown.

	Number of shares	Price per share	Charges
(a)	500	£1.24	£7.85
(b)	800	£1.67	£12.30
(c)	1 500	87p	£15.80
(d)	10 000	23p	£31.50
(e)	17 500	£3.47	£162.50

2 What will the seller receive for the following shares if the prices and brokerage charges are as shown below?

	Number of shares	Selling price per share	Brokerage charges
(a)	400	48p	£6.50
(b)	550	£1.64	£13.85
(c)	2 500	£2.13	£31.50
(d)	7 500	£1.04	£26.50
(e)	10 000	£4.24	£320.75

3 What profit or loss will be made in each case below on shares purchased at the first price and sold at the second price, given the brokerage charges as shown?

	Number of shares	Purchase price	Selling price	Brokerage on purchase	Brokerage on sale
(a)	250	23p	42p	£6.50	£6.50
(b)	750	£1.17	£1.95	£8.70	£12.35
(c)	1 600	£1.27	£1.21	£9.20	£9.12
(d)	2 400	£2.79	£3.21	£48.25	£63.40
(e)	12 000	£4.56	£4.43	£324.00	£308.00

30.4 Simple dealings in stocks

Stock can be dealt in to any amount, but it is usual to base the calculations on £100 of stock. £100 is regarded as the normal price or par value of any £100 unit of stock. If stock is changing hands at prices above £100 for £100 of stock, it is said to be 'above par' or at a premium, while if £100 of stock can be purchased for less than £100 it is said to be 'below par' or 'at a discount'.

The following matters are of interest in dealing with stocks:

(a) How much will we have to pay for stocks we buy?

(b) How much will we get for stocks we sell?

(c) What is the income on a stock—in other words the interest we will get from the stock?

(d) What is the yield per cent on the investment?

Let us consider each of these in turn.

Example (a): Mrs Jones wishes to buy £1500 worth of 9% Government stock at present selling at $109\frac{1}{4}$ (brokerage $\frac{1}{4}$). How much must she pay? What will she earn from the investment? What percentage interest is she earning on her investment?

The three questions above pose quite tricky points. First, she has to buy the stock at $109\frac{1}{4}$. This means that for every parcel of £100 stock she must pay $£109\frac{1}{4}$ and $£\frac{1}{4}$ brokerage on top. The price is therefore $£109\frac{1}{2}$ for every £100. As she wishes to buy £1500 worth of stock, she must pay:

$$£109\frac{1}{2} \times 15 = £1635 + £7.50 \text{ (the extra } \tfrac{1}{2}\text{)}$$

$$= \underline{\underline{£1642.50}}$$

$$
\begin{array}{r}
109 \\
15 \\
\hline
545 \\
1090 \\
\hline
1635 \\
\hline
\end{array}
$$

How much will she earn on the investment? The answer is that as she has 15 parcels of £100 and each £100 earns her £9 (a 9% stock) she will earn:

$$= 15 \times £9$$
$$\text{Earnings} = £135$$

What percentage interest is she earning on her investment? The answer is not 9%. Can you see why? If she had purchased the stock at par £100, she would be receiving £9 on every £100, which is 9%. As she purchased the stock at a premium she had to pay more than £100, and only earned £9 on every £109½. The yield on her investment is therefore £135 on £1642.50, which as a percentage is:

$$\text{Yield} = \frac{£135 \times 100}{£1642.50}$$

$$= \frac{£13\,500}{£1642\frac{1}{2}}$$

$$= \frac{£27\,000}{£3285}$$

$$= 8.22\%$$

$$
\begin{array}{r}
8.219 \\
3285\overline{)27000} \\
26280 \\
\hline
7200 \\
6570 \\
\hline
6300 \\
3285 \\
\hline
3015
\end{array}
$$

Of course, if the stock had been below par, so that the £1500 stock cost less than £1500, the yield on the investment would have been greater than 9%. Suppose the stock had been at 91¾ with ¼ brokerage, making 92 in all.

The price of £1500 stock at $92 = 15 \times 92$
$$= £1380$$

$$
\begin{array}{r}
92 \\
15 \\
\hline
460 \\
920 \\
\hline
1380
\end{array}
$$

The interest received would still be 9% on each £100 = £135.

The yield would therefore be

$$\frac{£135}{£1380} \times 100 \text{ (cancelling by 10)}$$

$$= \frac{£1350}{£138}$$

$$= 9.8\%$$

$$
\begin{array}{r}
9.78 \\
138\overline{)1350} \\
1242 \\
\hline
1080 \\
966 \\
\hline
1140 \\
1104 \\
\hline
36
\end{array}
$$

Example (b): An institutional investor has £25 000 of British Consols, earning 2½% per annum. They propose to sell them at 23¼ (brokerage ¼) and buy 9% Treasury Stock at 89¾ (brokerage ¼). In making this purchase they will purchase to the nearest £100 of stock, any small extra amount needed being contributed from other funds. What will be the increase or decrease in income?

Present income = 250 × £2.50 (every £100 gives £2.50)
$$= £625 \qquad (2\frac{1}{2} \times 250)$$

If sold at 23¼ (less brokerage ¼) the Consols will bring in cash available = 250 × £23 (every £100 sells for £23)

$$
\begin{array}{r}
250 \\
23 \\
\hline
750 \\
5000 \\
\hline
£5750
\end{array}
$$

$$= £5750$$

If reinvested at 89¾ (add brokerage ¼) this will purchase

$$\frac{£5750 \times 10\cancel{0}}{9\cancel{0}}$$

$$= \frac{£5750 \times 10}{9}$$

$$= \frac{£57500}{9}$$

$$= £6388.8$$

$$
\begin{array}{r}
9\overline{)57500} \\
6388.8
\end{array}
$$

Therefore they will purchase £6400 9% stock (the little extra money required will be contributed from other cash sources).

Income from £6400 9%
$$= £64 \times 9 \qquad \text{(each £100 earns 9%)}$$
$$= £576$$

Therefore there is a decrease in income: £625 − £576 = £49 decrease.

30.5 Exercises: calculations with stocks

1 What will an investor pay for stocks in each of the following cases?

	Quantity required	Price	Brokerage
(a)	£500	$98\frac{3}{4}$	$\frac{1}{4}$
(b)	£800	$112\frac{1}{4}$	$\frac{1}{4}$
(c)	£2 500	$76\frac{3}{4}$	$\frac{1}{4}$
(d)	£10 000	$91\frac{7}{8}$	$\frac{1}{8}$
(e)	£25 000	$103\frac{3}{8}$	$\frac{1}{8}$

2 What will an investor receive on selling the following amounts of stock at the rates shown?

	Amount of stock	Price	Brokerage charges
(a)	£150	$119\frac{3}{4}$	$\frac{1}{4}$
(b)	£350	$125\frac{1}{4}$	$\frac{1}{4}$
(c)	£1 350	$87\frac{3}{4}$	$\frac{1}{4}$
(d)	£7 800	$67\frac{3}{4}$	$\frac{1}{4}$
(e)	£12 250	$24\frac{1}{8}$	$\frac{1}{8}$

3 An investor buys £12 000 of 8% stock at $74\frac{3}{4}$ (brokerage $\frac{1}{4}$). (a) What will it cost him? (b) What will be the income from the stock? (c) What will be the yield per cent on the investment?

4 An institutional investor buys £150 000 of 7% stock at $77\frac{7}{8}$ (brokerage $\frac{1}{8}$). (a) What will it cost? (b) What will be the income from the stock? (c) What will be the yield per cent on the investment? (Answer correct to two decimal places.)

5 An investor at present holds £10 000 6% gilt-edged stock. She proposes to sell it and replace it with $2\frac{1}{2}$% Consols at $19\frac{3}{4}$ (brokerage $\frac{1}{4}$). The 6% stock is valued at present at $60\frac{1}{4}$, but brokerage is $\frac{1}{4}$. (a) What will the old stock realise? (b) How much Consol stock will she obtain? (c) What will be the change in income?

6 An investor holds £1500 $10\frac{1}{2}$% stock. At present it is selling at $110\frac{1}{4}$ on the market (brokerage $\frac{1}{4}$). The investor decides to sell it and replace it with a 7% stock selling at $82\frac{1}{4}$ (brokerage $\frac{1}{4}$). (a) What will he realise on the old stock? (b) How much of the new stock will he obtain? (c) What will be the change in income?

7 An institutional investor at present holds £18 000 $9\frac{1}{4}$% stock that was originally purchased at $121\frac{1}{2}$ some months ago. It is now proposed to sell it at 110 and invest the money in $3\frac{1}{2}$% War Loan at 33. (a) What is the yield per cent on the present investment? (b) What will the sale of the $9\frac{1}{4}$% stock realise in cash? (c) What quantity of War Loan will the investor be able to purchase? (d) What income will this earn? (e) What is the yield per cent on the new investment? (Ignore the brokerage. Answers correct to one decimal place where necessary.)

8 An institutional investor at present holds £25 000 8% stock which it purchased some time ago when it stood at 75. They propose to sell it, since it has fallen to 68, and use the money to buy 12% Treasury Stock at 85. (a) What was the yield per cent on the original investment? (b) What will be the amount of 12% Treasury Stock able to be purchased? (c) What will be the yield on this stock per cent? (Answer correct to one decimal place).

31

Compound Interest

31.1 Simple interest and compound interest

In Chapter 13 we studied simple interest, a method of paying interest where the interest due is actually paid to the lender of the money, who thus has control and use of the interest earned. We must now consider compound interest, where the interest earned is not paid to the lender of the money, but is simply added to the investment, and remains invested. This increased investment then earns interest in the next period. Compare the two investments of £1000 shown in Table 31.1, loaned by a depositor to a building society at 10% interest. The first is at simple interest, the second at compound interest.

Notice that by the beginning of Year 9 the original investment of £1000 at 10% has more than doubled to £2143.59. Even at $2\frac{1}{2}\%$ compound interest, money doubles itself in 25 years.

This idea of compound interest is much wider in its application than just the lending of money. For example, it is a popular view in economics that an annual increase in the standard of living of about $2\frac{1}{2}\%$ is a reasonable aim for mankind. As this growth in the national income is at compound interest ($2\frac{1}{2}\%$ growth each year on the previous year), to realise this growth we have to double the volume of goods and services we produce every 25 years. Even if it *is* a desirable increase, it does not mean we can achieve it.

Calculations with compound interest can be very long and very tedious, and we will only attempt simple calculations in this chapter.

31.2 Compound interest by the practice method

A simple way to do compound interest calculations is known as the 'practice method'. This is a method where each line of working follows simply from one of the earlier lines in the calculation, using the normal rules of arithmetic, addition, subtraction, multiplication or division. An example is the best way to follow the process.

Date of investment	Amount invested (£)	Interest (simple) (£) (paid to investor)	Amount invested (£)	Interest (compound) (£) (retained)
1 January Year 1	1000	—	1000	—
31 December Year 1	1000	100	1000	100
31 December Year 2	1000	100	1100	110
31 December Year 3	1000	100	1210	121
31 December Year 4	1000	100	1331	133.10
31 December Year 5	1000	100	1464.10	146.41
31 December Year 6	1000	100	1610.51	161.05
31 December Year 7	1000	100	1771.56	177.16
31 December Year 8	1000	100	1948.72	194.87
1 January Year 9	1000		2143.59	

Table 31.1

Example: (a) What will be the final amount of an investment of £3600 at $6\frac{1}{2}\%$ compound interest for 3 years?

The easy way to work out $6\frac{1}{2}\%$ interest is 1%, 5% and then $\frac{1}{2}\%$. The calculations are then as follows, if we correct up to three places of decimals.

		£
Initial investment	=	3600
1% interest	=	36
5% interest (5 × 1%)	=	180
$\frac{1}{2}\%$ interest ($\frac{1}{2}$ × 1%)	=	18
After one year investment	=	3834
1% interest (2nd year)	=	38.34
5% interest	=	191.70
$\frac{1}{2}\%$ interest	=	19.17
After two years investment	=	4083.21
1% interest (3rd year)	=	40.832
5% interest	=	204.160
$\frac{1}{2}\%$ interest	=	20.416
After three years investment	=	£4348.618

Therefore the final amount is £4348.62.

As with simple interest, the sum invested is called the **principal**, but we have a further concept now. The original principal becomes larger each year as a result of the re-investment of the interest. The term **'amount'** is used for this increased principal. Compound interest questions might therefore read as in the following example.

Example (b): What will be the amount of £5000 invested at $11\frac{1}{4}\%$ for $3\frac{1}{2}$ years?

		£
Principal	=	5000
Interest at 10%	=	500
Interest at 1%	=	50
Interest at $\frac{1}{4}\%$	=	12.50
Amount after one year	=	5562.50
Interest at 10%	=	556.25
Interest at 1%	=	55.625
Interest at $\frac{1}{4}\%$	=	13.906
Amount after two years	=	6188.281
Interest at 10%	=	618.828
Interest at 1%	=	61.883
Interest at $\frac{1}{4}\%$	=	15.471
Amount after three years	=	6884.463

Interest at 1%	=	68.845
Interest at 4%	=	275.380
Interest at $\frac{1}{2}\%$	=	34.422
Interest at $\frac{1}{8}\%$	=	8.606
Amount after $3\frac{1}{2}$ years	=	£7271.716

(*Note:* There is a method of calculating the interest for part of a year. In the last $\frac{1}{2}$ year of this example, the rate of interest is $11\frac{1}{4}\%$ for 1 year which is the same as $5\frac{5}{8}\%$ for a full year; we therefore calculate the interest at $5\frac{5}{8}\%$ by finding 1%, 4%, $\frac{1}{2}\%$ and $\frac{1}{8}\%$.)

31.3 Exercises: easy compound interest sums

1 What will be the final amount in each of the cases below if the sums shown are invested at 9% compound interest? (Calculations correct to the nearest penny.)

(a) £1000 for 2 years
(b) £1500 for 2 years
(c) £4250 for 2 years
(d) £7500 for 2 years
(e) £3850 for 3 years
(f) £4950 for 3 years
(g) £7250 for 3 years
(h) £15 000 for 3 years
(i) £25 000 for 4 years
(j) £35 500 for 4 years

2 What will be the final amount in each case if the following sums are invested at the rates shown for the length of time given, at compound interest? (Calculations correct to the nearest penny.)

	Principal (£)	Rate of interest (%)	Number of years
(a)	500	8	2
(b)	850	10	2
(c)	1 250	12	2
(d)	3 500	$7\frac{1}{2}$	3
(e)	3 850	$8\frac{1}{2}$	3
(f)	7 250	$11\frac{1}{2}$	3
(g)	8 750	$12\frac{1}{2}$	4
(h)	10 000	6	4
(i)	15 500	$6\frac{1}{2}$	5
(j)	27 500	$11\frac{1}{4}$	5

31.4 A compound interest formula

More advanced compound interest sums depend upon us using a formula, which is usually given as:

$$A = P(1.0r)^n$$

where A is the amount after the number of years, n; P is the principal; and r is the rate of interest.

Suppose we had applied this formula to the first year's calculations of Example (b) above. The calculations would have been as shown below, bearing in mind that the rate was $11\frac{1}{4}\%$, so that $1.0r = 1.1125$, and $n = 1$.

$$A = P(1.0r)^n$$
$$= £5000 \times (1.1125)^1$$
$$= £5 \times 1112.5$$
$$= £5562.50$$

This is the same answer as we found using the practice method. If we now apply this to the calculation for the third year in the same example we have:

$$A = P(1.0r)^n$$
$$= £5000 \times (1.1125)^3$$

At this point we have the difficulty of cubing 1.1125. This is $1.1125 \times 1.1125 \times 1.1125$.

We see now why compound interest sums can be long and tedious. Using a calculator, we get 1.3768925. Therefore:

$$A = £5000 \times 1.3768925$$
$$= 5 \times 1376.8925$$
$$= £6884.463$$

This is the same answer that we had in Example (b) at the end of Year 3.

Taking a different example suppose the question is as follows.

Example: (c) What will be the final amount of £12 500 invested at $8\frac{1}{2}\%$ over 10 years?

$$A = P(1.0r)^n$$
$$= £12\,500 \times (1.085)^{10}$$

We now have to multiply 1.085 by itself ten times. Using a calculator we find it is 2.260983. Continuing:

$$= £12\,500 \times 2.26093$$
$$= £28\,262.291$$

31.5 Exercises: compound interest using the formula method

(*Note:* For Question 1 you can do all the calculations on paper, but it will be much easier if you have a calculator. For Question 2 a calculator is essential or we could use logarithms. The study of logarithms is not appropriate to this elementary textbook.)

1 What will be the final amount if the following sums of money are invested at the rates of interest shown for the number of years indicated? (Answer correct to the nearest penny.)

	Principal (£)	Rate of interest (%)	Number of years
(a)	1 000	$7\frac{1}{2}$	2
(b)	2 500	$8\frac{1}{2}$	2
(c)	7 250	$11\frac{1}{4}$	2
(d)	12 500	$12\frac{1}{2}$	3
(e)	16 000	$9\frac{1}{2}$	3

2 What will be the final sum available to an investor in each of the following cases, if the principal is invested at compound interest at the rate shown for the number of years indicated? (Answer correct to the nearest *pound*.)

	Principal (£)	Rate of interest (%)	Number of years
(a)	500	6	3
(b)	800	8	3
(c)	1 450	$7\frac{1}{2}$	4
(d)	1 750	$9\frac{1}{2}$	4
(e)	2 500	$11\frac{1}{2}$	4
(f)	15 000	$12\frac{1}{4}$	5
(g)	18 000	$13\frac{1}{2}$	5
(h)	21 000	15	6
(i)	26 500	$16\frac{1}{2}$	10
(j)	32 000	$17\frac{1}{2}$	20

Appendix: Mental Arithmetic

This is a series of mental arithmetic exercises, graduated in difficulty, which should be worked from time-to-time as you work through the main text. Do not copy out the exercises at all. Simply take a slip of paper each time you do an exercise and fold a crease down the centre of it. On the left-hand side write the letters (a) to (j). The answers only are written next to these letters, but it is permissible to do a small amount of rough work jotting down partial answers if you feel this is helpful. This is done on the right-hand side of the page. A suggested layout is shown opposite.

Figure A.1 A suggested layout for mental work

Set no.1
  Answers   Rough working
(a)
(b)
(c)
(d)
(e)
(f)
(g)
(h)
(i)
(j)

Score out of 10 = ___

1 (a) $6 + 17 + 8 + 9 =$ (b) $394 \times 8 =$
   (c) $19 + 4 + 3 + 16 =$ (d) $781 \times 3 =$
   (e) $345 + 96 + 207 =$ (f) $211 \times 5 =$
   (g) $626 - 73 =$ (h) $336 \div 6 =$
   (i) $578 - 41 =$ (j) $924 \div 4 =$

2 (a) $95 + 48 + 62 + 3 =$ (b) $625 \times 7 =$
   (c) $33 + 78 + 56 + 9 =$ (d) $911 \times 4 =$
   (e) $218 + 555 + 127 =$ (f) $543 \times 3 =$
   (g) $412 - 52 =$ (h) $891 \div 9 =$
   (i) $706 - 33 =$ (j) $468 \div 6 =$

3 (a) $22 + 43 + 80 + 61 =$ (b) $481 \times 8 =$
   (c) $59 + 32 + 65 + 48 =$ (d) $962 \times 3 =$
   (e) $688 + 432 + 901 =$ (f) $549 \times 7 =$
   (g) $396 - 47 =$ (h) $312 \div 4 =$
   (i) $758 - 83 =$ (j) $576 \div 6 =$

4 (a) $25 + 86 + 450 =$ (b) $\frac{1}{2} \times \frac{2}{3} =$
   (c) $397 - 186 =$ (d) $\frac{3}{8} + \frac{1}{2} + \frac{1}{4} =$
   (e) $1938 \times 9 =$ (f) $\frac{5}{8} \times \frac{3}{5} =$
   (g) $3118 \div 7 =$ (h) $\frac{1}{2} \div \frac{1}{2} =$
   (i) $\frac{1}{2} \times \frac{1}{3} \times \frac{1}{4} =$ (j) $\frac{4}{5} \div \frac{2}{15} =$

5 (a) $2.8 + 3.56 + 6.18 =$
   (b) $2.4 \div 1.6 =$
   (c) $5.94 \times 0.6 =$
   (d) $4000 \div 250 =$
   (e) $\frac{3}{4} + \frac{2}{3} =$

   (f) $4\frac{1}{10} + 8\frac{1}{2} =$
   (g) $4\frac{3}{4} - 2\frac{7}{8} =$
   (h) What shall I pay altogether for 7 items at £35.00 each and 4 items at £12.00 each?
   (i) $3.9 \div 0.13 =$
   (j) $5.8 \div 0.029 =$

6 (a) $37.4 + 2.45 + 79.50 =$
   (b) $426.25 - 278.50 =$
   (c) $2500 \times 500 =$

(d) £6.75 ÷ 5 =

(e) How many $1\frac{1}{2}$-litre containers can be filled from a vat holding 30 000 litres?

(f) $2\frac{2}{3} + 3\frac{1}{4} + 4\frac{5}{8} =$

(g) Change 3.54 metres to centimetres.

(h) $\frac{5}{8} \times \frac{4}{5} \times \frac{9}{10} =$

(i) How many minutes are there in $4\frac{1}{2}$ hours?

(j) What shall I pay altogether for 6 items at 35p each and 7 items at 14p each?

7 (a) $274 + 132 + 1756 =$

(b) £53.30 + £27.60 + £41.10 =

(c) £351.00 − £180.15 =

(d) $8664 \times 9 =$

(e) £62.16 ÷ 8 =

(f) What is 30% of £420?

(g) What is 39% of £1200?

(h) Theatre tickets cost £8.50. What shall I pay for a party of 20?

(i) What is $\frac{3}{8}$ of $\frac{5}{6}$?

(j) VAT is set at 15%. What is the VAT on an item costing £850 exclusive of VAT?

8 (a) $2738 - 1857 =$

(b) Share up £390 equally among 12 claimants.

(c) How many days in November, December and January?

(d) How many 75 gram packets can be made up from 3 kilograms?

(e) How many centimetres are there in 7.5 metres?

(f) How many litres are there in 5.25 kilolitres?

(g) If 3 items cost £28.50, how much for 5?

(h) How many half-litre bottles can be filled from a vat holding 6 kilolitres if 150 litres are waste product?

(i) What is 35% of £400?

(j) What is the total cost of 3 articles at £63.00 each and 2 articles at £31.50?

9 (a) $38\,142 \div 9 =$

(b) £375.50 × 6 =

(c) $\frac{2}{3} \times \frac{3}{4} \times \frac{5}{9} =$

(d) What is a 40% discount on £350?

(e) $0.2 \times 0.3 =$

(f) $0.2 \div 0.3 =$

(g) How many days are there from February 9th to February 29th inclusive? (It is, of course, a leap year.)

(h) $3\frac{3}{5} + 6\frac{7}{8} + 1\frac{2}{5} =$

(i) $\frac{5}{6} \div \frac{2}{3} =$

(j) Share £6590 between Mrs Y and Mr Z in the ratio of 3:2.

10 (a) $7164 \times 7 =$

(b) £274.36 − £13.72 discount =

(c) How many days from 27th June–3rd August inclusive?

(d) The population of a town is 127 295. Express this to the nearest thousand.

(e) The population of a town is 135 500. Express this to the nearest thousand.

(f) If 12 items cost £150, how much for 7 of them?

(g) 29.5 ÷ 9. (Answer correct to 2 decimal places.)

(h) How many kilograms in $5\frac{1}{2}$ metric tonnes?

(i) If 3 men take 8 days to do a job, how long will it take 4 men at the same rate of working?

(j) If profits are shared out by partners in a ratio of 3:2:2, what will each receive on a transaction where an article costing £393 is sold for £610?

11 (a) Add together 12.65 metres, 13.89 metres and 14.5 metres.

(b) $3819 \div 19 =$

(c) $4175 \times 7 =$

(d) What is 15% VAT on £250?

(e) What is the average of 4, 7, 11, 13 and 15?

(f) Express $133\frac{1}{3}\%$ as a mixed number.

(g) $\frac{5}{6} \div \frac{2}{3} =$

(h) What is the average of 161, 165 and 172?

(i) If 4 similar items cost £12.80, what will 6 of them cost?

(j) If profits are shared out by partners in a ratio of $\frac{2}{3}$ to $\frac{1}{3}$, what will each receive out of total profits of £13 368?

12 (a) 3.6 m + 4.2 m + 12.7 m =

(b) £43.48 − £29.12 =

(c) £6945 ÷ 15 =

(d) $\frac{5}{6} \div \frac{10}{11} =$

(e) Share £6596 between Mrs Y and Mr Z in the ratio of 3:1.

(f) What is the profit on 18 items bought at £2.40 each and sold at £2.65 each?

(g) An article purchased for £5.50 is marked up by 20% on cost price. What is it sold for?

(h) What is the average of 1008, 1013 and 1015?

(i) A shopkeeper marks down an article priced at £15.20 by 10%. What is its sale price?

(j) An article purchased for £8.50 is marked up by 40% on cost price. What does it sell for?

13 (a) £53.30 + £27.60 + £41.40 =

(b) £351.00 − £186.15 =

(c) 8664 × 9 =

(d) £62.16 ÷ 8 =

(e) What is 30 per cent of £2635?

(f) What is the average of 5, 12, 19 and 20?

(g) Multiply 4.6 by 0.3.

(h) What is the simple interest on a loan of £250 for 2 years at 9 per cent per annum?

(i) What is the simple interest on £12 500 for $3\frac{1}{2}$ years at 8% per annum?

(j) What is the simple interest on £5000 for 4 years at $12\frac{1}{2}$% per annum?

14 (a) 288 + 349 + 622 =

(b) How many pence are there in £12.35?

(c) 300 × 450 =

(d) How many millilitres are there in 3.5 litres?

(e) How many minutes are there in 4 hours 26 minutes?

(f) How many days are there from 6th July to 8th October inclusive?

(g) How many pounds sterling shall I get for 35 000 pesetas, when 175 pesetas = £1?

(h) There are 1.35 United States dollars to £1 on the foreign exchange market. How much will an exporter get for 405 000 dollars earned by the sale of a ship?

(i) An English teacher in Singapore earns 6200 Singapore dollars per month. What is the equivalent salary in sterling when the rate of exchange is S$3.1 = £1?

(j) What will the simple interest be on £45 000 at 8% for $2\frac{1}{2}$ years?

15 (a) £10.60 + £7.40 + £15.80 =

(b) 12.69 × 4 =

(c) $3\frac{3}{8} + 6\frac{2}{5} + 4\frac{3}{20} =$

(d) How many 75 gram packets can be made up from 1.5 kilograms?

(e) How many centimetres are there in $7\frac{1}{2}$ metres?

(f) Divide up £9.80 in the ratio of 7:3.

(g) Write down $\frac{3}{8}$ as a decimal fraction.

(h) What is the average of £460, £470, £490 and £520?

(i) How many pounds sterling for 15 000 drachma at 75 drachma = £1?

(j) What shall I pay for 3850 units of electricity at 5p per unit?

16 (a) 3285 + 4271 + 3639 =

(b) 5.25 + 3.81 + 4.76 =

(c) 7263 ÷ 9 =

(d) How many $2\frac{1}{2}$-litre bottles can be filled from a barrel holding 8000 litres?

(e) How many seconds are there in $7\frac{1}{2}$ minutes?

(f) What is 5% of £180, when added to $12\frac{1}{2}$% of £64?

(g) If 450 Yen = £1, what shall I receive for 135 000 Yen?

(h) What is the VAT on an item costing £135 before tax, if the rate of tax is 15%?

(i) A penny rate in a certain town brings in £72 500. What rate must be raised to build a library costing £217 500?

(j) What was the cost price of an article selling at £16 after a mark-up of $33\frac{1}{3}$% on cost?

17 (a) 279 − 136 =

(b) £372.56 + £425.94 + £281.16 =

(c) 27.45 − 18.93 =

(d) $1\frac{1}{2} + 2\frac{2}{3} + 5\frac{1}{6} =$

(e) Change 560 krone to £ sterling at the exchange rate 11.2K = £1.

(f) What will a householder whose property is rated at £480 pay in rates if the rates are fixed at $87\frac{1}{2}$p in the £1?

(g) What will be the cost of 7 photocopying machines at £850 each?

(h) What was the cost price of an article selling at £25 after a mark-up of 25% on cost?

(i) Petrol to fill a car tank costs £11.66. If VAT is 10%, how much of the £11.66 is VAT?

(j) What is 20% of 360 metres?

18 (a) 3812 − 1584 =

(b) 37.65 × 0.05 =

(c) What is $16\frac{2}{3}$% of £5400?

(d) A chapter in a book is headed XLI. What does this mean in Arabic numbers?

(e) A retailer marks up a gold watch costing £800 by 20%. What is its selling price?

(f) $3\frac{7}{10} - 2\frac{4}{5} =$

(g) Three heiresses share £500 000 in the ratios of 8:3:1. How much does the girl entitled only to 1 share receive? (Answer correct to the nearest penny.)

(h) Change £20 000 sterling to lire at 2232 lire = £1.

(i) A telephone call to Singapore costs 79p per minute. How much for an $8\frac{1}{2}$ minute call? (Answer to the nearest penny.)

(j) What temperature Fahrenheit is the same as 20° Celsius?

19 (a) $4125 \div 5 =$

(b) £584.75 + £273.66 + £328.50 =

(c) How many seconds in $4\frac{3}{4}$ minutes?

(d) How many days in January, February and March in a non-leap year?

(e) What is the total cost of a job where materials cost £760, labour £1240 and overheads 40% on top of that?

(f) Books are loaned to 12 758 000 people in British libraries. Authors are paid 1p per loan, and overheads are 10% extra. What is the total sum required?

(g) Share up £150 000 in the ratio 3:2:1.

(h) What year was MCMLXXX?

(i) Share £12 500 in the ratio $2:1\frac{1}{2}:1\frac{1}{2}$.

(j) Change 27° Celsius to Fahrenheit.

20 (a) £4.75 + £2.23 + £3.68 =

(b) $3864 \div 8 =$

(c) $3.5 \times 0.08 =$

(d) How many days in July, August and September?

(e) Change 24 000 Dm to £ sterling at 4.8 Dm = £1.

(f) What is the selling price of an item purchased for £13.50 with a mark-up of $33\frac{1}{3}\%$?

(g) What is the simple interest on £800 for 3 years at 12%?

(h) Change $37\frac{1}{2}\%$ to a fraction.

(i) $1\frac{7}{12} + 2\frac{2}{3} + 3\frac{5}{8} =$

(j) An item is bought on hire purchase. The deposit is £26 and there are 12 instalments of £6.40. What is the total cost?

21 (a) 226 + 425 + 639 + 171 =

(b) £4295 − £3763.50 =

(c) $3\frac{1}{4} + 2\frac{1}{2} + 1\frac{7}{8} =$

(d) A debtor borrows £500 at simple interest of 10% per annum and has to repay £650 altogether. How many years did the loan last?

(e) Increase £7200 by 25%.

(f) An employee earns £112 per week but pays tax of £13.50 and other deductions of £5.80. What is his take-home pay?

(g) What is the simple interest on £600 for 6 months at 8%?

(h) An item costing £120 is offered on hire purchase terms for a deposit of 20% and 12 monthly payments of £9. How much money is the interest charge?

(i) $200 \times 300 \times 60 =$

(j) What will a firm pay in a quarter-year for telephones, if the charge is 5p per unit plus £84 hire of equipment? 60 000 units are used in the quarter.

22 (a) $3864 \div 3 =$

(b) $5943 \div 7 =$

(c) What is 12% of £2800?

(d) Express $22\frac{1}{2}\%$ as a fraction.

(e) $500 \times 400 \times 70 =$

(f) How many teaspoonfuls (each holding 5 millilitres) from a bottle of $\frac{1}{2}$ litre?

(g) What number is missing from the following 3:?::9:12?

(h) What is 30% of £5850?

(i) How many posts are required to support a fence in a straight line if there are seven panels?

(j) A petty cashier has £23.72 left from last week's funds. The weekly imprest is £75. How much should she draw from the chief cashier to restore the imprest?

23 (a) $125 \times 7 =$

(b) £27.50 − £13.85 =

(c) $0.08 \times 0.04 =$

(d) What temperature Celsius is equivalent to 104° F?

(e) How many pence in £27.38?

(f) Share up £18 000 among three partners in the ratio $2:1\frac{1}{2}:1$.

(g) What shall I pay for 8 reams of paper at £2.30 and 4 pads of notepaper at £1.15?

(h) A motor vehicle that cost £5800 on 1st January and is expected to last 5 years, and is then to be sold for £1000, is to be depreciated by the straight-line method. How much should be written off each year?

(i) If 7 labourers earn £84.00 per week, what is the total weekly wage bill?

(j) A lorry costing £23 500 is depreciated by 10%. What is its value on the books after depreciation?

24 (a) $1\frac{1}{2} + 2\frac{3}{4} + 5\frac{7}{8} =$

(b) $2765 - 399 =$

(c) $2486 \times 9 =$

(d) $0.002 \times 0.4 =$

(e) A holiday-maker returning from the United States changes $405 back to sterling at $1.35 = £1. How much does she receive?

(f) What is the average of 4008, 4012 and 4034?

(g) Telephone charges are $4\frac{1}{2}$p per unit plus a charge of £38 per quarter. What will the bill amount to if 5200 units are used in the quarter?

(h) What is the depreciation on a machine costing £2400 at $12\frac{1}{2}\%$ for the year?

(i) What is the area of a playing field 100 metres by 120 metres?

(j) What is the VAT on a purchase of £160 at 15 per cent?

25 (a) $13\,729 \times 3 =$

(b) Share £3584 among 32 people.

(c) Change £240 into pesetas at 199 pesetas to the £1.

(d) $1\frac{1}{3} \times 2\frac{1}{4} =$

(e) What rates will be raised in a town where the aggregate rateable value is £27 580 000 by a rate of a penny in the £1?

(f) Change 4.75 metres to millimetres.

(g) Partners share profits in the ratio 4:4:3. What will each receive out of profits of £77 000?

(h) A farmer's herd is valued this year at £68 000. Last year it was valued at £62 755. What is the change in value? Is it depreciation or appreciation?

(i) What is the formula for the circumference of a circle?

(j) If $\pi = 3\frac{1}{7}$, and a circle has a radius of 7 cm, what is its area?

26 (a) $256 + 384 + 423 + 625 =$

(b) $42.5 \times 0.3 =$

(c) £275.65 × 7 =

(d) What must I pay for 8 theatre tickets at £7.45 each?

(e) Share up £27 000 between A, B and C in the ratio 4:3:2.

(f) What is the average of 19, 20, 21, 23 and 24?

(g) What is the circumference of a circle whose diameter is 14 cm? (Use $\pi = 3\frac{1}{7}$.)

(h) What is the area of a rectangle $7\frac{1}{2}$ metres by $5\frac{1}{2}$ metres?

(i) A petty cashier spends £43.50 out of an imprest of £50, but collects £2.50 for staff telephone calls. How much must the chief cashier supply to restore the imprest?

(j) After one year a typewriter costing £580 is reduced by 20% for depreciation. What is it now worth on the books?

27 (a) $3275 \times 7 =$

(b) $286.9 \div 0.5 =$

(c) £381.42 ÷ 5. (Answer correct to the nearest penny.)

(d) A wheel revolves 100 times in going 110 metres. What is its circumference?

(e) What is the simple interest on £3500 for 3 years at 8%?

(f) Round off 735 to the nearest 100, and 750 to the nearest 100.

(g) A factory is rated at £4000 and the rates are £1.17 in the pound. How much is payable?

(h) What is the depreciation on a chemical plant costing £48 000 000 and estimated to last 15 years? Scrap value should be £3 000 000.

(i) Gas is 26p per therm. What shall I pay for 55 therms?

(j) A road haulier charges £7 per cubic metre for goods carried. What is the charge for a crate $3\,m \times 2\,m \times 2\frac{1}{2}\,m$?

28 (a) $1426 + 3856 + 2595 =$

(b) $2.7 \times 0.5 =$

(c) £4796.50 ÷ 12. (Answer correct to the nearest penny.)

(d) How many 25s in 1000?

(e) What will I pay for rates in a house with a rateable value of £480, if the rate is fixed at 75p in the £1?

(f) Change £20 to Greek drachma at 140 drachma = £1?

(g) What is the area of a circle radius $3\frac{1}{2}$ cm? (Use $\pi = 3\frac{1}{7}$.)

(h) Gas is 35p per therm. What shall I pay for 450 therms?

(i) What is the average score of a football team whose record shows as follows: 2, 5, 3, 4, 0, 0, 1, 2, 4, 6, 7, 3, 5, 3, 0.

(j) What will a town raise on a house valued at £800, if the rate is fixed at £1.15 in the £1?

29 (a) $2863 - 1795 =$

(b) $42.5 \div 2.5 =$

(c) $\frac{1}{2} \times \frac{3}{4} \times \frac{2}{3} =$

(d) Divide £24 000 between A and B so that A has twice as much as B.

(e) What is the area of a circle 7 metres in radius? (Use $\pi = 3\frac{1}{7}$.)

(f) What is the volume of a container 2.5 metres × 2.5 metres × 20 metres?

(g) What is the median of 15, 18, 19, 20, 23, 24, 25, 26, 30?

(h) A car cost £8400. It is estimated to last six years and at the end of its useful life to fetch a trade-in price of £1200. What is the depreciation per annum?

(i) A swimming pool is to cost £2 million. The rate yield in the town is £250 000 per penny rate. How much will it cost on the rates to build the pool?

(j) A bowler takes the following wickets in a series of matches: 2, 3, 5, 0, 1, 4, 3, 3, 5, 2. What is his modal number of wickets?

30 (a) $4756 \div 4 =$

(b) $£125.65 - £88.74 =$

(c) What is the area of a rectangle 16 metres × 8.5 metres?

(d) What shall I pay for 10 000 units of electricity at 4.5p per unit?

(e) What is the arithmetic mean of 199, 205 and 217?

(f) What is the formula for the surface area of a cylinder, including both ends?

(g) What is the yield of a penny rate in a town where the aggregate rateable value is £7 265 440?

(h) I purchase £1000 stock at $91\frac{1}{8}$. How much do I pay if brokerage is $\frac{1}{8}$?

(i) A $\frac{1}{2}$% sample of motorists driving a particular model is to be interviewed about design features. 185 000 have been sold. How many interviews must be held?

(j) What shall I pay for 500 shares in Universal Supplies Ltd, at 69p per share, if charges are £8.50?

31 (a) $3295 - 2864 =$

(b) A circle has a radius of 70 cm. What is its circumference if $\pi = 3\frac{1}{7}$?

(c) What is the arithmetic mean of 27, 36, 45 and 52?

(d) What is the formula for the volume of a sphere?

(e) How many small cubes 2 cm square can I get into a cubic box 6 cm × 6 cm × 6 cm?

(f) What is the volume of a rectangular solid 4 m × 4 m × 20 m?

(g) 240 motorists out of 10 000 checked are not wearing seat belts. What percentage is that?

(h) What is the compound interest on £100 invested for 2 years at 10% per annum?

(i) I purchase 500 shares at £1.75. The charges are £9.25. What must I pay altogether?

(j) What is the compound interest on £1000 invested at 10% for three years?

Answers

Chapter 2

2.3 (a) 1723; (b) 1158; (c) 1095; (d) 1513; (e) 11 285;
(f) 12 867; (g) 11 989; (h) 9717; (i) 1 763 010; (j) 13 833 298

2.6 1 (a) Subtotals 2393, 1851, 2377; Total 6621
(b) Subtotals 2849, 2324, 2562; Total 7735
(c) Subtotals 29 300, 31 422, 30 493; Total 91 215
(d) Subtotals 23 147, 25 059, 35 237; Total 83 443
(e) Subtotals 28 642, 26 692, 30 805; Total 86 139
(f) Subtotals 186 162, 346 071, 161 594; Total 693 827

2 (a) 25; (b) 82; (c) 789; (d) 3335; (e) 7227; (f) 5490

3 (a) 29; (b) 116; (c) 559; (d) 8305; (e) 110 105

4 (a) Jan. 58 141; Feb. 91 791; Mar. 86 552; Apr. 67 198; May 107 611; June 113 837
(b) Europe 260 681; Africa 101 954; Far East 114 640; USA 47 855
(c) Grand total 525 130

2.8 1 (a) 283; (b) 332; (c) 9; (d) 222; (e) 571; (f) 7389; (g) 6606; (h) 2810; (i) 2328; (j) 45 132

2 (a) 2734; (b) 2369; (c) 7138; (d) 13 460; (e) 3650; (f) 522 108; (g) 9975; (h) 320 613; (i) 777 877; (j) 50 302

3 (a) 3; (b) 17; (c) 8; (d) 43; (e) 23; (f) 9; (g) 16; (h) 15; (i) 43; (j) 36

Chapter 3

3.2 1 (a) 6692; (b) 9620; (c) 1844; (d) 3452; (e) 28 496; (f) 53 028; (g) 28 662; (h) 14 556; (i) 5335; (j) 56 052

2 (a) 32 274; (b) 54 175; (c) 29 925; (d) 58 272; (e) 50 052; (f) 41 285; (g) 152 940; (h) 323 076; (i) 64 552; (j) 349 074

3.5 1 (a) 4522; (b) 4446; (c) 12 502; (d) 31 122; (e) 129 074; (f) 117 342; (g) 179 388; (h) 573 615; (i) 241 542; (j) 93 528

2 (a) 451 326; (b) 648 159; (c) 1 146 596; (d) 2 763 075; (e) 496 392; (f) 877 752; (g) 2 033 664; (h) 3 497 615; (i) 13 640 176; (j) 53 064 432

3.6 1 27 433
2 645 939
3 147 840
4 21 877

3.9 1 (a) 139; (b) 183; (c) 106; (d) 318; (e) 106; (f) 598; (g) 811; (h) 1048; (i) 661; (j) 626

2 (a) 66; (b) $61\frac{1}{2}$; (c) $232\frac{10}{11}$; (d) $424\frac{1}{9}$; (e) $675\frac{1}{2}$; (f) $1166\frac{2}{5}$; (g) $1213\frac{1}{2}$; (h) $649\frac{1}{6}$; (i) $1495\frac{1}{2}$; (j) $477\frac{1}{8}$

3.11 1 (a) 163; (b) 895; (c) 99; (d) 234; (e) 987; (f) 456; (g) 547; (h) 999; (i) 412; (j) $201\frac{7}{22}$

2 (a) $369\frac{4}{85}$; (b) $842\frac{7}{51}$; (c) $1023\frac{23}{63}$; (d) $5574\frac{5}{8}$; (e) $3772\frac{1}{16}$; (f) 1516; (g) $384\frac{53}{92}$; (h) $2597\frac{19}{33}$; (i) $987\frac{16}{19}$; (j) $1046\frac{7}{27}$

3.12 1 69 tonnes to each customer, 21 tonnes to charity
2 830 students
3 235 bags
4 14 buses
5 13 journeys

Chapter 4

4.2 1 (a) $1\frac{1}{2}$; (b) 2; (c) $2\frac{1}{2}$; (d) $1\frac{1}{3}$; (e) $2\frac{1}{3}$; (f) $1\frac{1}{4}$; (g) $1\frac{3}{4}$; (h) $2\frac{3}{4}$; (i) $1\frac{3}{5}$; (j) $2\frac{3}{5}$; (k) $1\frac{5}{6}$; (l) $2\frac{5}{6}$; (m) $1\frac{1}{8}$; (n) $1\frac{1}{12}$; (o) $2\frac{5}{12}$; (p) $4\frac{1}{11}$

2 (a) $\frac{7}{4}$; (b) $\frac{8}{5}$; (c) $\frac{5}{2}$; (d) $\frac{11}{4}$; (e) $\frac{23}{8}$; (f) $\frac{35}{12}$; (g) $\frac{10}{3}$; (h) $\frac{15}{4}$; (i) $\frac{23}{6}$; (j) $\frac{47}{10}$; (k) $\frac{47}{8}$; (l) $\frac{38}{5}$; (m) $\frac{33}{4}$; (n) $\frac{28}{3}$; (o) $\frac{95}{12}$; (p) $\frac{69}{8}$

4.4 1 (a) $\frac{1}{2}$; (b) $\frac{2}{3}$; (c) $\frac{1}{4}$; (d) $\frac{1}{2}$; (e) $\frac{3}{4}$; (f) $\frac{1}{2}$; (g) $\frac{1}{4}$; (h) $\frac{1}{3}$; (i) $\frac{1}{2}$; (j) $\frac{2}{3}$; (k) $\frac{5}{6}$; (l) $\frac{1}{2}$

2 (a) $\frac{1}{2}$; (b) $\frac{3}{4}$; (c) $\frac{4}{9}$; (d) $\frac{1}{2}$; (e) $\frac{1}{2}$; (f) $\frac{5}{9}$; (g) $\frac{3}{4}$; (h) $\frac{2}{3}$; (i) $\frac{1}{4}$; (j) $\frac{1}{2}$; (k) $\frac{1}{3}$; (l) $\frac{9}{16}$

4.6 1 1, 2, 3, 5, 7
2 23, 29
3 (a) 3; (b) 19; (c) 5, 13; (d) 7; (e) 11; (f) 29; (g) 7; (h) 5, 17, 1; (i) 1; (j) 11, 3

4 (a) 2, 4, 7, 14; (b) 3, 7, 9, 21; (c) 3, 5; (d) 3, 7; (e) 2, 3, 4, 6, 8, 12, 16, 24; (f) 2, 3, 6, 9, 18, 27; (g) 2, 3, 4, 6, 9, 12, 18; (h) 2, 3, 4, 6, 8, 12, 16, 24, 32, 48; (i) 2, 3, 6, 9; (j) 2, 3, 4, 5, 6, 10, 12, 15, 20, 30

5 (a) 3; (b) 17; (c) 3, 5, 15; (d) 2, 4; (e) 2, 3, 4, 6, 8, 12, 24; (f) 2, 3, 4, 6, 12; (g) 2, 4; (h) 7; (i) 2, 4; (j) 2, 3, 6

6 *Note:* There are, of course, many common multiples besides the following: (a) 14; (b) 44; (c) 15; (d) 315; (e) 8; (f) 120; (g) 18; (h) 42; (i) 12; (j) 180

4.8 1 (a) $1\frac{7}{15}$; (b) $1\frac{7}{20}$; (c) $1\frac{9}{20}$; (d) $\frac{49}{60}$; (e) $1\frac{7}{16}$; (f) $2\frac{3}{20}$; (g) $2\frac{1}{8}$; (h) $1\frac{17}{20}$; (i) $2\frac{1}{20}$; (j) $1\frac{19}{24}$; (k) $2\frac{3}{140}$; (l) $1\frac{5}{6}$

2 (a) $8\frac{3}{4}$; (b) $18\frac{7}{15}$; (c) 12; (d) $14\frac{9}{10}$; (e) $9\frac{11}{15}$; (f) $10\frac{23}{40}$; (g) $8\frac{19}{20}$; (h) $11\frac{59}{70}$; (i) $11\frac{19}{24}$; (j) $16\frac{5}{12}$; (k) $9\frac{33}{40}$; (l) $11\frac{11}{12}$

4.10 1 (a) $\frac{1}{4}$; (b) $\frac{13}{30}$; (c) $\frac{13}{24}$; (d) $\frac{9}{20}$; (e) $\frac{23}{35}$; (f) $\frac{5}{14}$; (g) $\frac{7}{60}$; (h) $\frac{2}{3}$; (i) $\frac{8}{15}$; (j) $\frac{5}{18}$

2 (a) $1\frac{1}{6}$; (b) $1\frac{7}{30}$; (c) $6\frac{11}{12}$; (d) $3\frac{47}{60}$; (e) $2\frac{13}{30}$; (f) $12\frac{1}{8}$; (g) $3\frac{3}{4}$; (h) $5\frac{97}{120}$; (i) $15\frac{19}{24}$; (j) $1\frac{13}{14}$; (k) $2\frac{13}{24}$; (l) $2\frac{7}{20}$; (m) $6\frac{2}{6}$; (n) $5\frac{1}{35}$

4.12 1 (a) $\frac{2}{5}$; (b) $\frac{3}{5}$; (c) $\frac{2}{5}$; (d) $\frac{11}{14}$; (e) $\frac{5}{8}$; (f) $\frac{16}{33}$; (g) $\frac{1}{12}$; (h) $\frac{4}{57}$; (i) $\frac{17}{35}$; (j) $\frac{5}{14}$

2 (a) $\frac{5}{16}$; (b) $\frac{49}{100}$; (c) $\frac{8}{35}$; (d) $\frac{20}{63}$; (e) $\frac{1}{4}$; (f) $\frac{7}{27}$; (g) $\frac{7}{24}$; (h) $\frac{1}{36}$; (i) $\frac{3}{14}$; (j) $\frac{3}{10}$; (k) $\frac{27}{100}$; (l) $\frac{6}{25}$

3 (a) $7\frac{1}{4}$; (b) $3\frac{27}{55}$; (c) $67\frac{5}{20}$; (d) $10\frac{5}{6}$; (e) $7\frac{17}{21}$; (f) $27\frac{1}{12}$; (g) $40\frac{5}{48}$; (h) $23\frac{5}{6}$; (i) $35\frac{5}{24}$; (j) $32\frac{2}{5}$

4 (a) $68\frac{1}{16}$; (b) $124\frac{1}{5}$; (c) $82\frac{1}{16}$; (d) $49\frac{3}{5}$; (e) 336; (f) $55\frac{5}{9}$; (g) $14\frac{1}{4}$; (h) $12\frac{5}{6}$; (i) $5\frac{1}{3}$; (j) $18\frac{3}{8}$; (k) $113\frac{3}{4}$; (l) $18\frac{3}{4}$; (m) $4\frac{1}{2}$; (n) $7\frac{1}{3}$

4.14 1 (a) $1\frac{1}{5}$; (b) $1\frac{1}{2}$; (c) $\frac{7}{8}$; (d) $\frac{5}{12}$; (e) $2\frac{4}{9}$; (f) $1\frac{1}{3}$; (g) $\frac{25}{36}$; (h) $\frac{1}{6}$; (i) 4; (j) $1\frac{1}{7}$

2 (a) $3\frac{1}{3}$; (b) $3\frac{3}{7}$; (c) 2; (d) $1\frac{1}{4}$; (e) $2\frac{4}{5}$; (f) $2\frac{2}{5}$; (g) $1\frac{1}{3}$; (h) $1\frac{1}{2}$; (i) $\frac{3}{5}$; (j) $1\frac{1}{4}$

4.15 1 (a) $\frac{8}{15}$; (b) $\frac{13}{24}$; (c) $1\frac{1}{4}$; (d) $\frac{11}{42}$; (e) $\frac{23}{24}$; (f) $1\frac{1}{12}$; (g) $1\frac{8}{63}$; (h) $\frac{9}{28}$; (i) $\frac{5}{8}$; (j) $1\frac{2}{3}$

2 (a) $\frac{5}{8}$; (b) $\frac{7}{8}$; (c) $5\frac{11}{24}$; (d) $1\frac{7}{12}$; (e) $1\frac{3}{5}$; (f) $1\frac{9}{23}$; (g) 19; (h) $2\frac{18}{35}$; (i) $2\frac{7}{40}$; (j) $9\frac{3}{4}$

Chapter 5

5.3 1 (a) 48.66; (b) 253.96; (c) 257.692; (d) 446.84; (e) 378.302; (f) 1338.585; (g) 627.0659; (h) 261.9026; (i) 576.546; (j) 7162.02

2 (a) 3954.01075; (b) 614.27085; (c) 463.7666

5.5 1 (a) 24.421; (b) 392.019; (c) 19.062; (d) 33.88; (e) 134.921; (f) 114.747; (g) 102.15; (h) 744.284; (i) 305.496; (j) 52.3145

2 (a) 137.1463; (b) 34.72472; (c) 452.8424; (d) 468.2375; (e) 237.92175; (f) 356.43355

5.7 1 (a) 2.86; (b) 24.38; (c) 34.888; (d) 22.761; (e) 140.7; (f) 94.528; (g) 1034.045; (h) 164.6325; (i) 1264.052; (j) 157.2675

2 (a) 19.435; (b) 125.587; (c) 2425.5; (d) 276.013; (e) 311.7425; (f) 76.128; (g) 180.46278; (h) 72.318; (i) 98.8839; (j) 171.306

5.11 1 (a) 27.1; (b) 27.2; (c) 27.6; (d) 27.7; (e) 27.6; (f) 27.6; (g) 27.5; (h) 27.3; (i) 27.1; (j) 27.0

2 (a) 2.957; (b) 2.958; (c) 2.958; (d) 2.958; (e) 3.813; (f) 3.813; (g) 3.812; (h) 3.812; (i) 3.979; (j) 3.978

5.12 1 (a) 7.5; (b) 4.4; (c) 67.0; (d) 5.5; (e) 20.3; (f) 426.8; (g) 21.6; (h) 9.0; (i) 160.4; (j) 28.2

2 (a) 53.19; (b) 77.68; (c) 11321.43; (d) 111.92; (e) 903.61; (f) 27.91; (g) 2642. 31; (h) 31.69; (i) 20795.17; (j) 61.56

Chapter 6

6.3 1 (a) £23.68; (b) £29.82; (c) £46.42; (d) £42.29; (e) £35.43; (f) £71.48; (g) £4741.38; (h) £5100.66; (i) £5324.40; (j) £8747.89

2 (a) £10.71; (b) £86.32; (c) £109.46; (d) £71.75; (e) £934.39; (f) £306.52; (g) £2102.85; (h) £11 081.67; (i) £5922.81; (j) £10 080.82

3 Monday £449.79, Tuesday £565.09, Wednesday £385.39, Thursday £240.13, Friday £674.20, Saturday £718.13; Confectionery £1818.30, Newsagency £1214.43; Grand total £3032.73

4 (a) 37p; (b) £7.17; (c) £8.23; (d) £13.28; (e) £7.50; (f) £145.50; (g) £111; (h) £206.50; (i) £112.50; (j) £259.50

5 (a) £33.75; (b) £23.08; (c) £539.52; (d) £324.81; (e) £231.05; (f) £4455.46; (g) £366.46; (h) £2437.50; (i) £415.59; (j) £3307.34

6.5 1 (a) £22; (b) £32.85; (c) £169.40; (d) £363.25; (e) £7510.08; (f) £5155.15; (g) £18 965.25; (h) £38 155.36; (i) £30 214.32; (j) £25 469.25

2 £75.74

3 £565.44

4 £179 691.60

5 (a) Yes; (b) £1057.80 per annum

6.7 1 (a) £1.52; (b) £5.95; (c) £71.83; (d) £57.84, remainder 6p; (e) £658.84, remainder 8p; (f) £428.01, remainder 12p; (g) £851.66, remainder 10p; (h) £226.01, remainder 11p; (i) £493.78, remainder 16p; (j) £2162.68, remainder 2p

2 (a) £228 each; (b) £16

3 £11.75

4 (a) £251; (b) £37 148

5 £428 826

Chapter 7

7.2 1 (a) £10; (b) £1; (c) 10p; (d) £5; (e) £2.50; (f) £2;

(g) £1.70; (h) 85p; (i) 55p; (j) 35p
2 (a) £30; (b) £27; (c) £18; (d) £9.45; (e) £11.10;
   (f) £4.65; (g) £5.40; (h) £63; (i) £41.25; (j) £26.25
3 (a) £80; (b) £172.50; (c) £111.25; (d) £4.13;
   (e) £2456.25; (f) £427.50; (g) £546.88; (h) £624;
   (i) £352.80; (j) £2749.50

7.4 1 (a) $\frac{7}{10}$; (b) $\frac{1}{2}$; (c) $\frac{23}{100}$; (d) $\frac{47}{50}$; (e) $\frac{33}{50}$; (f) $\frac{1}{4}$; (g) $\frac{17}{40}$;
   (h) $\frac{13}{16}$; (i) $\frac{19}{40}$; (j) $\frac{19}{20}$; (k) $\frac{31}{40}$; (l) $\frac{2}{3}$
2 (a) $\frac{9}{20}$; (b) $\frac{27}{40}$; (c) $\frac{17}{20}$; (d) $\frac{27}{50}$; (e) $\frac{57}{80}$; (f) $\frac{1}{3}$; (g) $\frac{67}{80}$;
   (h) $\frac{77}{80}$; (i) $\frac{11}{20}$; (j) $\frac{29}{40}$; (k) $\frac{4}{5}$; (l) $\frac{7}{25}$
3 (a) 75%; (b) 50%; (c) 37.5%; (d) 62.5%;
   (e) 60%; (f) 40%; (g) 85%; (h) 15%; (i) 33.3%;
   (j) 66.7%; (k) 14.3%; (l) 42.9%
4 (a) 380%; (b) 250%; (c) 487.5%; (d) 535%;
   (e) 675%; (f) 180%; (g) 340%; (h) 287.5%;
   (i) 728%; (j) 466.6%; (k) 562.5%; (l) 410%

7.6 1 (a) 0.36; (b) 0.48; (c) 0.86; (d) 0.365; (e) 0.72;
   (f) 0.92; (g) 0.025; (h) 0.4875; (i) 1.44; (j) 1.5;
   (k) 2.25; (l) 5.9; (m) 0.855; (n) 0.6̇; (o) 0.083;
   (p) 0.2725
2 (a) 46%; (b) 87%; (c) 54%; (d) 63%; (e) 91%;
   (f) 35%; (g) 72%; (h) 48%; (i) 65%; (j) 50.7%;
   (k) 74.3%; (l) 86.9%; (m) 425%; (n) 387.5%;
   (o) 425%; (p) 85%

7.8 1 (a) £115; (b) £230; (c) £575; (d) £34.50;
   (e) £74.75; (f) £55.20; (g) £27.60; (h) £14.38;
   (i) £9.89; (j) £6.15
2 (a) £74; (b) £82.25; (c) £1050; (d) £467.50;
   (e) £693.75
3 (a) £1.35; (b) £40; (c) £0.88; (d) £64; (e) £4.20;
   (f) £18; (g) £4.12; (h) £0.12; (i) £1; (j) £0.12
4 £269.34
5 £647.90
6 £237.66

Chapter 8

8.4 1 (a) 1640 kilometres; (b) £223.04
2 £134.13
3 293.7 km
4 £17 501.38
5 8680 small packets
6 4405 bags, 130 gm left
7 120 000 cartons
8 19 500 bags
9 378 000 cartons
10 90 litres

8.6 1 (a) 3.218 km, 321 800 cm; (b) 4.852 km,
   485 200 cm; (c) 5.8923 km, 589 230 cm;
   (d) 6.38425 km, 638 425 cm; (e) 85.167 589 km,
   8516 758.9 cm; (f) 0.678 219 km, 67 821.9 cm
2 (a) 93.781 kg, 93 781 000 mg; (b) 7.3129 kg,
   7312 900 mg; (c) 5.683 246 kg, 5 683 246 mg;

(d) 4.593 668 kg, 4 593 668 mg; (e) 76.543 2 kg,
   76 543 200 mg; (f) 216.712 458 kg, 216 712 458 mg
3 (a) 3600 ml, 36 dl; (b) 9300 ml, 93 dl;
   (c) 58 900 ml, 589 dl; (d) 41 700 ml, 417 dl;
   (e) 9322 ml, 93.22 dl; (f) 6313 ml, 63.13 dl

8.8 1 13 days
2 26 days
3 22 days
4 33 days
5 63 days
6 60 days

Chapter 9

9.2 1 (a) 1:15; (b) 1:7; (c) 1:3; (d) 1:2; (e) 1:10;
   (f) 1:3; (g) 1:3; (h) 1:2; (i) 4:1; (j) 20:1
2 (a) 3:50; (b) 1:100; (c) 1:300; (d) 1:7; (e) 12:1;
   (f) 1:300; (g) 80:1; (h) 1:15; (i) 1:5000; (j) 1:400
3 (a) 1:5.3; (b) 1:333.3; (c) 1:2.3; (d) 1:3.8;
   (e) 1:13.8; (f) 1:13.9 (g) 1:2.8; (h) 1:128.6;
   (i) 1:666.7; (j) 1:34.3
4 Department B (only 1 unit out of 3000 is
   defective)
5 1:1.23

9.4 1 (a) £4375 and £1875; (b) £8400 and £4200;
   (c) £7932, £5288 and £5288; (d) £2430, £810 and
   £810; (e) £9300 and £6200; (f) £3440, £2580,
   £1720 and £860; (g) £2812, £2109 and £1406;
   (h) £6400, £5120 and £3840; (i) £5652, £2826
   and £1413; (j) £8309, £7122 and £3561
2 (a) 544 kg and 408 kg; (b) 1050 kg and 525 kg;
   (c) 3126 kg, 2084 kg and 1042 kg; (d) 2500 kg,
   2000 kg and 1500 kg; (e) 1885 tonnes,
   1885 tonnes and 1508 tonnes; (f) 1026 tonnes,
   1026 tonnes and 513 tonnes; (g) 2421 litres,
   2421 litres and 807 litres; (h) 2750 litres,
   1100 litres and 550 litres; (i) 9100 litres, 3900
   litres and 2600 litres; (j) 80 000 eggs, 80 000 eggs
   and 100 000 eggs

9.6 1 (a) 24p; (b) 15p; (c) 18p; (d) 12 p; (e) 96p;
   (f) 16p; (g) £365; (h) £248; (i) £147; (j) £120
2 (a) £237.50; (b) £720; (c) £1056; (d) £78;
   (e) £90; (f) £7.26; (g) £1182.24; (h) £48
3 (a) 495 days; (b) 49$\frac{1}{2}$ days
4 4$\frac{1}{5}$ days
5 1750 men

9.10 1 A receives £1605; B receives £4815 and C
   receives £535
2 W receives £1100, X receives £550, Y receives
   £550 and Z receives £1650
3 A = 140, B = 92, C = 56
4 (a) 30 marks; (b) 15 marks; (c) 8 marks
5 A receives £184.50, B £61.50 and C £123

6 (a) Ratio is 2:6:9 (this could be shown as
1 : 3 : 4.5); (b) gallery £460, circle £1380 and
stalls £2070

7 (a) £1860; (b) 186 stall seats

8 (a) £341.25; (b) £1.75 and £1.05

Chapter 10

10.4 1 (a) 9; (b) 8; (c) 8; (d) 12; (e) 16; (f) 9; (g) 10;
(h) 11; (i) 560; (j) 903

2 (a) 38 kg; (b) 42 kg; (c) 19 hrs $2\frac{1}{2}$ mins;
(d) 511 litres; (e) 53.9 m; (f) 28.9 tonnes

3 (a) 7009; (b) 24 304; (c) 50 300; (d) 49 730;
(e) 16 888

4 (a) 4.7; (b) 6.5; (c) 17.35; (d) 36.4; (e) 19.92

10.6 1 166.5 cm

2 1.97 kg

3 £142.11

4 35 kg

5 62.9

Chapter 11

11.2 1 (a) £2.44; (b) £1.77; (c) £127.50; (d) £46.80;
(e) £5.04; (f) £23.60; (g) £5.39; (h) £78.60;
(i) £141.30; (j) £41.40

2 (a) £21.49; (b) £12.61; (c) £75.50; (d) £30.37;
(e) £243.20

11.4 1 (a) £937.44; (b) £188.00; (c) £4774;
(d) £5350.40; (e) £1157.52

2 (a) £200.20; (b) £144.40; (c) £66; (d) £87.56;
(e) £121.80

3 (a) £531.38; (b) £119.70; (c) £530.88;
(d) £271.42; (e) £635.94

Chapter 12

12.2 1 (a) £1.20; (b) £2; (c) £3.20; (d) £33.60;
(e) £51.60; (f) £74; (g) £104; (h) £126.56;
(i) £171.40; (j) £222

2 (a) £1.95; (b) £3.10; (c) £5.32; (d) £7.88;
(e) £8.12; (f) £10.53; (g) £11.60; (h) £36.90;
(i) £46.25; (j) £170.01

12.4 1 £4987.65

2 £15 258.25

3 Shortage of £122.80; confirm appointment as it
is a very small percentage of total

4 £12 259.25

5 £14 019.10

12.6 1 (a) £6; (b) £24; (c) £9.60; (d) £17.60; (e) £39;
(f) £49.20

2 (a) £4; (b) £33.75; (c) £22.50; (d) £28; (e) £29;
(f) £68; (g) £175; (h) £52.50; (i) £96; (j) £34

12.8 1 (a) £10, $33\frac{1}{3}\%$; (b) £16, $33\frac{1}{3}\%$; (c) £1.20, 25%;
(d) £90, 25%; (e) £80, 20%; (f) £4.48, 20%;
(g) £10, $16\frac{2}{3}\%$; (h) £60, $16\frac{2}{3}\%$; (i) £32, $11\frac{1}{9}\%$;
(j) £80, $11\frac{1}{9}\%$

2 (a) £2, 23.1%; (b) £3, 28.6%; (c) £20, 37.5%;
(d) £4.50, 37.5%; (e) £12, 31.0%; (f) £24,
35.5%

3 £400

4 £250

5 £142

Chapter 13

13.4 1 (a) £60; (b) £126; (c) £378; (d) £2160; (e) £390

2 (a) £297.50; (b) £1501.50; (c) £1147.50;
(d) £19 237.50; (e) £429.69

3 (a) £173.25; (b) £582.90; (c) £687.70;
(d) £336.88; (e) £477.95

4 (a) £148.50; (b) £149.62; (c) £315; (d) £234;
(e) £27

13.6 1 (a) £559.55; (b) £2244.38; (c) £182.81;
(d) £49.50; (e) £1434.38

2 (a) £912.50; (b) £5000; (c) £1000; (d) £400;
(e) £2240

3 (a) $12\frac{1}{2}\%$; (b) 10%; (c) $7\frac{1}{2}\%$; (d) 8%; (e) 12%

4 (a) $2\frac{1}{2}$ years; (b) $6\frac{1}{2}$ years; (c) $2\frac{1}{2}$ years;
(d) $3\frac{1}{5}$ years; (e) 3 years

Chapter 14

14.3 1 (a) 766 DM; (b) 330 Naira; (c) US$296;
(d) 5040 Swiss francs; (e) A $3120; (f) 675
dinars; (g) 78 960 French francs; (h) 17 400
Swiss francs; (i) 675 000 pesos; (j) 63 120
markkha

2 (a) £2453.99; (b) £18.68; (c) £327.10;
(d) £35.43; (e) £9.26; (f) £91.25; (g) £340.13;
(h) £83.92; (i) £44 444.44; (j) £75.78

3 (a) US$7301; (b) 3 378 320 yen;
(c) 81 952.50 kroner; (d) 18 809 400 lire;
(e) 961 700 Belgian francs

4 £12 000

5 £7600

6 £465

7 43 992 DM

8 £2980.39

14.5 1 (a) £2000; (b) £10 000; (c) £30 000;
(d) £49 019.61; (e) £612 745.09

2 (a) £500; (b) £4000; (c) £300; (d) £8833.92;
(e) £19 876.32

3 (a) £1793.72; (b) £78.94 profit
4 (a) £50 000; (b) £4952.83 profit
5 (a) £1600; (b) £66.67 profit

Chapter 15

15.3 1 (a) £181.94; (b) £167; (c) £150.22; (d) £97.64; (e) £198.45
    2 (a) £490.10; (b) £319.16; (c) £691.28; (d) £1074.84; (e) £575.92
    3 (a) £1314.68; (b) £3402.53; (c) £2359.38; (d) £2810.80; (e) £3789.05
15.5 1 (a) £109.32; (b) £138.94; (c) £118.92; (d) £191.82; (e) £84.28
    2 (a) £212.95; (b) £485.62; (c) £637.82; (d) £310.12; (e) £758.36
    3 (a) £4595.25; (b) £4642; (c) £6036; (d) £6696; (e) £11 084
15.7 1 (a) 15°C; (b) 25°C; (c) 35°C; (d) 28.9°C; (e) 40.6°C; (f) 52.2°C; (g) 42.8°C; (h) 49.4°C; (i) 58.9°C; (j) 78.9°C
    2 (a) 68°F; (b) 77°F; (c) 86°F; (d) 62.6°F; (e) 75.2°F; (f) 80.6°F; (g) 111.2°F; (h) 118.4°F; (i) 125.6°F; (j) 179.6°F

Chapter 16

16.2 1 (a) £1.20; (b) £1.65; (c) £2.40; (d) £2.65; (e) £3.80; (f) £4.55; (g) £7.60; (h) £8.50; (i) £9.84; (j) £23.25
    2 (a) £121.80; (b) £160.95; (c) £191.40; (d) £213.15; (e) £304.50; (f) £337.56; (g) £631.62; (h) £735.15; (i) £870; (j) £1087.50
    3 (a) £243.20; (b) £425.60; (c) £133; (d) £638.40; (e) £1033.60; (f) £18 810; (g) £7144; (h) £20 900; (i) £3678.40; (j) £27 360
    4 (a) £2600; (b) £3852.40; (c) £7600; (d) £6856; (e) £24 273.50; (f) £35 008.50; (g) £47 208.50; (h) £97 263.40; (i) £243 867.25; (j) £337 284.48
16.4 1 (a) £280.80; (b) £175.50; (c) £436.80; (d) £747.50; (e) £631.80; (f) £1 150; (g) £822.80; (h) £1712.50; (i) £975; (j) £3513.60
    2 (a) 7.6p; (b) 4.0p; (c) 0.3p; (d) 1.6p; (e) 5.3p
    3 (a) 46.9p; (b) 69.5p; (c) 111.0p; (d) 82.4p; (e) 124.0p
    4 12.4p
    5 (a) £881 438; (b) extra rate 9.3p
    6 (a) 2.6p; (b) 0.4p
    7 (a) £378 500; (b) £11 385 276; (c) 30p
    8 43p

Chapter 17

17.2 1 (a) £20.83; (b) £29.27; (c) £34.70; (d) £38.68; (e) £47.59
    2 (a) 10.8p; (b) 11.3p; (c) 12.0p; (d) 9.6p; (e) 11.2p
    3 (a) £3104.50; (b) 10.3p
    4 (a) £2150; (b) 9.0p
    5 Vehicle (c) may be operated improperly
    6 Vehicle (c) has higher average costs per kilometre than the other vehicles

Chapter 18

18.2 1 (a) £68.18; (b) £82.12; (c) £250.36; (d) £311.36; (e) £1347.01
    2 (a) £113.39; (b) 246.48; (c) £368.22; (d) £744.37; (e) £1131.94
18.4 1 (a) £225.80; (b) £549.29; (c) £530.87; (d) £615.61; (e) £836.38
    2 (a) £291.45; (b) £650.31; (c) £537.29; (d) £642.67; (e) £1029.89

Chapter 19

19.5 1 (a) £74.10; (b) £125.55; (c) £121.24; (d) £179.55; (e) £220.50
    2 (a) £93.60; (b) £159.60; (c) £132.30; (d) £231; (e) £220.50
19.7 1 (a) £616; (b) £1899; (c) £1984; (d) £2261; (e) £426.50; (f) £148.70; (g) £339; (h) £134.20; (i) £109.28; (j) £132.08
    2 (a) £710; (b) £835; (c) £630; (d) £592.50; (e) £521.25
    3 (a) £814; (b) £665; (c) £668; (d) £545; (e) £632.50
    4 (a) £203.50; (b) £173.30; (c) £252.10; (d) £288.90; (e) £219.75; Miss P earns the highest and Mr N the lowest
    5 (a) £697.50; (b) £821.40; (c) £883.80; (d) £746.70; (e) £652.50
19.9 1 Gross pay £622.00; Pay for tax purposes £572.24; Gross pay to date for tax purposes £1415; Free pay £392.25; Taxable pay to date £1022.75; Tax due to date £306.60; Tax to be deducted £24.10; Total deductions £82.86; Amount due as net pay £489.38; Total amount in pay packet after refund of fares £507.83; Total due to National Insurance £124.40
    2 Gross pay £558.28; Pay for tax purposes £524.78; Gross pay to date for tax purposes

£1745.22; Free pay £712.26; Taxable pay to date £1032.96; Tax due to date £309.60; Tax to be refunded £30.40; Total deductions £60.75; Take-home pay £494.43; Total to National Insurance £111.66

3 Gross pay £757.25; Pay for tax purposes £681.52; Gross pay to date for tax purposes £1533.75; Free pay £489.75; Taxable pay to date £1044; Tax due to date £313.20; Tax to be deducted £23.20; Total deductions £95.15; Take-home pay £586.37; Total to National Insurance £151.45

4 Gross pay £501.00; Pay for tax purposes £460.12; Gross pay to date for tax purposes £1680.12; Free pay £642.27; Taxable pay to date £1037.85; Tax due to date £311.10; Tax to be deducted £122.50; Total deductions £170.51; Take home pay £314.61; Total to National Insurance £102.20

Chapter 20

20.2 1 (a) £7.19; (b) £9.60; (c) £12.50; (d) £18.28; (e) £7.20
2 (a) Deposit £1300, instalment £93.89;
(b) Deposit £1500, instalment £108.33;
(c) Deposit £1600, instalment £115.56;
(d) Deposit £2526.67, instalment £182.48;
(e) Deposit £1739.33, instalment £125.62
3 (a) £18.23; (b) £20.75; (c) £43.12; (d) £75.52; (e) £112.12; (f) £32.34; (g) £63.27; (h) £11.49; (i) £12.45;; (j) £18.38
4 Deposit £66.92, instalment £5.79
5 £37.11

Chapter 21

21.3 1 Balance at end of day = £146.22
2 Balance at end of day = £172.22
3 Balance at end of week = £229.40
21.6 1 Balance at end of day = £1763.84
2 Balance at end of day = £2122.55
3 Balance at end of week = £3636.60

Chapter 22

22.2 1 Balance at end of week = £23.18
2 Balance at end of week = £10.45
3 Balance = £31.85; Imprest restored with £68.15
4 Balance = £19.45; Imprest restored with £80.55
5 Balance = £14.10; Imprest restored with £85.90

Chapter 23

23.3 1 (a) £1400; (b) £5500; (c) £1400; (d) £238; (e) £200
2 (a) £1667; (b) £8000; (c) £1255; (d) £147 000; (e) £1 633 333
23.6 1 (a) Yr 1 £247, Yr 2 £164, Yr 3 £110, Final value £219
(b) Yr 1 £1223, Yr 2 £816, Yr 3 £544, Final value £1087
(c) Yr 1 £1847, Yr 2 £1231, Yr 3 £821, Final value £1641
(d) Yr 1 £6300, Yr 2 £4200, Yr 3 £2800, Final value £5600
(e) Yr 1 £8973, Yr 2 £5982, Yr 3 £3988, Final value £7977
2 (a) Yr 1 £110, Yr 2 £88, Yr 3 £70, Final value £282
(b) Yr 1 £176, Yr 2 £141, Yr 3 £113, Final value £450
(c) Yr 1 £312, Yr 2 £234, Yr 3 £176, Final value £528
(d) Yr 1 £688, Yr 2 £516, Yr 3 £386, Final value £1160
(e) Yr 1 £16 500, Yr 2 £11 550, Yr 3 £8085, Final value £18 865
3 (a) Yr 1 £58, Yr 2 £100, Yr 3 £76, Final value £226
(b) Yr 1 £288, Yr 2 £503, Yr 3 £377, Final value £1132
(c) Yr 1 £475, Yr 2 £1742, Yr 3 £1161, Final value £2322
(d) Yr 1 £767, Yr 2 £2811, Yr 3 £1874, Final value £3748
(e) Yr 1 £3918, Yr 2 £3917, Yr 3 £2612, Final value £5223
4 £13 800 depreciation
5 £58 200 appreciation. Animals Account final figure £531 000. The other £5200 would be in Insurance Claims Due Account. It would only be added to Animals Account if actually spent on further animals, at a later date.

Chapter 24

24.3 1 (a) 28 cm; (b) 48 cm; (c) 60 cm; (d) 6 m; (e) 17 m; (f) 400 m
2 (a) 34 cm; (b) 60 cm; (c) 26 m; (d) 68 m; (e) 440 m; (f) 300 m
3 Breadth is 70 metres
4 Length is 300 metres
5 (a) 25 cm^2; (b) 81 cm^2; (c) 169 cm^2; (d) 400 cm^2; (e) 17.64 m^2; (f) 33.64 m^2

6 (a) 930 cm^2; (b) 432 cm^2; (c) 2970 cm^2;
   (d) 3465 cm^2; (e) 3$\frac{1}{2}$ m^2; (f) 10 m^2; (g) 104 m^2;
   (h) 160 m^2; (i) 49 000 m^2; (j) 172 800 m^2

24.5 1 (i) 32.42 m^2; (ii) 61.06 m^2; (iii) 35.09 m^2;
   (iv) 33.82 m^2

2 12.25 m^2

3 14 m^2

4 (a) 4800 m^2; (b) 6624 m^2; (c) 1824 m^2

5 (a) 1024 m^2; (b) 345 m^2; (c) 231 m^2

6 Perimeter is 520 metres

7 Perimeter is 260 metres

8 (a) 128 m; (b) 148 m; (c) 160 m

9 (a) 274 m^2; (b) 318 m^2; (c) 894 m^2; (d) 280 m^2

24.7 1 65 m^2

2 (a) 9 m^2; (b) 27 m^2

3 44 m^2

4 90 m^2

5 £129.96

6 (a) 24; (b) £79.20

7 (a) £160.65; (b) £16.50; (c) 71.75 m^2; (d) £51

8 Tiles £108.68; Wallpaper £27.60; Paint £15.50;
   Total cost £236.78

24.9 1 (a) 10 cm^2; (b) 31.5 cm^2; (c) 48 cm^2; (d) 90 cm^2;
   (e) 135 cm^2

2 (a) 3.75 m^2; (b) 9 m^2; (c) 33.6 m^2; (d) 32.5 m^2;
   (e) 57 m^2

24.11 1 (a) 0.072 m^3; (b) 0.648 m^3; (c) 0.35 m^3;
   (d) 2.304 m^3; (e) 1.248 m^3; (f) 1.008 m^3;
   (g) 1.36 m^3; (h) 1.44 m^3; (i) 3.51 m^3;
   (j) 3.168 m^3

2 (a) 50 000; (b) 61 250; (c) 60 000; (d) 31 500;
   (e) 26 250

3 (a) 304 cm^3; (b) 1048 cm^3; (c) 4000 cm^3;
   (d) 1160 cm^3

4 Height is 1.5 m

5 Height is $\frac{1}{2}$ m

Chapter 25

25.2 1 (a) 22 cm; (b) 11 cm; (c) 15.7 cm; (d) 28.3 cm;
   (e) 44 m; (f) 31.4 m; (g) 33 m; (h) 88 m;
   (i) 154 cm; (j) 2.2 m

2 (a) 25.1 cm; (b) 37.7 cm; (c) 75.4 cm;
   (d) 113.1 cm; (e) 132 m; (f) 345.7 m; (g) 154 m;
   (h) 220 m; (i) 440 m; (j) 528 m

3 14.08 metres

4 30 000 revolutions

5 (a) 4.396 m; (b) 8143 revolutions

6 7980 metres

25.4 1 (a) 154 cm^2; (b) 616 cm^2; (c) 3850 cm^2;
   (d) 346$\frac{1}{2}$ cm^2; (e) 1386 cm^2; (f) 452$\frac{4}{7}$ cm^2;
   (g) 3422$\frac{4}{7}$ cm^2; (h) 6650$\frac{2}{7}$ cm^2; (i) 2291$\frac{1}{7}$ cm^2;
   (j) 8498$\frac{2}{7}$ cm^2

2 (a) 38$\frac{1}{2}$ cm^2; (b) 154 cm^2; (c) 452$\frac{4}{7}$ cm^2;
   (d) 616 m^2; (e) 707$\frac{1}{7}$ m^2; (f) 28$\frac{2}{7}$ m^2; (g) 176$\frac{11}{14}$ m^2;
   (h) 2828$\frac{4}{7}$ m^2; (i) 4419$\frac{9}{14}$ m^2; (j) 61 600 m^2

3 (a) 75.4 cm^2; (b) 163.3 cm^2; (c) 169.6 cm^2;
   (d) 392.5 m^2; (e) 19 782 m^2

25.6 1 (a) 1.57 cm^3; (b) 283 cm^3; (c) 668 cm^3;
   (d) 942 cm^3; (e) 2384 cm^3; (f) 3815 cm^3

2 (a) 6.6 m^3; (b) 27.2 m^3; (c) 51.5 m^3;
   (d) 134.6 m^3; (e) 721.4 m^3

3 (a) 111.5 cm^2; (b) 307.5 cm^2; (c) 427.3 cm^2;
   (d) 1483.6 cm^2; (e) 2025.7 cm^2

4 (a) 471 m^3; (b) 2412 m^3; (c) 5652 m^3;
   (d) 9043 m^3; (e) 16 956 m^3

5 (a) 113.1 cm^3; (b) 1437.3 cm^3; (c) 14142.9 cm^3;
   (d) 11.5 m^3; (e) 179.7 m^3

Chapter 26

26.5 1 £24 m, £12 m, £8 m, £6 m; 48%, 24%, 16%,
   12%

2 2675, 4272, 19 821, 7382; Total 34 150

3 1, 3, 6, 4, 4, 2, Total 20; 5% 15%, 30%, 20%,
   20%, 10%

4 No numerical answer required

5 636, 38, 74, 29, 777; 81.9%, 4.9%, 9.5%, 3.7%

6 (a) Passengers: set down 41 220 and picked up
   40 485, Total 81 705 (thousands)
   (b) Freight: set down 324 and picked up 396,
   Total 720 (thousand tonnes)
   (c) Mail: set down 24 and picked up 34, Total 58
   (thousand tonnes)

7 Total outlets 228 077; Total sales £58 485 m;
   31.0%, 6.6%, 14.5%, 48.0%, 100%
   (percentages do not sum to 100% because of
   rounding)

8 6, 3, 1, 9, 0, 3, 6, 4, 6, 2; 15%, 7.5%, 2.5%,
   22.5%, 0%, 7.5%, 15%, 10%, 15%, 5%

Chapter 27

27.3 No numerical answers required

27.5 No numerical answers required

27.8 1 No numerical answers required

2 (a) 5.3 hours; (b) 165 km

3 (a) £113.75; (b) 44 items

4 (a) £141.60; (b) 7 hours

Chapter 28

28.2 No numerical answers required

28.5 No numerical answers required

28.7 No numerical answers required

Chapter 29

29.3 1 9
    2 31
    3 59.8
    4 £101.17
    5 £366.33
29.5 1 476 hours
    2 £12 938.50
    3 125 280 tonnes
    4 £206.50
29.7 1 A = 2, B = 0, C = 2
    2 8 guests
    3 A = 2; B = bi-modal, 2 wickets and 4 wickets;
      C = bi-modal, 2 wickets and 4 wickets; D = 7
    4 32 tonnes

Chapter 30

30.3 1 (a) £627.85; (b) £1348.30; (c) £1320.80;
    (d) £2331.50; (e) £60 887.50
    2 (a) £185.50; (b) £888.15; (c) £5293.50;
    (d) £7773.50; (e) £42 079.25
    3 (a) Profit £34.50; (b) Profit £563.95; (c) Loss
    £114.32, (d) Profit £896.35; (e) Loss £2192
30.5 1 (a) £495; (b) £900; (c) £1925; (d) £9200;
    (e) £25 875
    2 (a) £179.25; (b) £437.50; (c) £1181.25;
    (d) £5265; (e) £2940
    3 (a) £9000; (b) £960; (c) $10\frac{2}{3}$%
    4 (a) £117 000; (b) £10 500; (c) 8.97%
    5 (a) £6000; (b) £30 000; (c) An increase of £150
    6 (a) £1650; (b) £2000; (c) £17.50 fall in income
    7 (a) 7.6%; (b) £19 800; (c) £60 000; (d) £2100;
    (e) 10.6%
    8 (a) 10.7%; (b) £20 000; (c) 14.1%

Chapter 31

31.3 1 (a) £1188.10; (b) £1782.15; (c) £5049.42;
    (d) £8910.75; (e) £4985.86; (f) £6410.39;
    (g) £9388.96; (h) £19 425.44; (i) £35 289.54;
    (j) £50 111.15
    2 (a) £583.20; (b) £1028.50; (c) £1568;
    (d) £4348.04; (e) £4917.56; (f) £10 049.92;
    (g) £14 015.81; (h) £12 624.77; (i) £21 236.34;
    (j) £46 863.29
31.5 1 (a) £1155.62; (b) £2943.06; (c) £9013.38;
    (d) £17 797.85; (e) £21 006.92
    2 (a) £596; (b) £1008; (c) £1936; (d) £2516;
    (e) £3864; (f) £26 731; (g) £33 904; (h) £48 574;
    (i) £122 041; (j) £805 207

Appendix: mental arithmetic

1 (a) 40; (b) 3152; (c) 42; (d) 2343; (e) 648; (f) 1055;
  (g) 553; (h) 56; (i) 537; (j) 231
2 (a) 208; (b) 4375; (c) 176; (d) 3644; (e) 900; (f) 1629;
  (g) 360; (h) 99; (i) 673; (j) 78
3 (a) 206; (b) 3848; (c) 204; (d) 2886; (e) 2021;
  (f) 3843; (g) 349; (h) 78; (i) 675; (j) 96
4 (a) 561; (b) $\frac{1}{3}$; (c) 211; (d) $1\frac{1}{8}$; (e) 17 442; (f) $\frac{3}{8}$;
  (g) $445\frac{3}{7}$; (h) 1; (i) $\frac{1}{24}$; (j) 6
5 (a) 12.54; (b) 1.5; (c) 3.564; (d) 16; (e) $1\frac{5}{12}$; (f) $12\frac{3}{5}$;
  (g) $1\frac{7}{8}$; (h) £293; (i) 30; (j) 200
6 (a) 119.35; (b) 147.75; (c) 1 250 000; (d) £1.35;
  (e) 20 000; (f) $10\frac{13}{24}$; (g) 354 cm; (h) $\frac{9}{20}$; (i) 270;
  (j) £3.08
7 (a) 2162; (b) £122; (c) £170.85; (d) 77 976; (e) £7.77;
  (f) £126; (g) £468; (h) £170; (i) $\frac{5}{16}$; (j) £127.50
8 (a) 881; (b) £32.50; (c) 92; (d) 40; (e) 750; (f) 5250;
  (g) £47.50; (h) 11 700; (i) £140; (j) £252
9 (a) 4238; (b) £2253; (c) $\frac{5}{18}$; (d) £140; (e) 0.06; (f) $\frac{2}{3}$;
  (g) 21; (h) $11\frac{7}{8}$; (i) $1\frac{1}{4}$; (j) Mrs Y £3954, Mr Z £2636
10 (a) 50 148; (b) £260.64; (c) 38 days; (d) 127 000;
  (e) 136 000; (f) £87.50; (g) 3.28; (h) 5500; (i) 6 days;
  (j) £93, £62, £62
11 (a) 41.04 metres; (b) 201; (c) 29 225; (d) £37.50;
  (e) 10; (f) $1\frac{1}{3}$; (g) $1\frac{1}{4}$; (h) 166; (i) £19.20; (j) £8912,
  £4456
12 (a) 20.5 m; (b) £14.36; (c) £463; (d) $\frac{11}{12}$; (e) £4947,
  £1649; (f) £4.50; (g) £6.60; (h) 1012; (i) £13.68;
  (j) £11.90
13 (a) £122.30; (b) £164.85; (c) 77 976; (d) £7.77;
  (e) £790.50; (f) 14; (g) 1.38; (h) £45; (i) £3500;
  (j) £2500
14 (a) 1259; (b) 1235; (c) 135 000; (d) 3500;
  (e) 266 minutes; (f) 95 days; (g) £200; (h) £300 000;
  (i) £2000; (j) £9000
15 (a) £33.80; (b) 50.76; (c) $13\frac{37}{40}$; (d) 20; (e) 750;
  (f) £6.86, £2.94; (g) 0.375; (h) £485; (i) £200;
  (j) £192.50
16 (a) 11 195; (b) 13.82; (c) 807; (d) 3200 bottles;
  (e) 450 seconds; (f) £17; (g) £300; (h) £20.25;
  (i) a 3p rate; (j) £12
17 (a) 143; (b) £1079.66; (c) 8.52; (d) $9\frac{1}{3}$; (e) £50;
  (f) £420; (g) £5950; (h) £20; (i) £1.06;
  (j) 72 metres
18 (a) 2228; (b) 1.8825; (c) £900; (d) 41; (e) £960;
  (f) $\frac{9}{10}$; (g) £41 666.67; (h) 44 640 000 lire; (i) £6.72;
  (j) 68°F
19 (a) 825; (b) £1186.91; (c) 285 seconds; (d) 90;
  (e) £2800; (f) £140 338; (g) £75 000, £50 000,
  £25 000; (h) 1980; (i) £5000, £3750, £3750;
  (j) 80.6° Fahrenheit
20 (a) £10.66; (b) 483; (c) 0.28; (d) 92; (e) £5000;
  (f) £18; (g) £288; (h) $\frac{3}{8}$; (i) $7\frac{7}{8}$; (j) £102.80

21 (a) £1461; (b) £531.50; (c) $7\frac{5}{8}$; (d) 3 years; (e) £9000; (f) £92.70; (g) £24; (h) £12; (i) 3 600 000; (j) £3084

22 (a) 1288; (b) 849; (c) £336; (d) $\frac{9}{40}$; (e) 14 000 000; (f) 100 spoonfuls; (g) 4; (h) £1755; (i) 8; (j) £51.28

23 (a) 875; (b) £13.65; (c) 0.0032; (d) 40°C; (e) 2738; (f) £8000, £6000, £4000; (g) £23; (h) £960; (i) £588; (j) £21 150

24 (a) $10\frac{1}{8}$; (b) 2366; (c) 22 374; (d) 0.0008; (e) £300; (f) 4018; (g) £272; (h) £300; (i) 12 000 m^2; (j) £24

25 (a) 41 187; (b) £112; (c) 47 760 pesetas; (d) 3; (e) £275 800; (f) 4750 mm; (g) £28 000, £28 000, £21 000; (h) £5245 appreciation; (i) $2\pi r$ or πD; (j) 154 cm^2

26 (a) 1688; (b) 12.75; (c) £1929.55; (d) £59.60;

(e) £12 000, £9000, £6000; (f) 21.4; (g) 44 cm; (h) 41.25 m^2; (i) £41; (j) £464

27 (a) 22 925; (b) 573.8; (c) £76.28; (d) 1.1 metres; (e) £840; (f) 700 and 800; (g) £4680; (h) £3 million; (i) £14.30; (j) £105

28 (a) 7877; (b) 1.35; (c) £399.71; (d) 40; (e) £360; (f) 2800 drachmas; (g) 38.5 cm^2; (h) £157.50; (i) 3; (j) £920

29 (a) 1068; (b) 17; (c) $\frac{1}{4}$; (d) A £16 000, B £8000; (e) 154 m^2; (f) 125 m^3; (g) 23; (h) £1200; (i) 8p; (j) 3

30 (a) 1189; (b) £36.91; (c) 136 m^2; (d) £450; (e) 207; (f) $2\pi r\,(r+h)$; (g) £72 654.40; (h) £912.50; (i) 925; (j) £353.50

31 (a) 431; (b) 4.4 metres; (c) 40; (d) $\frac{4}{3}\pi r^3$; (e) 27; (f) 320 m^3; (g) 2.4%; (h) £21; (i) £884.25; (j) £331